ECONOMIC DOCTRINES
A Book of Readings
Volume 2
THE ECONOMY AND ITS PROBLEMS
By HOWARD L. BALSLEY

About the Author

1. *Position and Qualifications:* Professor and Head, Department of Business and Economic Research, Louisiana Polytechnic Institute. Educated at Indiana University, The Johns Hopkins University, and The University of Chicago. Awarded the Ph.D. degree in Economics at Indiana University in 1950. Member of Phi Beta Kappa.

2. *Publications:* Coauthor with James Gemmell of *Principles of Economics* (D. C. Health, 1953; 589 pp.), a college textbook. Author of monographs and periodical articles on taxation, natural resources, and the teaching of economics.

About the Book

1. A scholarly collection of the most important economic doctrines of the ages, as originally stated by the great philosophers who created them.

2. Illuminating descriptions of the doctrines and their authors included at the beginning of each reading, to place the philosopher and his doctrine in point of time and place and importance.

3. Readings on both sides of controversial economic issues included, presenting the most powerful thought of the leaders of pro and con groups on such questions as "the planned economy" and "free trade."

LITTLEFIELD QUALITY PAPERBACKS

A. W. LITTLEFIELD, General Editor

ACCOUNTING, COST
ACCOUNTING (CPA EXAMS)
ACCOUNTING, ELEMENTARY
ADMINISTRATION, BASIC
ADMINISTRATION, PUBLIC
ADVERTISING, Principles
ALGEBRA, COLLEGE
ANATOMY, HUMAN, ATLAS
ANTHROPOLOGY, DICTIONARY*
ASTRONOMY and ASTRONAUTICS, DICT.*
BENTHAM'S FICTIONS, THEORY†
BIOLOGY, General
BUSINESS COMMUNICATION
BUSINESS ORGANIZATION
CALCULUS
CHEMISTRY, Elementary
CHEMISTRY, General*
CHILD'S CONCEPTION of Phys. Causality†
CHILD'S CONCEPTION OF WORLD†
CHILD, JUDGMENT, REASONING†
CITIZENSHIP, Tools for Good
COMMUNICATION FOR NURSES N
CONSTITUTION, ANALYZED
CONSTITUTION, LEADING CASES
CONSTITUTIONS, MODERN
CORPORATE FINANCE
CREDITS AND COLLECTIONS
DISASTER NURSING N
DOCUMENTS, BASIC AMERICAN
ECONOMIC HISTORY OF U. S.*
ECONOMICS, Principles
ECONOMICS, DICTIONARY
EDUCATION, PHILOSOPHY OF*
EDUCATORS, SOCIAL IDEAS, AMER.*
ENGLISH ESSENTIALS
ETHICAL RELATIVITY†
ETHICAL THEORY, FIVE TYPES†
FICTION, MODERN WORLD
FIGURES THAT COUNT (Math. for Nurses) N
FOREIGN POLICY, AMER.*
GOVERNMENT, AMERICAN
GOVERNMENT, AMER., DICT.*
GOVERNMENT, COMPARATIVE*
GOVERNMENT, U. S. (Visual)*
GRAMMAR, AMER., DICT.*
HISTORY, AMER., DICT.*
HISTORY, AMER., to 1865*
HISTORY, AMER., Since 1865*
HISTORY, AMERICAN, Before 1877
HISTORY, AMERICAN, After 1865
HISTORY, ANCIENT*
HISTORY, CIVILIZATION, Before 1648
HISTORY, CIVILIZATION, After 1500
HISTORY OF ENGLAND
HISTORY, EUROPE, 1500-1848
HISTORY, EUROPE, After 1815
HISTORY, FAR EAST
HISTORY, MEDIEVAL*
HISTORY, U. S. DIPLOMATIC
INDUCTION AND PROBABILITY†

INSURANCE, DICTIONARY
INSURANCE, General Principles
INTELLIGENCE, NATURE OF†
INTELLIGENCE, PSYCHOLOGY OF†
LANGUAGE, LOGICAL SYNTAX†
LAW FOR THE NURSE N
LITERATURE, AMERICAN
LITERATURE, AMERICAN, DICT.*
LITERATURE, ENGLISH, Vol. I
LITERATURE, ENGLISH, Vol. II
LITERATURE, RECENT AMERICAN
LITERATURE, RUSSIAN, DICTIONARY*
LITERATURE, SPANISH, HISTORY
LITERATURE, WORLD, DICTIONARY*
MARKETING
MATERNAL AND CHILD HEALTH N
MATHEMATICS, FOUNDATIONS OF†
MATHEMATICS, NATURE OF†
MATHEMATICS TABLES
MIND, GROWTH OF THE†
MIND, ITS PLACE IN NATURE†
MONEY AND BANKING
PHARMACOLOLGY FOR NURSES N
PHILOSOPHICAL STUDIES†
PHILOSOPHICAL SYSTEMS*
PHILOSOPHY*
PHILOSOPHY, DICTIONARY OF*
PHILOSOPHY, LIVING SCHOOLS*
PHILOSOPHY, WORLD TREASURY*
PLATO'S WORKS, ABRIDGED*
POLITICAL SCIENCE
POSITIVISM, LOGICAL, AN EXAM. OF†
PSYCHOLOGICAL TERMS, HANDBOOK
PSYCHOLOGY, ABNORMAL*
PSYCHOLOGY, ABNORMAL, R'D'GS
PSYCHOLOGY, EDUC.
PSYCHOLOGY, EDUC., R'D'GS
PSYCHOLOGY, GENERAL
PSYCHOLOGY, INDIVIDUAL†
PSYCHOLOGY, MODERN
READING, RAPID
RELIGION, ENCYCLOPEDIA*
RELIGIONS, LIVING SCHOOLS*
SALESMANSHIP
SAVAGE SOCIETY, CRIME, CUSTOM†
SHAKESPEARE'S PLAYS, SYNOPSES
SCIENCE, DICTIONARY*
SLIDE RULE, UNDERSTANDING THE
SCIENTIFIC METHODS†
SOCIOLOGY, An Introduction
SOCIOLOGY, DICTIONARY OF*
STATISTICAL PRESENTATION
SYNONYMS, AMERICAN, DICT.*
THERMODYNAMICS, ENGINEERING
THESES, TYPED MSS., PREP.
THESIS WRITING
THOUGHT, SCIENTIFIC†
WESTERN CIVILIZATION, READINGS
WORD ORGINS, DICTIONARY OF*

* Asterisk indicates titles in the new Students Outline Series.
† Dagger indicates titles in the International Library of Psychology, Philosophy and Scientific Method.
N Indicates Nurses Handbook Series.
  All others are Littlefield College Outlines.

ECONOMIC DOCTRINES
A Book of Readings

VOLUME 2
The Economy and Its Problems

By

HOWARD L. BALSLEY, Ph.D.

Head, Department of Business and Economic Research
Louisiana Polytechnic Institute

CHRISTIAN COLLEGE LIBRARY
COLUMBIA, MISSOURI

1961

LITTLEFIELD, ADAMS & CO.
PATERSON, NEW JERSEY

22342

CONTENTS

PREFACE

This compilation serves as an introduction to the great literature of economics. The author has felt that in economics courses the students should be brought into contact not only with the doctrines and principles of economics but with the sources of those doctrines; that there should be some acquaintanceship made with the great economists and philosophers who divined the ideas and also with the background of philosophy of those great figures. Such an approach to the teaching of economics takes the direction of the attainment of a true "liberal" education.

The great ideas in economics are essentially simple ideas. They were discovered or delineated by men who recognized this simplicity; and these men, fortunately, have often expressed themselves in simple language. This book consists chiefly of readings from the great contributions of economists and philosophers up to the present. In all cases of the readings selected, the original source of the doctrine or principle of economics has been searched out in so far as possible and either the original statement or the clearest statement made to date has been selected. The book, it is expected, may be of considerable use for source materials in advanced courses and may prove of use to students studying the history of economic ideas.

Some of the readings in this book explain concepts usually found in basic textbooks, but as originally stated by the discoverer of the idea. The use of such readings is a powerful teaching technique, resulting in an emphasis that stimulates thought and comparison and that serves to register the importance of the principle upon the student's mind. In this book in many instances—on controversial items—arguments for and against a stand on an economic question are given. Thus the attitudes of two important authorities like Friedrich List and Fréderic Bastiat which should be familiar to the student are presented. In every reading an introductory paragraph has been included to place the author, both in point of time and in importance, as well as the significance of the reading.

The readings in this book, selected according to the criteria outlined, have been carefully screened. The total number of readings included is sixty-seven, fewer than is found in other compilations. The author has felt that a few concepts well learned are far more valuable than a hodgepodge of innumerable items superficially scanned. To this end, no fragmentary readings are included. The shortest reading in the book is two pages. Such shorter readings have been included where the principle dealt with was of a lesser importance or was stated most succinctly in that short a space. Most of the readings are from ten to twenty pages in length. Such excerpts are neither too long for an undergraduate to read pleasurably and profitably, nor too short to enable him to gain an insight into the philosophy of the writer.

There has been no editing of the materials in this book, since most of the selections are masterpieces in their own right. Where context has been omitted within a reading, space breaks have been made between paragraphs; the use of ellipses has been kept at a minimum. Students have complained of ellipses as interrupting the train of thought, and teachers have expressed the same opinion. Ordinarily, footnotes in the context have been omitted except for quoted materials.

This compilation of readings was made possible through the generous assistance of the Carnegie Foundation for the Advancement of Teaching. While the author takes full responsibility for the final selections, a number of professors made valuable suggestions and criticisms: Mark C. Mills, Taulman C. Miller, and the late James E. Moffat of Indiana University; Tjalling C. Koopmans of Yale University; Earl J. Hamilton of the University of Chicago; Clifford L. James of the Ohio State University; Tipton R. Snavely of the University of Virginia; Edward C. Atwood of Washington and Lee University; and Jack N. Behrman of the University of Delaware.

HOWARD L. BALSLEY

Louisiana Polytechnic Institute

PART I

THE NATURE OF

THE ECONOMY

READING 1

The Social Contract

THE ESSENCE OF SOCIETY is that individuals contract to respect each other's persons and possessions. To live together, therefore, man sets up conventions by way of laws and customs, binding himself as an individual to certain methods of conduct which we call morality. There can be no morality where man exists as a perfectly independent being, for there is then no standard by which he can be judged.

The following reading, Rousseau's *Social Contract,* is a masterful statement of this situation. Rousseau explains why and how man lives in groups. The right of man to own property is a central feature of society, for man could not own anything except through an agreement by which such ownership is respected. The final authority of the sovereign (the will of the people) over all property is precisely formulated; we recognize this final authority in our doctrine of *eminent domain,* by which government may seize private property for the welfare of society. Fundamentally the doctrine of eminent domain rests upon the proposition that, since the right of private ownership is conferred upon individuals by the sovereign (the will of the people) resulting from the social contract voluntarily entered upon, the sovereign has the power to rescind the right of private ownership in individual cases.

Jean Jacques Rousseau (1712-1778) was a French political philosopher of the pre-Revolutionary era. His writing influenced the thought and attitudes leading to the French and American Revolutions. The reading is in Book I, pp. 3-22, from the book *The Social Contract and Other Discourses* by Jean Jacques Rousseau, translated by G. D. H. Cole. Everyman's Library. Reprinted by permission of E. P. Dutton & Co., Inc.

CHAPTER I

Subject of the First Book

Man is born free; and everywhere he is in chains. One thinks himself the master of others, and still remains a greater slave than they. How did this change come about? I do not know. What can make it legitimate? That question I think I can answer.

If I took into account only force, and the effects derived from it, I should say: "As long as a people is compelled to obey, and obeys, it does well; as soon as it can shake off the yoke, and shakes it off, it does still better; for, regaining its liberty by the same right as took it away, either it is justified in resuming it, or there was no justification for those who took it away." But the social order is a sacred right which is the basis of all other rights. Nevertheless, this right does not come from nature, and must therefore be founded on conventions. Before coming to that, I have to prove what I have just asserted.

CHAPTER II

The First Societies

The most ancient of all societies, and the only one that is natural, is the family: and even so the children remain attached to the father only so long as they need him for their preservation. As soon as this need ceases, the natural bond is dissolved. The children, released from the obedience they owed to the father, and the father, released from the care he owed his children, return equally to independence. If they remain united, they continue so no longer naturally, but voluntarily; and the family itself is then maintained only by convention.

This common liberty results from the nature of man. His first law is to provide for his own preservation, his first cares are those which he owes to himself; and, as soon as he reaches years of discretion, he is the sole judge of the proper means of preserving himself, and consequently becomes his own master.

The family then may be called the first model of political

societies: the ruler corresponds to the father, and the people to the children; and all, being born free and equal, alienate their liberty only for their own advantage. The whole difference is that, in the family, the love of the father for his children repays him for the care he takes of them, while, in the State, the pleasure of commanding takes the place of the love which the chief cannot have for the peoples under him.

Grotius denies that all human power is established in favour of the governed, and quotes slavery as an example. His usual method of reasoning is constantly to establish right by fact. It would be possible to employ a more logical method, but none could be more favourable to tyrants.

It is then, according to Grotius, doubtful whether the human race belongs to a hundred men, or that hundred men to the human race: and, throughout his book, he seems to incline to the former alternative, which is also the view of Hobbes. On this showing, the human species is divided into so many herds of cattle, each with its ruler, who keeps guard over them for the purpose of devouring them.

As a shepherd is of a nature superior to that of his flock, the shepherds of men, *i.e.* their rulers, are of a nature superior to that of the peoples under them. Thus, Philo tells us, the Emperor Caligula reasoned, concluding equally well either that kings were gods, or that men were beasts.

The reasoning of Caligula agrees with that of Hobbes and Grotius. Aristotle, before any of them, had said that men are by no means equal naturally, but that some are born for slavery, and others for dominion.

Aristotle was right; but he took the effect for the cause. Nothing can be more certain than that every man born in slavery is born for slavery. Slaves lose everything in their chains, even the desire of escaping from them: they love their servitude, as the comrades of Ulysses loved their brutish condition. If then there are slaves by nature, it is because there have been slaves against nature. Force made the first slaves, and their cowardice perpetuated the condition.

I have said nothing of King Adam, or Emperor Noah, father of the three great monarchs who shared out the universe, like the children of Saturn, whom some scholars have recognised in them. I trust to getting due thanks for my moderation; for, being a direct descendant of one of these princes, perhaps of the eldest branch, how do I know that a verification of titles might not leave me the legitimate king of the human race? In any case, there can be no doubt that Adam was sovereign of the world, as Robinson Crusoe was of his island, as long as he was its only inhabitant; and this empire had the advantage that the monarch, safe on his throne, had no rebellions, wars, or conspirators to fear.

CHAPTER III

The Right of the Strongest

The strongest is never strong enough to be always the master, unless he transforms strength into right, and obedience into duty. Hence the right of the strongest, which, though to all seeming meant ironically, is really laid down as a fundamental principle. But are we never to have an explanation of this phrase? Force is a physical power, and I fail to see what moral effect it can have. To yield to force is an act of necessity, not of will—at the most, an act of prudence. In what sense can it be a duty?

Suppose for a moment that this so-called "right" exists. I maintain that the sole result is a mass of inexplicable nonsense. For, if force creates right, the effect changes with the cause: every force that is greater than the first succeeds to its right. As soon as it is possible to disobey with impunity, disobedience is legitimate; and, the strongest being always in the right, the only thing that matters is to act so as to become the strongest. But what kind of right is that which perishes when force fails? If we must obey perforce, there is no need to obey because we ought; and if we are not forced to obey, we are under no obligation to do so. Clearly, the word "right" adds nothing to force: in this connection, it means absolutely nothing.

Obey the powers that be. If this means yield to force, it is a good precept, but superfluous: I can answer for its never being violated. All power comes from God, I admit; but so does all sickness: does that mean that we are forbidden to call in the doctor? A brigand surprises me at the edge of a wood: must I not merely surrender my purse on compulsion; but, even if I could withhold it, am I in conscience bound to give it up? For certainly the pistol he holds is also a power.

Let us then admit that force does not create right, and that we are obliged to obey only legitimate powers. In that case, my original question recurs.

CHAPTER IV

Slavery

Since no man has a natural authority over his fellow, and force creates no right, we must conclude that conventions form the basis of all legitimate authority among men.

If an individual, says Grotius, can alienate his liberty and make himself the slave of a master, why could not a whole people do the same and make itself subject to a king? There are in this passage plenty of ambiguous words which would need explaining; but let us confine ourselves to the word *alienate*. To alienate is to give or to sell. Now, a man who becomes the slave of another does not give himself; he sells himself, at the least for his subsistence: but for what does a people sell itself? A king is so far from furnishing his subjects with their subsistence that he gets his own only from them; and, according to Rabelais, kings do not live on nothing. Do subjects then give their persons on condition that the king takes their goods also? I fail to see what they have left to preserve.

It will be said that the despot assures his subjects civil tranquillity. Granted; but what do they gain, if the wars his ambition brings down upon them, his insatiable avidity, and the vexatious conduct of his ministers press harder on them than their own dissensions would have done? What do they gain, if the very tranquillity they enjoy is one of their miseries? Tranquillity is found also in dungeons; but is that enough to make them desirable places to live in? The Greeks imprisoned in the case of the Cyclops lived there very tranquilly, while they were awaiting their turn to be devoured.

To say that a man gives himself gratuitously, is to say what is absurd and inconceivable; such an act is null and illegitimate, from the mere fact that he who does it is out of his mind. To say the same of a whole people is to suppose a people of madmen; and madness creates no right.

Even if each man could alienate himself, he could not alienate his children: they are born men and free; their liberty belongs to them, and no one but they has the right to dispose of it. Before they come to years of discretion, the father can, in their name, lay down conditions for their preservation and well-being, but he cannot give them irrevocably and without conditions: such

a gift is contrary to the ends of nature, and exceeds the rights of
paternity. It would therefore be necessary, in order to legitimise
an arbitrary government, that in every generation the people
should be in a position to accept or reject it; but, were this so,
the government would be no longer arbitrary.

To renounce liberty is to renounce being a man, to surrender
the rights of humanity and even its duties. For him who re-
nounces everything no indemnity is possible. Such a renunciation
is incompatible with man's nature; to remove all liberty from
his will is to remove all morality from his acts. Finally, it is an
empty and contradictory convention that sets up, on the one
side, absolute authority, and, on the other, unlimited obedience.
Is it not clear that we can be under no obligation to a person
from whom we have the right to exact everything? Does not this
condition alone, in the absence of equivalence or exchange, in
itself involve the nullity of the act? For what right can my slave
have against me, when all that he has belongs to me, and, his
right being mine, this right of mine against myself is a phrase
devoid of meaning?

Grotius and the rest find in war another origin for the so-
called right of slavery. The victor having, as they hold, the right
of killing the vanquished, the latter can buy back his life at the
price of his liberty; and this convention is the more legitimate
because it is to the advantage of both parties.

But it is clear that this supposed right to kill the conquered
is by no means deducible from the state of war. Men, from the
mere fact that, while they are living in their primitive independence, they have no mutual relations stable enough to constitute either the state of peace or the state of war, cannot be
naturally enemies. War is constituted by a relation between
things, and not between persons; and, as the state of war cannot
arise out of simple personal relations, but only out of real
relations, private war, or war of man with man, can exist neither
in the state of nature, where there is no constant property, nor
in the social state, where everything is under the authority of
the laws.

Individual combats, duels and encounters, are acts which
cannot constitute a state; while the private wars, authorised by
the Establishments of Louis IX, King of France, and suspended
by the Peace of God, are abuses of feudalism, in itself an absurd
system if ever there was one, and contrary to the principles of
natural right and to all good polity.

War then is a relation, not between man and man, but

between State and State, and individuals are enemies only accidentally, not as men, nor even as citizens, but as soldiers; not as members of their country, but as its defenders. Finally, each State can have for enemies only other States, and not men; for between things disparate in nature there can be no real relation.

Furthermore, this principle is in conformity with the established rules of all times and the constant practice of all civilised peoples. Declarations of war are intimations less to powers than to their subjects. The foreigner, whether king, individual, or people, who robs, kills or detains the subjects, without declaring war on the prince, is not an enemy, but a brigand. Even in real war, a just prince, while laying hands, in the enemy's country, on all that belongs to the public, respects the lives and goods of individuals: he respects rights on which his own are founded. The object of the war being the destruction of the hostile State, the other side has a right to kill its defenders, while they are bearing arms; but as soon as they lay them down and surrender, they cease to be enemies or instruments of the enemy, and become once more merely men, whose life no one has any right to take. Sometimes it is possible to kill the State without killing a single one of its members; and war gives no right which is not necessary to the gaining of its object. These principles are not those of Grotius: they are not based on the authority of poets, but derived from the nature of reality and based on reason.

The right of conquest has no foundation other than the right of the strongest. If war does not give the conqueror the right to massacre the conquered peoples, the right to enslave them cannot be based upon a right which does not exist. No one has a right to kill an enemy except when he cannot make him a slave, and the right to enslave him cannot therefore be derived from the right to kill him. It is accordingly an unfair exchange to make him buy at the price of his liberty his life, over which the victor holds no right. Is it not clear that there is a vicious circle in founding the right of life and death on the right of slavery, and the right of slavery on the right of life and death?

Even if we assume this terrible right to kill everybody, I maintain that a slave made in war, or a conquered people, is under no obligation to a master, except to obey him as far as he is compelled to do so. By taking an equivalent for his life, the victor has not done him a favour; instead of killing him without profit, he has killed him usefully. So far then is he from acquiring over him any authority in addition to that of force, that the state of war continues to subsist between them: their mutual relation is the effect of it, and the usage of the right of war does not imply a treaty of peace. A convention has indeed been made; but this convention, so far from destroying the state of war, pre-supposes its continuance.

So, from whatever aspect we regard the question, the right of slavery is null and void, not only as being illegitimate, but also because it is absurd and meaningless. The words *slave* and *right* contradict each other, and are mutually exclusive. It will always be equally foolish for a man to say to a man or to a people: "I make with you a convention wholly at your expense and wholly to my advantage; I shall keep it as long as I like, and you will keep it as long as I like."

CHAPTER V

That We Must Always Go Back to a First Convention

Even if I granted all that I have been refuting, the friends of despotism would be no better off. There will always be a great difference between subduing a multitude and ruling a society. Even if scattered individuals were successively enslaved by one man, however numerous they might be, I still see no more than a master and his slaves, and certainly not a people and its ruler; I see what may be termed an aggregation, but not an association; there is as yet neither public good nor body politic. The man in question, even if he has enslaved half the world, is still only an individual; his interest, apart from that of others, is still a purely private interest. If this same man comes to die, his empire, after him, remains scattered and without unity, as an oak falls and dissolves into a heap of ashes when the fire has consumed it.

A people, says Grotius, can give itself to a king. Then, according to Grotius, a people is a people before it gives itself. The gift is itself a civil act, and implies public deliberation. It would be better, before examining the act by which a people gives itself to a king, to examine that by which it has become a people; for this act, being necessarily prior to the other, is the true foundation of society.

Indeed, if there were no prior convention, where, unless the election were unanimous, would be the obligation on the minor-ity to submit to the choice of the majority? How have a hundred men who wish for a master the right to vote on behalf of ten who do not? The law of majority voting is itself something established by convention, and presupposes unanimity, on one occasion at least.

CHAPTER VI

The Social Compact

I suppose men to have reached the point at which the obstacles in the way of their preservation in the state of nature show their power of resistance to be greater than the resources at the disposal of each individual for his maintenance in that state. That primitive condition can then subsist no longer; and the human race would perish unless it changed its manner of existence.

But, as men cannot engender new forces, but only unite and direct existing ones, they have no other means of preserving themselves than the formation, by aggregation, of a sum of forces great enough to overcome the resistance. These they have to bring into play by means of a single motive power, and cause to act in concert.

This sum of forces can arise only where several persons come together: but, as the force and liberty of each man are the chief instruments of his self-preservation, how can he pledge them without harming his own interests, and neglecting the care he owes to himself? This difficulty, in its bearing on my present subject, may be stated in the following terms—

"The problem is to find a form of association which will defend and protect with the whole common force the person and goods of each associate, and in which each, while uniting himself with all, may still obey himself alone, and remain as free as before." This is the fundamental problem of which the *Social Contract* provides the solution.

The clauses of this contract are so determined by the nature of the act that the slightest modification would make them vain and ineffective; so that, although they have perhaps never been formally set forth, they are everywhere the same and everywhere tacitly admitted and recognised, until, on the violation of the social compact, each regains his original rights and resumes his natural liberty, while losing the conventional liberty in favour of which he renounced it.

These clauses, properly understood, may be reduced to one—

the total alienation of each associate, together with all his rights, to the whole community; for, in the first place, as each gives himself absolutely, the conditions are the same for all; and, this being so, no one has any interest in making them burdensome to others.

Moreover, the alienation being without reserve, the union is as perfect as it can be, and no associate has anything more to demand: for, if the individuals retained certain rights, as there would be no common superior to decide between them and the public, each, being on one point his own judge, would ask to be so on all; the state of nature would thus continue, and the association would necessarily become inoperative or tyrannical.

Finally, each man, in giving himself to all, gives himself to nobody; and as there is no associate over whom he does not acquire the same right as he yields others over himself, he gains an equivalent for everything he loses, and an increase of force for the preservation of what he has.

If then we discard from the social compact what is not of its essence, we shall find that it reduces itself to the following terms—

"Each of us puts his person and all his power in common under the supreme direction of the general will, and, in our corporate capacity, we receive each member as an indivisible part of the whole."

At once, in place of the individual personality of each contracting party, this act of association creates a moral and collective body, composed of as many members as the assembly contains votes, and receiving from this act its unity, its common identity, its life and its will. This public person, so formed by the union of all other persons, formerly took the name of *city*, and now takes that of *Republic* or *body politic*; it is called by its members *State* when passive, *Sovereign* when active, and *Power* when compared with others like itself. Those who are associated in it take collectively the name of *people*, and severally are called *citizens*, as sharing in the sovereign power, and *subjects*, as being under the laws of the State. But these terms are often confused and taken one for another: it is enough to know how to distinguish them when they are being used with precision.

CHAPTER VII

The Sovereign

This formula shows us that the act of association comprises a mutual undertaking between the public and the individuals, and that each individual, in making a contract, as we may say, with himself, is bound in a double capacity; as a member of the Sovereign he is bound to the individuals, and as a member of the State to the Sovereign. But the maxim of civil right, that no one is bound by undertakings made to himself, does not apply in this case; for there is a great difference between incurring an obligation to yourself and incurring one to a whole of which you form a part.

Attention must further be called to the fact that public deliberation, while competent to bind all the subjects to the Sovereign, because of the two different capacities in which each of them may be regarded, cannot, for the opposite reason, bind the Sovereign to itself; and that it is consequently against the nature of the body politic for the Sovereign to impose on itself a law which it cannot infringe. Being able to regard itself in only one capacity, it is in the position of an individual who makes a contract with himself; and this makes it clear that there neither is nor can be any kind of fundamental law binding on the body of the people—not even the social contract itself. This does not mean that the body politic cannot enter into undertakings with others, provided the contract is not infringed by them; for in relation to what is external to it, it becomes a simple being, an individual.

But the body politic or the Sovereign, drawing its being wholly from the sanctity of the contract, can never bind itself, even to an outsider, to do anything derogatory to the original act, for instance, to alienate any part of itself, or to submit to another Sovereign. Violation of the act by which it exists would be self-annihilation; and that which is itself nothing can create nothing.

As soon as this multitude is so united in one body, it is impossible to offend against one of the members without attacking the body, and still more to offend against the body without the members resenting it. Duty and interest therefore equally oblige the two contracting parties to give each other help; and the same men should seek to combine, in their double capacity, all the advantages dependent upon that capacity.

Again, the Sovereign, being formed wholly of the individuals who compose it, neither has nor can have any interest contrary to theirs; and consequently the sovereign power need give no guarantee to its subjects, because it is impossible for the body to wish to hurt all its members. We shall also see later on that it cannot hurt any in particular. The Sovereign, merely by virtue of what it is, is always what it should be.

This, however, is not the case with the relation of the subjects to the Sovereign, which, despite the common interest, would have no security that they would fulfill their undertakings, unless it found means to assure itself of their fidelity.

In fact, each individual, as a man, may have a particular will contrary or dissimilar to the general will which he has as a citizen. His particular interest may speak to him quite differently from the common interest: his absolute and naturally independent existence may make him look upon what he owes to the common cause as a gratuitous contribution, the loss of which do less harm to others than the payment of it is burdensome to himself; and, regarding the moral person who constitutes the State as a *persona ficta,* because not a man, he may wish to enjoy the rights of citizenship without being ready to fulfil the duties of a subject. The continuance of such an injustice could not but prove the undoing of the body politic.

In order then that the social compact may not be an empty formula, it tacitly includes the undertaking, which alone can give force to the rest, that whoever refuses to obey the general will shall be compelled to do so by the whole body. This means nothing less than that he will be forced to be free; for this is the condition which, by giving each citizen to his country, secures him against all personal dependence. In this lies the key to the working of the political machine; this alone legitimises civil undertakings, which, without it, would be absurd, tyrannical, and liable to the most frightful abuses.

CHAPTER VIII

The Civil State

The passage from the state of nature to the civil state produces a very remarkable change in man, by substituting justice for instinct in his conduct, and giving his actions the morality they had formerly lacked. Then only, when the voice of duty takes the place of physical impulses and right of appetite, does man, who so far had considered only himself, find that he is forced to act on different principles, and to consult his reason before listening to his inclinations. Although, in this state, he deprives himself of some advantages which he got from nature, he gains in return others so great, his faculties are so stimulated and developed, his ideas so extended, his feelings so ennobled, and his whole soul so uplifted, that, did not the abuses of this new condition often degrade him below that which he left, he would be bound to bless continually the happy moment which took him from it for ever, and, instead of a stupid and unimaginative animal, made him an intelligent being and a man.

Let us draw up the whole account in terms easily commensurable. What man loses by the social contract is his natural liberty and an unlimited right to everything he tries to get and succeeds in getting; what he gains is civil liberty and the proprietorship of all he possesses. If we are to avoid mistake in weighing one against the other, we must clearly distinguish natural liberty, which is bounded only by the strength of the individual, from civil liberty, which is limited by the general will; and possession, which is merely the effect of force or the right of the first occupier, from property, which can be founded only on a positive title.

We might, over and above all this, add, to what man acquires in the civil state, moral liberty, which alone makes him truly master of himself; for the mere impulse of appetite is slavery, while obedience to a law which we prescribe to ourselves is liberty. But I have already said too much on this head, and the philosophical meaning of the word liberty does not now concern us.

CHAPTER IX

Real Property

Each member of the community gives himself to it, at the moment of its foundation, just as he is, with all the resources at his command, including the goods he possesses. This act does not make possession, in changing hands, change its nature, and become property in the hands of the Sovereign; but, as the forces

of the city are incomparably greater than those of an individual,
public possession is also, in fact, stronger and more irrevocable,
without being any more legitimate, at any rate from the point of
view of foreigners. For the State, in relation to its members, is
master of all their goods by the social contract, which, within
the State, is the basis of all rights; but, in relation to other
powers, it is so only by the right of the first occupier, which it
holds from its members.

The right of the first occupier, though more real than the
right of the strongest, becomes a real right only when the right
of property has already been established. Every man has naturally
a right to everything he needs; but the positive act which makes
him proprietor of one thing excludes him from everything else.
Having his share, he ought to keep to it, and can have no further
right against the community. This is why the right of the first
occupier, which in the state of nature is so weak, claims the
respect of every man in civil society. In this right we are respecting not so much what belongs to another as what does not belong
to ourselves.

In general, to establish the right of the first occupier over a
plot of ground, the following conditions are necessary: first, the
land must not yet be inhabited; secondly, a man must occupy
only the amount he needs for his subsistence; and, in the third
place, possession must be taken, not by an empty ceremony, but
by labour and cultivation, the only sign of proprietorship that
should be respected by others, in default of a legal title.

In granting the right of first occupancy to necessity and
labour, are we not really stretching it as far as it can go? Is it
possible to leave such a right unlimited? Is it to be enough to set
foot on a plot of common ground, in order to be able to call
yourself at once the master of it? Is it to be enough that a man
has the strength to expel others for a moment, in order to establish his right to prevent them from ever returning? How can
a man or a people seize an immense territory and keep it from
the rest of the world except by a punishable usurpation, since
all others are being robbed, by such an act, of the place of
habitation and the means of subsistence which nature gave them
in common? When Nunez Balbao, standing on the sea-shore,
took possession of the South Seas and the whole of South America
in the name of the crown of Castille, was that enough to dis-
possess all their actual inhabitants, and to shut out from them all
the princes of the world? On such a showing, these ceremonies
are idly multiplied, and the Catholic King need only take

possession all at once, from his apartment, of the whole universe, merely making a subsequent reservation about what was already in the possession of other princes.

We can imagine how the lands of individuals, where they were contiguous and came to be united, became the public territory, and how the right of Sovereignty, extending from the subjects over the lands they held, became at once real and personal. The possessors were thus made more dependent, and the forces at their command used to guarantee their fidelity. The advantage of this does not seem to have been felt by ancient monarchs, who called themselves King of the Persians, Scythians, or Macedonians, and seemed to regard themselves more as rulers of men than as masters of a country. Those of the present day more cleverly call themselves Kings of France, Spain, England, etc.: thus holding the land, they are quite confident of holding the inhabitants.

The peculiar fact about this alienation is that, in taking over the goods of individuals, the community, so far from despoiling them, only assures them legitimate possession, and changes usurpation into a true right and enjoyment into proprietorship. Thus the possessors, being regarded as depositaries of the public good, and having their rights respected by all the members of the State and maintained against foreign aggression by all its forces, have, by a cession which benefits both the public and still more themselves, acquired, so to speak, all that they gave up. This paradox may easily be explained by the distinction between the rights which the Sovereign and the proprietor have over the same estate, as we shall see later on.

It may also happen that men begin to unite one with another before they possess anything, and that, subsequently occupying a tract of country which is enough for all, they enjoy it in common, or share it out among themselves, either equally or according to a scale fixed by the Sovereign. However the acquisition be made, the right which each individual has to his own estate is always subordinate to the right which the community has over all: without this, there would be neither stability in the social tie, nor real force in the exercise of Sovereignty.

I shall end this chapter and this book by remarking on a fact on which the whole social system should rest: *i.e.* that, instead of destroying natural inequality, the fundamental compact substitutes, for such physical inequality as nature may have set up between men, an equality that is moral and legitimate, and that men, who may be unequal in strength or intelligence, become every one equal by convention and legal right.

READING 2

Representative Government

THE SOVEREIGN, OR GOVERNMENT, or "will of the people" may exist in many forms, for example, monarchy, aristocracy, or democracy. The case for representative government, which may be defined as a "republic," or "representative democracy," is here stated by Mill.

John Stuart Mill (1806-1873) was, with Adam Smith, Thomas Malthus, and David Ricardo, one of the four great "classical" economists. His father, James Mill, a famous economist himself, tutored John Stuart, so that the son received no school education. John Stuart Mill was an accomplished genius: At eight years of age he was a Greek scholar; at thirteen, an economist of reputation. He was employed by the East India Company for three decades. The latter part of his life was devoted chiefly to economic study and writing. His principal economic work was *Principles of Political Economy* (1848), a reformulation of classical economic doctrine. The reading is in Chapter III, "That the Ideally Best Form of Government Is, Representative Government," pp. 278-283, 287-290, 291-292, from the book *Utilitarianism; On Liberty; and, Representative Government* by John Stuart Mill. Everyman's Library. Reprinted by permission of E. P. Dutton & Co., Inc.

There is no difficulty in showing that the ideally best form of government is that in which the sovereignty, or supreme controlling power in the last resort, is vested in the entire aggregate of the community; every citizen not only having a voice in the exercise of that ultimate sovereignty, but being, at least occasionally, called on to take an actual part in the government, by the personal discharge of some public function, local or general.

To test this proposition, it has to be examined in reference to the two branches into which, as pointed out in the last chapter, the inquiry into the goodness of a government conveniently divides itself, namely, how far it promotes the good management of the affairs of society by means of the existing faculties, moral, intellectual, and active, of its various members, and what is its effect in improving or deteriorating those faculties.

The ideally best form of government, it is scarcely necessary to say, does not mean one which is practicable or eligible in all states of civilisation, but the one which, in the circumstances in which it is practicable and eligible, is attended with the greatest amount of beneficial consequences, immediate and prospective. A completely popular government is the only polity which can make out any claim to this character. It is pre-eminent in both the departments between which the excellence of a political constitution is divided. It is both more favourable to present good government, and promotes a better and higher form of national character, than any other polity whatsoever.

Its superiority in reference to present well-being rests upon two principles, of as universal truth and applicability as any general propositions which can be laid down respecting human affairs. The first is, that the rights and interests of every or any person are only secure from being disregarded when the person interested is himself able, and habitually disposed, to stand up for them. The second is, that the general prosperity attains a greater height, and is more widely diffused, in proportion to the amount and variety of the personal energies enlisted in promoting it.

Putting these two propositions into a shape more special to their present application; human beings are only secure from evil at the hands of others in proportion as they have the power of being, and are, self-*protecting*; and they only achieve a high degree of success in their struggle with Nature in proportion as they are self-*dependent,* relying on what they themselves can do, either separately or in concert, rather than on what others do for them.

The former proposition—that each is the only safe guardian of his own rights and interests—is one of those elementary maxims of prudence, which every person, capable of conducting his own affairs, implicitly acts upon, wherever he himself is interested. Many, indeed, have a great dislike to it as a political doctrine, and are fond of holding it up to obloquy, as a doctrine of universal selfishness. To which we may answer, that whenever it ceases to be true that mankind, as a rule, prefer themselves to others, and those nearest to them to those more remote, from that moment Communism is not only practicable, but the only defensible form of society; and will, when that time arrives, be assuredly carried into effect. For my own part, not believing in universal selfishness, I have no difficulty in admitting that Communism would even now be practicable among the *elite* of mankind, and may become so among the rest. But as this opinion is anything but popular with those defenders of existing institutions who find fault with the doctrine of the general predominance of self-interest, I am inclined to think they do in reality believe that most men consider themselves before other people. It is not, however, necessary to affirm even thus much in order to support the claim of all to participate in the sovereign power. We need not suppose that when power resides in an exclusive class, that class will knowingly and deliberately sacrifice the other classes to themselves: it suffices that, in the absence of its natural defenders, the interest of the excluded is always in danger of being overlooked; and, when looked at, is seen with very different eyes from those of the persons whom it directly concerns. In this country, for example, what are called the working classes may be considered as excluded from all direct participation in the government. I do not believe that the classes who do participate in it have in general any intention of sacrificing the working classes to themselves. They once had that intention; witness the persevering attempts so long made to keep down wages by law. But in the present day their ordinary disposition is the very opposite: they willingly make considerable sacrifices, especially of their pecuniary interest, for the benefit of the working classes, and err rather by too lavish and indiscriminating beneficence; nor do I believe that any rulers in history have been actuated by a more sincere desire to do their duty towards the poorer portion of their countrymen. Yet does Parliament, or almost any of the members composing it, ever for an instant look at any question with the eyes of a working man? When a subject arises in which the labourers as such have an interest, is it regarded from any point of view but that of the employers of labour? I do not say that the working men's view of these questions is in general nearer to the truth than the other: but it is sometimes quite as near; and in any case it ought to be respectfully listened to, instead of being, as it is, not merely turned away from, but ignored. On the question of strikes, for instance, it is doubtful if there is so much as one among the leading members of either House who is not firmly convinced that the reason of the matter is unqualifiedly on the side of the masters, and that the men's view of it is simply absurd. Those who have studied the question know well how far this is from being the case; and in how different, and how infinitely less superficial a manner the point would have to be argued, if the classes who strike were able to make themselves heard in Parliament.

It is an adherent condition of human affairs that no intention, however sincere, of protecting the interests of others can make it safe or salutary to tie up their own hands. Still more obviously true is it, that by their own hands only can any positive and durable improvement of their circumstances in life be worked out. Through the joint influence of these two principles, all free communities have both been more exempt from social injustice and crime, and have attained more brilliant prosperity, than any others, or than they themselves after they lost their freedom. Contrast the free states of the world, while their freedom lasted, with the cotemporary subjects of monarchical or oligarchical despotism: the Greek cities with the Persian satrapies; the Italian republics and the free towns of Flanders and Germany, with the feudal monarchies of Europe; Switzerland, Holland, and England, with Austria or ante-revolutionary France. Their superior prosperity was too obvious ever to have been gainsaid: while their superiority in good government and social relations is proved by the prosperity, and is manifest besides in every page of history. If we compare, not one age with another, but the different governments which co-existed in the same age, no amount of disorder which exaggeration itself can pretend to have existed amidst the publicity of the free states can be compared for a moment with the contemptuous trampling upon the mass of the people which pervaded the whole life of the monarchical countries, or the disgusting individual tyranny which was of more than daily occurrence under the systems of plunder which they called fiscal arrangements, and in the secrecy of their frightful courts of justice.

It must be acknowledged that the benefits of freedom, so far as they have hitherto been enjoyed, were obtained by the extension of its privileges to a part only of the community; and that a government in which they are extended impartially to all is a desideratum still unrealised. But though every approach to this has an independent value, and in many cases more than an approach could not, in the existing state of general improvement, be made, the participation of all in these benefits is the ideally perfect conception of free government. In proportion as any, no matter who, are excluded from it, the interests of the excluded are left without the guarantee accorded to the rest, and they themselves have less scope and encouragement than they might otherwise have to that exertion of their energies for the good of themselves and of the community, to which the general prosperity is always proportioned.

Thus stands the case as regards present well-being; the good management of the affairs of the existing generation. If we now pass to the influence of the form of government upon character, we shall find the superiority of popular government over every other to be, if possible, still more decided and indisputable.

This question really depends upon a still more fundamental one, viz., which of two common types of character, for the general good of humanity, it is most desirable should predominate—the active, or the passive type; that which struggles against evils, or that which endures them; that which bends to circumstances, or that which endeavours to make circumstances bend to itself.

The commonplaces of moralists, and the general sympathies of mankind, are in favour of the passive type. Energetic characters may be admired, but the acquiescent and submissive are those which most men personally prefer. The passiveness of our neighbours increases our sense of security, and plays into the hands of our wilfulness. Passive characters, if we do not happen to need their activity, seem an obstruction the less in our own path. A contented character is not a dangerous rival. Yet nothing is more certain than that improvement in human affairs is wholly the work of the uncontented characters; and, moreover, that it is much easier for an active mind to acquire the virtues of patience than for a passive one to assume those of energy.

*   *   *

The striving, go-ahead character of England and the United States is only a fit subject of disapproving criticism on account of the very secondary objects on which it commonly expends its strength. In itself it is the foundation of the best hopes for the general improvement of mankind. It has been acutely remarked that whenever anything goes amiss the habitual impulse of French people is to say, "Il faut de la patience;" and of English people, "What a shame." The people who think it a shame when anything goes wrong—who rush to the conclusion that the evil could and ought to have been prevented, are those who, in the long run, do most to make the world better. If the desires are low placed, if they extend to little beyond physical comfort, and the show of riches, the immediate results of the energy will not be much more than the continual extension of man's power over material objects; but even this makes room, and prepares the mechanical appliances, for the greatest intellectual and social achievements; and while the energy is there, some persons will apply it, and it will be applied more and more, to the perfecting not of outward circumstances alone, but of man's inward nature. Inactivity, unaspiringness, absence of desire, are a more fatal hindrance to improvement than any misdirection of energy; and are that through which alone, when existing in the mass, any very formidable misdirection by an energetic few becomes possible. It is this, mainly, which retains in a savage or semi-savage state the great majority of the human race.

Now there can be no kind of doubt that the passive type of character is favoured by the government of one or a few, and the active self-helping type by that of the Many. Irresponsible rulers need the quiescence of the ruled more than they need any activity but that which they can compel. Submissiveness to the prescriptions of men as necessities of nature is the lesson inculcated by all governments upon those who are wholly without participation in them. The will of superiors, and the law as the will of superiors, must be passively yielded to. But no men are mere instruments or materials in the hands of their rulers who have will or spirit or a spring of internal activity in the rest of their proceedings: and any manifestation of these qualities, instead of receiving encouragement from despots, has to get itself forgiven by them. Even when irresponsible rulers are not sufficiently conscious of danger from the mental activity of their subjects to be desirous of repressing it, the position itself is a repression. Endeavour is even more effectually restrained by the certainty of its impotence than by any positive discouragement. Between subjection to the will of others, and the virtues of self-help and self-government, there is a natural incompatibility. This is more or less complete, according as the bondage is strained or relaxed. Rulers differ very much in the length to which they carry the control of the free agency of their subjects, or the supersession of it by managing their business for them. But the difference is in degree, not in principle; and the best despots often go the greatest lengths in chaining up the free agency of their subjects. A bad despot, when his own personal indulgences have been provided for, may sometimes be willing to let the people alone; but a good despot insists on doing them good, by making them do their own business in a better way than they themselves know of. The regulations which restricted to fixed processes all the leading branches of French manufactures were the work of the great Colbert.

Very different is the state of the human faculties where a human being feels himself under no other external restraint than the necessities of nature, or mandates of society which he has his share in imposing, and which it is open to him, if he thinks them wrong, publicly to dissent from, and exert himself actively to get altered. No doubt, under a government partially popular, this freedom may be exercised even by those who are not partakers in the full privileges of citizenship. But it is a great additional stimulus to any one's self-help and self-reliance when he starts from even ground, and has not to feel that his success depends on the impression he can make upon the sentiments and dispositions of a body of whom he is not one. It is a great discouragement to an individual, and a still greater one to a class, to be left out of the constitution; to be reduced to plead from outside the door to the arbiters of their destiny, not taken into consultation within. The maximum of the invigorating effect of freedom upon the character is only obtained when the person acted on either is, or is looking forward to becoming, a citizen as fully privileged as any other. What is still more important than even this matter of feeling is the practical discipline which the character obtains from the occasional demand made upon the citizens to exercise, for a time and in their turn, some social function. It is not sufficiently considered how little there is in most men's ordinary life to give any largeness either to their conceptions or to their sentiments. Their work is a routine; not a labour of love, but of self-interest in the most elementary form, the satisfaction of daily wants; neither the thing done, nor the process of doing it, introduces the mind to thoughts or feelings extending beyond individuals; if instructive books are within their reach, there is no stimulus to read them; and in most cases the individual has no access to any person of cultivation much superior to his own. Giving him something to do for the public, supplies, in a measure, all these deficiencies. If circumstances allow the amount of public duty assigned him to be considerable, it makes him an educated man.

* * *

From these accumulated considerations it is evident that the only government which can fully satisfy all the exigencies of the social state is one in which the whole people participate;

that any participation, even in the smallest public function, is useful; that the participation should everywhere be as great as the general degree of improvement of the community will allow; and that nothing less can be ultimately desirable than the admission of all to a share in the sovereign power of the state. But since all cannot, in a community exceeding a single small town, participate personally in any but some very minor portions of the public business, it follows that the ideal type of a perfect government must be representative.

READING 3

The "Just" Price

THE INFLUENCE OF Christian ethics permeates the modern economy. Our laws concerning "fair trade practices," our doctrines of "fair wages" and "fair prices" stem essentially from ethical judgments as to fair treatment by each man of his neighbor. The doctrine that a "just price" should exist for each article offered for sale was stated most aptly by Thomas Aquinas during the Middle Ages.

The "just price" for an article was considered its cost of production represented chiefly by labor cost. A man adding usefulness to an article may charge, therefore, a higher price than he had paid for it—the difference rewarding him for his labor. A higher price could be charged for a good than was paid for it to compensate for the adding of time and place utilities as well as for the adding of form utilities. On the other hand, however, it was considered unethical to sell a thing for more than its original cost plus the value added to it. Aquinas' stand, therefore, was that goods that are sold for "as much as the market will bear" are sold at "unfair," or "unjust," prices.

Thomas Aquinas attempted, and was successful to a marked degree, to weld the teachings of the Bible and the teachings of Aristotle into a single body of thought which would give humanity rules by which to act on all occasions. The pattern Aquinas used in presenting his doctrines is illustrated in the following reading. He states a question and then a series of objections to the statement implied in the question. Following the objections he states his own position. The proof of his position is then presented in his replies to the objections.

Thomas Aquinas (1227?-1274), the "prince of scholasticists," was educated in a monastery in Italy, following which he studied at the University of Naples, Cologne, and Paris. His teacher was the great theologian, Albertus Magnus. He wrote extensively, but his chief work was the monumental *Summa Theologica*. His work exerted not only a great influence upon men's actions during the Middle Ages, but has served as standards of morality to the present day. The reading is from *The Summa Theologica of Saint Thomas Aquinas,* literally translated by Fathers of the English Dominican Province, Part II (Second Part), Volume 10 (London: Burns Oates & Washbourne Ltd., 1912-25), pp. 317-320, 326-328. Reprinted by permission of Benziger Brothers, Inc., publishers, New York.

Question LXXVII.

OF CHEATING, WHICH IS COMMITTED IN BUYING AND SELLING.

First Article.

Whether It is Lawful to Sell a Thing for More Than Its [sic] Worth?

We proceed thus to the First Article:—

Objection 1. It would seem that it is lawful to sell a thing for more than its worth. In the commutations of human life, civil laws determine that which is just. Now according to these laws it is just for buyer and seller to deceive one another (Cod., IV., xliv., *De Rescind. Vend.* 8, 15): and this occurs by the seller selling a thing for more than its worth, and the buyer buying a thing for less than its worth. Therefore it is lawful to sell a thing for more than its worth.

Obj. 2. Further, That which is common to all would seem to be natural and not sinful. Now Augustine relates that the saying of a certain jester was accepted by all, *You wish to buy for a song and to sell at a premium,* which agrees with the saying of Prov. xx. 14, *It is naught, it is naught, saith every buyer: and when he is gone away, then he will boast.* Therefore it is lawful to sell a thing for more than its worth.

Obj. 3. Further, It does not seem unlawful if that which honesty demands be done by mutual agreement. Now, according to the Philosopher [Aristotle] (*Ethic.* viii. 13), in the friendship which is based on utility, the amount of the recompense for a favour received should depend on the utility accruing to the receiver: and this utility sometimes is worth more than the thing given, for instance if the receiver be in great need of that thing, whether for the purpose of avoiding a danger, or of deriving some particular benefit. Therefore, in contracts of buying and selling, it is lawful to give a thing in return for more than its worth.

On the contrary, It is written (Matth. vii. 12): *All things . . . whatsoever you would that men should do to you, do you also to them.* But no man wishes to buy a thing for more than its worth. Therefore no man should sell a thing to another man for more than its worth.

I answer that, It is altogether sinful to have recourse to deceit in order to sell a thing for more than its just price, because this is to deceive one's neighbour so as to injure him. Hence Tully says (*De Offic.* iii. 15): *Contracts should be entirely free from double-dealing; the seller must not impose upon the bidder, nor the buyer upon one that bids against him.*

But, apart from fraud, we may speak of buying and selling in two ways. First, as considered in themselves, and from this point of view, buying and selling seem to be established for the common advantage of both parties, one of whom requires that which belongs to the other, and vice versa, as the Philosopher states (*Polit.* i. 3). Now whatever is established for the common advantage, should not be more of a burden to one party than to another, and consequently all contracts between them should observe equality of thing and thing. Again, the quality of a thing that comes into human use is measured by the price given for it, for which purpose money was invented, as stated in *Ethic.* v. 5. Therefore if either the price exceed the quantity of the thing's worth, or, conversely, the thing exceed the price, there is no longer the equality of justice: and consequently, to sell a thing for more than its worth, or to buy it for less than its worth, is in itself unjust and unlawful.

Secondly we may speak of buying and selling, considered as

accidentally tending to the advantage of one party, and to the disadvantage of the other: for instance, when a man has great need of a certain thing, while another man will suffer if he be without it. In such a case the just price will depend not only on the thing sold, but on the loss which the sale brings on the seller. And thus it will be lawful to sell a thing for more than it is worth in itself, though the price paid be not more than it is worth to the owner. Yet if the one man derive a great advantage by becoming possessed of the other man's property, and the seller be not at a loss through being without that thing, the latter ought not to raise the price, because the advantage accruing to the buyer, is not due to the seller, but to a circumstance affecting the buyer. Now no man should sell what is not his, though he may charge for the loss he suffers.

On the other hand if a man find that he derives great advantage from something he has bought, he may, of his own accord, pay the seller something over and above: and this pertains to his honesty.

Reply Obj. 1. As stated above (I.-II., Q. XCVI., A. 2) human law is given to the people among whom there are many lacking virtue, and it is not given to the virtuous alone. Hence human law was unable to forbid all that is contrary to virtue; and it suffices for it to prohibit whatever is destructive of human intercourse, while it treats other matters as though they were lawful, not by approving of them, but by not punishing them. Accordingly, if without employing deceit the seller disposes of his goods for more than their worth, or the buyer obtain them for less than their worth, the law looks upon this as licit, and provides no punishment for so doing, unless the excess be too great, because then even human law demands restitution to be made, for instance if a man be deceived in regard of more than half the amount of the just price of a thing.

On the other hand the Divine law leaves nothing unpunished that is contrary to virtue. Hence, according to the Divine law, it is reckoned unlawful if the equality of justice be not observed in buying and selling: and he who has received more than he ought must make compensation to him that has suffered loss, if the loss be considerable. I add this condition, because the just price of things is not fixed with mathematical precision, but depends on a kind of estimate, so that a slight addition or subtraction would not seem to destroy the equality of justice.

Reply Obj. 2. As Augustine says (*ibid.*) *this jester, either by looking into himself or by his experience of others, thought that all men are inclined to wish to buy for a song and sell at a premium. But since in reality this is wicked, it is in every man's power to acquire that justice whereby he may resist and overcome this inclination.* And then he gives the example of a man who gave the just price for a book to a man who through ignorance asked a low price for it. Hence it is evident that this common desire is not from nature but from vice, wherefore it is common to many who walk along the broad road of sin.

Reply Obj. 3. In commutative justice we consider chiefly real equality. On the other hand, in friendship based on utility we consider equality of usefulness, so that the recompense should depend on the usefulness accruing, whereas in buying it should be equal to the thing bought.

*   *   *

Fourth Article.

Whether, in Trading, It Is Lawful to Sell a Thing at a Higher Price than What Was Paid for It?

We proceed thus to the Fourth Article:—

Objection 1. It would seem that it is not lawful, in trading, to sell a thing for a higher price than we paid for it. For Chrysostom[1] says on Matth. xxi. 12: *He that buys a thing in order that he may sell it, entire and unchanged, at a profit, is the trader who is cast out of God's temple.* Cassiodorus speaks in the same sense in his commentary on Ps. lxx. 15, *Because I have not known learning,* or *trading according to another version:*[2] *What is trade,* says he, *but buying at a cheap price with the purpose of retailing at a higher price?* and he adds: *Such were the tradesmen whom Our Lord cast out of the temple.* Now no man is cast out of the temple except for a sin. Therefore suchlike trading is sinful.

Obj. 2. Further, It is contrary to justice to sell goods at a higher price than their worth, or to buy them for less than their value, as shown above (A. 1). Now if you sell a thing for a higher price than you paid for it, you must either have bought it for

---

[1] *Hom.* xxxviii. in the *Opus Imperfectum,* falsely ascribed to S. John Chrysostom.
[2] The Septuagint.

less than its value, or sell it for more than its value. Therefore this cannot be done without sin.

Obj. 3. Further, Jerome says (*Ep. ad Nepot.* lii.): *Shun, as you would the plague, a cleric who from being poor has become wealthy, or who, from being a nobody has become a celebrity.* Now trading would not seem to be forbidden to clerics except on account of its sinfulness. Therefore it is a sin in trading, to buy at a low price and to sell at a higher price.

On the contrary, Augustine commenting on Ps. lxx. 15, *Because I have not known learning*, says: *The greedy tradesman blasphemes over his losses; he lies and perjures himself over the price of his wares. But these are vices of the man, not of the craft, which can be exercised without these vices.* Therefore trading is not in itself unlawful.

I answer that, A tradesman is one whose business consists in the exchange of things. According to the Philosopher (*Polit.* i. 3), exchange of things is twofold; one, natural as it were, and necessary, whereby one commodity is exchanged for another, or money taken in exchange for a commodity, in order to satisfy the needs of life. Suchlike trading, properly speaking, does not belong to tradesmen, but rather to housekeepers or civil servants who have to provide the household or the state with the necessaries of life. The other kind of exchange is either that of money for money, or of any commodity for money, not on account of the necessities of life, but for profit, and this kind of exchange, properly speaking, regards tradesmen, according to the Philosopher (*Polit.* i. 3). The former kind of exchange is commendable because it supplies a natural need: but the latter is justly deserving of blame, because, considered in itself, it satisfies the greed for gain, which knows no limit and tends to infinity. Hence trading, considered in itself, has a certain debasement attaching thereto, in so far as, by its very nature, it does not imply a virtuous or necessary end. Nevertheless gain which is the end of trading, though not implying, by its nature, anything virtuous or necessary, does not, in itself, connote anything sinful or contrary to virtue: wherefore nothing prevents gain from being directed to some necessary or even virtuous end, and thus trading becomes lawful. Thus, for instance, a man may intend the moderate gain which he seeks to acquire by trading for the upkeep of his household, or for the assistance of the needy: or again, a man may take to trade for some public advantage, for instance, lest his country lack the necessaries of life, and seek gain, not as an end, but as payment for his labour.

Reply Obj. 1. The saying of Chrysostom refers to the trading which seeks gain as a last end. This is especially the case where a man sells something at a higher price without its undergoing any change. For if he sells at a higher price something that has changed for the better, he would seem to receive the reward of his labour. Nevertheless the gain itself may be lawfully intended, not as a last end, but for the sake of some other end which is necessary or virtuous, as stated above.

Reply Obj. 2. Not everyone that sells at a higher price than he bought is a tradesman, but only he who buys that he may sell at a profit. If, on the contrary, he buys not for sale but for possession, and afterwards, for some reason wishes to sell, it is not a trade transaction even if he sell at a profit. For he may lawfully do this, either because he has bettered the thing, or because the value of the thing has changed with the change of place or time, or on account of the danger he incurs in transferring the thing from one place to another, or again in having it carried by another. In this sense neither buying nor selling is unjust.

Reply Obj. 3. Clerics should abstain not only from things that are evil in themselves, but even from those that have an appearance of evil. This happens in trading, both because it is directed to worldly gain, which clerics should despise, and because trading is open to so many vices, since *a merchant is hardly free from sins of the lips* (Ecclus. xxvi. 28). There is also another reason, because trading engages the mind too much with worldly cares, and consequently withdraws it from spiritual cares; wherefore the Apostle says (2 Tim. ii. 4): *No man being a soldier to God entangleth himself with secular businesses.* Nevertheless it is lawful for clerics to engage in the first mentioned kind of exchange, which is directed to supply the necessaries of life, either by buying or by selling.

READING 4

Utility

THE POWERFUL STATEMENT by Jeremy Bentham of the principle
of utility, variously called the "doctrine of pleasure and pain,"
"utilitarianism," and "hedonism," is here given as stated in 1789.
This principle is fundamental to understanding "economic man,"
that individual who supposedly acts in the ordinary business of
life in his own "self-interest." It is fundamental to an understanding of "laissez-faire" economics, of "individualism," indeed of
economics from Adam Smith to the present day.

Hedonism has been vastly criticized and belabored as an
"un-Christian" ethic and as a statement of the dismal aspect of
mankind. The idea is indeed one that is in some part responsible
for economics being designated "that dismal science." Certainly
a man acting always to maximize his pleasures (meaning happiness, well-being, etc.) or to minimize his pains (misfortunes, etc.)
would seem anything but a Godlike creature. But Bentham does
not maintain this: he does not say "always" or "invariably"; he
implies "usually." We can perhaps think of examples in which
individuals have chosen the painful course; but Bentham would
often be able to point out that the alternative was possibly worse,
and his principle still valid. Thus, for example, the Christian
martyr in the lion's den who had chosen death—might not the
alternative to death have been even more painful to him?

Jeremy Bentham (1748-1832) was an English philosopher.
Having inherited wealth, he spent his life in study and writing.
Although trained in law, he never practiced. His essays on law
and government had considerable influence in England. In economics his chief contribution was in "utilitarianism." The reading is from *An Introduction to the Principles of Morals and
Legislation* (Oxford: The Clarendon Press, 1907, a reprint of the
author's last edition of 1823, 378 pp.), Chapter I, "Of the Principle of Utility," pp. 1-7. Reprinted by permission.

Nature has placed mankind under the governance of two sovereign masters, *pain* and *pleasure*. It is for them alone to point out what we ought to do as well as to determine what we shall do. On the one hand the standard of right and wrong, on the other the chain of causes and effects, are fastened to their throne. They govern us in all we do, in all we say, in all we think: every effort we can make to throw off our subjection, will serve but to demonstrate and confirm it. In words a man may pretend to abjure their empire: but in reality he will remain subject to it all the while. The *principle of utility* recognises this subjection, and assumes it for the foundation of that system, the object of which is to rear the fabric of felicity by the hands of reason and law. Systems which attempt to question it, deal in sounds instead of sense, in caprice instead of reason, in darkness instead of light.

But enough of metaphor and declamation: it is not by such means that moral science is to be improved.

The principle of utility is the foundation of the present work: it will be proper therefore at the outset to give an explicit and determinate account of what is meant by it. By the principle of utility is meant that principle which approves or disapproves of every action whatsoever, according to the tendency which it appears to have to augment or diminish the happiness of the party whose interest is in question: or, what is the same thing in other words, to promote or to oppose that happiness. I say of every action whatsoever; and therefore not only of every action of a private individual, but of every measure of government.

By utility is meant that property in any object, whereby it tends to produce benefit, advantage, pleasure, good, or happiness, (all this in the present case comes to the same thing) or (what comes again to the same thing) to prevent the happening of mischief, pain, evil, or unhappiness to the party whose interest is considered: if that party be the community in general, then the happiness of the community: if a particular individual, then the happiness of that individual.

The interest of the community is one of the most general expressions that can occur in the phraseology of morals: no wonder that the meaning of it is often lost. When it has a meaning, it is this. The community is a fictitious *body*, composed of the individual persons who are considered as constituting as it were its *members*. The interest of the community then is, what?—the sum of the interests of the several members who compose it.

It is in vain to talk of the interest of the community, without understanding what is the interest of the individual. A thing is said to promote the interest, or to be *for* the interest, of an individual, when it tends to add to the sum total of his pleasures: or, what comes to the same thing, to diminish the sum total of his pains.

An action then may be said to be conformable to the principle of utility, or, for shortness sake, to utility, (meaning with respect to the community at large) when the tendency it has to augment the happiness of the community is greater than any it has to diminish it.

A measure of government (which is but a particular kind of action, performed by a particular person or persons) may be said to be conformable to or dictated by the principle of utility, when in like manner the tendency which it has to augment the happiness of the community is greater than any which it has to diminish it.

When an action, or in particular a measure of government, is supposed by a man to be conformable to the principle of utility, it may be convenient, for the purposes of discourse, to imagine a kind of law or dictate, called a law or dictate of utility: and to speak of the action in question, as being conformable to such law or dictate.

A man may be said to be a partizan of the principle of utility, when the approbation or disapprobation he annexes to any action, or to any measure, is determined by and proportioned to the tendency which he conceives it to have to augment or to diminish the happiness of the community: or in other words, to its conformity or unconformity to the laws or dictates of utility.

Of an action that is conformable to the principle of utility one may always say either that it is one that ought to be done, or at least that it is not one that ought not to be done. One may say also, that it is right it should be done; at least that it is not wrong it should be done: that it is a right action; at least that it is not a wrong action. When thus interpreted, the words *ought*, and *right* and *wrong*, and others of that stamp, have a meaning: when otherwise, they have none.

Has the rectitude of this principle been ever formally contested? It should seem that it had, by those who have not known what they have been meaning. Is it susceptible of any direct proof? it should seem not: for that which is used to prove every thing else, cannot itself be proved: a chain of proofs must have their commencement somewhere. To give such proof is as impossible as it is needless.

Not that there is or ever has been that human creature breathing, however stupid or perverse, who has not on many, perhaps on most occasions of his life, deferred to it. By the natural constitution of the human frame, on most occasions of their lives men in general embrace this principle, without thinking of it: if not for the ordering of their own actions, yet for the trying of their own actions, as well as those of other men. There have been, at the same time, not many, perhaps, even of the most intelligent, who have been disposed to embrace it purely and without reserve. There are even few who have not taken some occasion or other to quarrel with it, either on account of their not understanding always how to apply it, or on account of some prejudice or other which they were afraid to examine into, or could not bear to part with. For such is the stuff that man is made of: in principle and in practice, in a right track and in a wrong one, the rarest of all human qualities is consistency.

When a man attempts to combat the principle of utility, it is with reasons drawn, without his being aware of it, from that very principle itself. His arguments, if they prove any thing, prove not that the principle is *wrong,* but that, according to the applications he supposes to be made of it, it is *misapplied.* Is it possible for a man to move the earth? Yes; but he must first find out another earth to stand upon.

To disprove the propriety of it by arguments is impossible; but, from the causes that have been mentioned, or from some confused or partial view of it, a man may happen to be disposed not to relish it. Where this is the case, if he thinks the settling of his opinions on such a subject worth the trouble, let him take the following steps, and at length, perhaps, he may come to reconcile himself to it.

1. Let him settle with himself, whether he would wish to discard this principle altogether; if so, let him consider what it is that all his reasonings (in matters of politics especially) can amount to?

2. If he would, let him settle with himself, whether he would judge and act without any principle, or whether there is any other he would judge and act by?

3. If there be, let him examine and satisfy himself whether

the principle he thinks he has found is really any separate intelligible principle; or whether it be not a mere principle in words, a kind of phrase, which at bottom expresses neither more nor less than the mere averment of his own unfounded sentiments; that is, what in another person he might be apt to call caprice?

4. If he is inclined to think that his own approbation or disapprobation, annexed to the idea of an act, without any regard to its consequences, is a sufficient foundation for him to judge and act upon, let him ask himself whether his sentiment is to be a standard of right and wrong, with respect to every other man, or whether every man's sentiment has the same privilege of being a standard to itself?

5. In the first case, let him ask himself whether his principle is not despotical, and hostile to all the rest of human race?

6. In the second case, whether it is not anarchial, and whether at this rate there are not as many different standards of right and wrong as there are men? and whether even to the same man, the same thing, which is right to-day, may not (without the least change in its nature) be wrong to-morrow? and whether the same thing is not right and wrong in the same place at the same time? and in either case, whether all argument is not at an end? and whether, when two men have said, 'I like this,' and 'I don't like it,' then can (upon such a principle) have any thing more to say?

7. If he should have said to himself, No: for that the sentiment which he proposes as a standard must be grounded on reflection, let him say on what particulars the reflection is to turn? If on particulars having relation to the utility of the act, then let him say whether this is not deserting his own principle, and borrowing assistance from that very one in opposition to which he sets it up: or if not on those particulars, on what other particulars?

8. If he should be for compounding the matter, and adopting his own principle in part, and the principle of utility in part, let him say how far he will adopt it?

9. When he has settled with himself where he will stop, then let him ask himself how he justifies to himself the adopting it so far? and why he will not adopt it any farther?

10. Admitting any other principle than the principle of utility to be a right principle, a principle that it is right for a man to pursue; admitting (what is not true) that the word *right* can have a meaning without reference to utility, let him say whether

there is any such thing as a *motive* that a man can have to
pursue the dictates of it: if there is, let him say what that motive
is, and how it is to be distinguished from those which enforce
the dictates of utility: if not, then lastly let him say what it is this
other principle can be good for?

READING 5

Scarcity

THE VALUE OF A COMMODITY can be *measured* only in terms of
other commodities, since values are relative. Such values are
usually expressed in terms of money (money being an option on
the purchase of all other commodities) which we call "prices."
To *possess* value, however, a commodity must be desired by man
and it must be scarce. The importance of scarcity to mankind
cannot be overestimated. It is basic to the "economic problem,"
or the "economic calculus," which is the problem man faces in
attempting to satisfy his wants with means that are scarce. His
wants represent demand, and the scarce means to satisfy them
represent supply. Here, then, is the fundamental source of the
laws of demand and supply: desire and scarcity. In this reading
the possible variations in value are explored, and the great importance of scarcity made clear.

James Maitland, Eighth Earl of Lauderdale (1759-1839) was
a Scottish economist active in British politics. A member of
Parliament for many years, in his early life he was a liberal,
becoming reactionary in his later policies. His chief economic
work was in critical rebuttal of Adam Smith's principles. The
reading is from his most important work, *An Inquiry into the
Nature and Origin of Public Wealth, and into the Means and
Causes of Its Increase* (Edinburgh: Arch. Constable & Co., 1804,
and T. N. Longman & O. Rees, London, 482 pp.), Chapter I,
"Of Value, and the possibility of an accurate Measure of Value,"
pp. 12-21; Chapter II, "Of Public Wealth, of Individual Riches,
and the relation they bear to each other," pp. 43-49.

Experience shews us, that every thing is uniformly considered as valuable which, to the possession of qualities, that make it the object of the desire of man, adds the circumstance of existing in scarcity. To confer value, therefore, two things appear requisite: 1. That the commodity, as being useful or delightful to man, should be an object of his desire: 2. That it should exist in a degree of scarcity.

With respect to the variations in value, of which every thing valuable is susceptible, if we could for a moment suppose that any substance possessed intrinsic and fixed value, so as to render an assumed quantity of it constantly, under all circumstances, of equal value; then the degree of value of all things, ascertained by such a fixed standard, would vary according to the proportion betwixt the quantity of them and the demand for them, and every commodity would of course be subject to a variation in its value from four different circumstances.

1. It would be subject to an increase of its value, from a diminution of its quantity.

2. To a diminution of its value, from an augmentation of its quantity.

3. It might suffer an augmentation in its value, from the circumstance of an increased demand.

4. Its value might be diminished, by a failure of demand.

As it will, however, clearly appear, that no commodity can possess fixed and intrinsic value, so as to qualify it for a measure of the value of other commodities, mankind are reduced to select, as a practical measure of value, that which appears the least liable to any of these four fources of variation, which are the sole causes of alteration of value.

When in common language, therefore, we express the *value* of any commodity, it may vary at one period from what it is at another, in consequence of eight different contingencies.

1. From the four circumstances above stated, in relation to the commodity of which we mean to express the value. And,

2. From the same four circumstances, in relation to the commodity we have adopted as a measure of value.

As the value, therefore, of all commodities depends upon the possession of a quality that makes them the object of man's desire, and the circumstance of their existing in a certain degree of scarcity; it follows that the variation of all value must depend upon the alteration of the proportion betwixt the demand for, and the quantity of, the commodity, occasioned by the occurrence of one of the four circumstances above stated; and that a variation in the expression of value, may be occasioned by the occurrence of any of the eight circumstances we have alluded to. The truth of these propositions may be variously illustrated.

Water, it has been observed, is one of the things most useful to man, yet it seldom possesses any value; and the reason of this is evident: it rarely occurs, that to its quality of utility, is added the circumstance of existing in scarcity: but if, in the course of a siege, or a sea-voyage, it becomes scarce, it instantly acquires value; and its value is subject to the same rule of variation as that of other commodities.

Gold is no where to be found in abundance; but scarcity alone cannot give it value, any more than utility alone can confer value on water. We are accordingly told, that the poor inhabitants of Cuba and St Domingo, when first discovered by the Spaniards, not knowing the use of gold, considered it as little bits of pebble, just worth the picking up, but not worth the refusing to any body that asked it; and that they in reality gave it to their new guests at the first request. But the knowledge of its utility by the Spaniards, and its possessing therefore qualities, that to them made it an object of desire, added to the circumstance of its scarcity, soon gave it value; and the degree of its value came speedily to be fixed even in the minds of the natives, on the same principle as that of food, and of all other commodities.

Though the scarcity of gold and silver, and the demand for them, have made them what is called *most precious,* that is, under the general circumstances of mankind, commodities of the greatest value; yet particular circumstances may occasion such a scarcity of, and demand for, things of a very ordinary nature, as to make them, for a time, of a value superior even to those metals. Thus, as Mr Locke well observes, in a man of war, silver may not be of equal value to gunpowder, and a famine may certainly occasion gold's not being worth its weight in bran.

The value of every thing is so completely dependent upon the proportion betwixt the demand for it and the quantity of it, that the possession of no quality, whatever excellence it might add to a commodity, could produce any material alteration in its value, if it did not affect either the demand for it, or the quantity of it. Supposing there could be conferred on Corn the important attribute, that one grain, when given to an infant on the day of its birth, should secure a century of robust health; (though it is certain there could not be added to it a qualification more to the general taste of mankind), yet, as this would produce no alteration in the quantity of grain, and, from the small quantity that would be thus consumed, hardly any perceptible increase in the demand for it, we should not be able to discern any variation in its value.

So little has the quality of things to do with their value, that it very often happens, when a commodity possesses, in the highest degree of perfection, all the qualities which make it desirable, its value is the lowest; and when, on the contrary, it possesses them in a very inferior degree, its value is the highest. This is almost constantly the case with Grain. In a fine season it is always of a superior, in a bad season of an inferior quality; yet, as the fine season generally produces an increased, and a bad season a diminished quantity; with a thorough contempt of the quality, the value of the corn is always regulated on the principle here stated; and the greatness of the quantity, though of superior quality, reduces its value; whilst the diminution of its quantity, though of very inferior quality, increases the value in the market.

The value of Cattle, though the recommendations with regard to bread, fatness, and every other quality that renders them desirable, and even the number of them should remain unaltered, is always found to vary in proportion to the scarcity or abundance of the food on which they are nourished. The value of certain inferior species of grain is also often increased, without any alteration either of the quantity or quality of it, but merely in consequence of an augmentation of demand, arising from a scarcity of the better sorts of grain, which usually form the bread of the community.

We have often occasion to observe that, whilst a web of cloth or a piece of silk have sold at very considerable prices, if there remains a small quantity of them, this Remnant, as it is called, brings a very inferior price to what was given for the greater part of the same cloth, and of the same piece of silk. On the other hand, a small quantity of stock, in the 3 or 4 *per cents,* is uniformly sold in the Alley above the market-price of the commodity; and yet the small pieces of silk and cloth are of the same quality with the whole of the respective webs, and the stock is exactly productive of the same advantages with any other portion of stock; the variations depending, in these cases, totally upon alterations in the degree of demand; there being few people who wish for so small a piece of cloth, and many who, in consequence of wills and trusts, are obliged to purchase smaller portions of stock for accumulation than are usually exposed in the market.

*   *   *

It must, then, appear, that a commodity being useful or delightful to man, cannot alone give it value; that to obtain value, or to be qualified to constitute a portion of private riches, it must combine with that quality, the circumstance of existing in a certain degree of scarcity. Yet the common sense of mankind would revolt at a proposal for augmenting the wealth of a nation, by creating a scarcity of any commodity generally useful and necessary to man. For example, let us suppose a country possessing abundance of the necessaries and conveniencies of life, and universally accommodated with the purest streams of water:— what opinion would be entertained of the understanding of a man, who, as the means of increasing the wealth of such a country, should propose to create a scarcity of water, the abundance of which was deservedly considered as one of the greatest blessings incident to the community? It is certain, however, that such a projector would, by this means, succeed in increasing the mass of individual riches; for to the water, which would still retain the quality of being useful and desirable, he would add the circumstance of existing in scarcity, which of course must confer upon it value; and, when it once obtained value, the same circumstances that fix the value of its produce for a certain number of years, as the price of the possession of land which produces food, would equally fix the value of the produce of springs for a certain number of years, as the price of the possession of that which produced drink; and thus the individual riches of the country would be increased, in a sum equal to the value of the fee-simple of all the wells.

But further to illustrate this proposition, that the wealth of the nation, and the mass of individual riches, cannot be regarded as in every respect the same, let us for a moment suppose it possible to create as great an abundance of any species of food as there exists of water: what would be thought of the advice of a man, who should cautiously recommend, even at the moment of the pressure of scarcity, to beware of creating this boasted abundance? for, however flattering it might appear as a remedy for the immediate evil, it would inevitably diminish the wealth of the nation. Yet ridiculous as this opinion might appear, as every thing, which partakes of the abundance of water or air, must at once cease to possess value; it follows that, by occasioning such an abundance, the sum-total of individual riches would most certainly be diminished, to an extent equal to the total value of that species of food, whose value would by this means be destroyed.

When we reflect on the situation of this country, it appears, indeed, almost self-evident, that the sum-total of individual riches cannot be considered as affording an accurate statement of public wealth.

At present, the capital of the national debt amounts nearly to five hundred millions. We have seen, and know, that war, even in the course of the first year, may sink the value of this capital twenty *per cent.*; that is, that it may diminish the mass of individual fortunes one hundred millions; and thus impose upon any man, who made up the account of public wealth on the principle, that an accurate statement of it was to be derived from adding together the fortunes of individuals, the necessity of saying, that one hundred millions of our wealth had vanished.

But this is not all. The value of many things sinks at the same time. In the value of land, in particular, we have seen a considerable diminution, which would create the necessity of a further reduction in this statement of public wealth. Yet the surface of the national territory remains unaltered; the landlord receives the same rent; the stockholder is paid the same interest; and there is no one thing, on which a man can lay his hand as an article of national wealth, which does not appear, to retain the same qualities that rendered it either useful or desirable, and to be in every respect unaltered.

It seems, therefore, apparent, that an increase in the mass of individual riches does not necessarily increase the national wealth: that it is possible to imagine a very important increase of national wealth, which must diminish the mass of individual riches; and that the practice of considering the sum-total of individual riches, as calculated to convey an accurate idea of national wealth, must be regarded as erroneous.

Indeed, a little further consideration makes it evident, that, if we could suppose Nature to bestow on any community, or Art to procure for them, such an abundance, that every individual should find himself in possession of whatever his appetites could want, or his imagination wish or desire, they would possess the greatest possible degree of national wealth; though, under such circumstances, it is impossible that any commodity could obtain the attribute of value: for, like water and air, all commodities, that partake of their abundance, must at once be divested of value, or of the possibility of constituting any part of individual riches. The inhabitants of a country thus abounding in all that man can desire, would, without the possibility of possessing riches, enjoy all the wealth and comforts which the largest fortunes can secure. Diminish this supposed abundance, it is obvious you will impoverish the community; but you will, by such diminution, infallibly confer value on the commodities used or desired by man, and of course create individual riches. Subsequent, however, to this diminution, which occasions the existence of riches, those who remain possessed, even of the largest fortunes, cannot enjoy a greater quantity of the objects of their desire, than the community at large possessed, in that supposed state of society where abundance precluded the existence of value, and of course the possibility of individual riches.

READING 6

Laissez Faire

THE CENTRAL DOCTRINE OF "laissez faire, laissez passez" is by no economist better stated than by Adam Smith. The belief that that economy functions best in which the government keeps "hands off" economic matters is supported by Adam Smith by the following argument: If the economy is free of governmental influence, then each man will naturally seek his own self-interest; in seeking his own self-interest, he will be led "as by an invisible hand" to achieve the betterment of the entire economy. The implication is that society will be better off as a result than it would had the government taken direct measures to improve society.

We may criticize Adam Smith's belief that each man pursuing his own self-interest will achieve the best national economy: in the preceding reading the Earl of Lauderdale explained the basic importance of *scarcity:* national wealth, he said, could be increased by individuals' making goods scarce, thus raising the values; when all such values which have been increased by consciously causing scarcity are added together, it would seem that national wealth is increased; but is national wealth increased when society has less goods than it had before? Thus the doctrine of the "invisible hand" can be severely brought to task.

Adam Smith (1723-1790) has often been called the "founder of political economy." His great work, *The Wealth of Nations*, was the first comprehensive statement explaining an economic "system." His work consisted chiefly in a selection from and a tying together of all preceding fragmentary works on economics. From these ideas that had gone before, he erected a system of economics which we call "classical economics." Three other economists are usually included among the great "classical" economists: David Ricardo, Thomas Malthus, and John Stuart Mill.

Smith was a Scottish philosopher who was Professor of Moral Philosophy at the University of Glasgow. Later he was appointed Commissioner of Customs in Scotland, a post which he held in Edinburgh until his death. The reading is taken from his great work, *An Inquiry Into the Nature and Causes of the Wealth of Nations* (New York: Random House, Inc., Cannan Edition, 1937, 976 pp.), Book IV, "Of Systems of political Oeconomy," Chapter II, "Of Restraints upon the Importation From Foreign Countries of Such Goods as Can Be Produced at Home," pp. 421 and 423, and Chapter IX, "Of the Agricultural Systems, or of Those Systems of Political Economy, which Represent the Produce of Land as Either the Sole or the Principal Source of the Revenue and Wealth of Every Country," pp. 650-651.

The general industry of the society never can exceed what the capital of the society can employ. As the number of workmen that can be kept in employment by any particular person must bear a certain proportion to his capital, so the number of those that can be continually employed by all the members of a great society, must bear a certain proportion to the whole capital of that society, and never can exceed that proportion. No regulation of commerce [by government] can increase the quantity of industry in any society beyond what its capital can maintain. It can only divert a part of it into a direction into which it might not otherwise have gone; and it is by no means certain that this artificial direction is likely to be more advantageous to the society than that into which it would have gone of its own accord.

Every individual is continually exerting himself to find out the most advantageous employment for whatever capital he can command. It is his own advantage, indeed, and not that of the society, which he has in view. But the study of his own advantage naturally, or rather necessarily leads him to prefer that employment which is most advantageous to the society.

* * *

The produce of industry is what it adds to the subject or materials upon which it is employed. In proportion as the value of this produce is great or small, so will likewise be the profits of the employer. But it is only for the sake of profit that any man employs a capital in the support of industry; and he will always, therefore, endeavour to employ it in the support of that industry of which the produce is likely to be of the greatest value, or to exchange for the greatest quantity either of money or of other goods.

But the annual revenue of every society is always precisely equal to the exchangeable value of the whole annual produce of its industry, or rather is precisely the same thing with that exchangeable value. As every individual, therefore, endeavours as much as he can both to employ his capital in the support of domestic industry, and so to direct that industry that its produce may be of the greatest value; every individual necessarily labours to render the annual revenue of the society as great as he can. He generally, indeed, neither intends to promote the public interest, nor knows how much he is promoting it. By preferring the support of domestic to that of foreign industry, he intends only his own security; and by directing that industry in such a manner as its produce may be of the greatest value, he intends only his own gain, and he is in this, as in many other cases, led by an invisible hand to promote an end which was no part of his intention. Nor is it always the worse for the society that it was no part of it. By pursuing his own interest he frequently promotes that of the society more effectually than when he really intends to promote it. I have never known much good done by those who affected to trade for the public good. It is an affectation, indeed, not very common among merchants, and very few words need be employed in dissuading them from it.

What is the species of domestic industry which his capital can employ, and of which the produce is likely to be of the greatest value, every individual, it is evident, can, in his local situation, judge much better than any statesman or lawgiver can do for him. The statesman, who should attempt to direct private people in what manner they ought to employ their capitals, would not only load himself with a most unnecessary attention, but assume an authority which could safely be trusted, not only to no single person, but to no council or senate whatever, and which would nowhere be so dangerous as in the hands of a man who had folly and presumption enough to fancy himself fit to exercise it.

It is thus that every system [of government] which endeavours, either, by extraordinary encouragements, to draw towards a particular species of industry a greater share of the capital of the society than what would naturally go to it; or, by extraordinary restraints, to force from a particular species of industry some share of the capital which would otherwise be employed in it; is in reality subversive of the great purpose which it means to promote. It retards, instead of accelerating, the progress of the society towards real wealth and greatness; and diminishes, instead of increasing, the real value of the annual produce of its land and labour.

All systems either of preference or of restraint, therefore, being thus completely taken away, the obvious and simple system of natural liberty establishes itself of its own accord. Every man, as long as he does not violate the laws of justice, is left perfectly free to pursue his own interest his own way, and to bring both his industry and capital into competition with those of any other man, or order of men. The sovereign is completely discharged from a duty, in the attempting to perform which he must always be exposed to innumerable delusions, and for the proper performance of which no human wisdom or knowledge could ever be sufficient; the duty of superintending the industry of private people, and of directing it towards the employments most suitable to the interest of the society. According to the system of natural liberty, the sovereign has only three duties to attend to; three duties of great importance, indeed, but plain and intelligible to common understandings; first, the duty of protecting the society from the violence and invasion of other independent societies; secondly, the duty of protecting, as far as possible, every member of the society from the injustice or oppression of every other member of it, or the duty of establishing an exact administration of justice; and, thirdly, the duty of erecting and maintaining certain public works and certain public institutions, which it can never be for the interest of any individual, or small number of individuals, to erect and maintain; because the profit could never repay the expence to any individual or small number of individuals, though it may frequently do much more than repay it to a great society.

READING 7

The Profit Motive

THE SEARCH FOR PROFITS is probably the most important single motivating force in modern business. Undoubtedly many businessmen experience other impulses in the daily affairs of their business than the sheer desire to make profit: the desire to retain an old and faithful employee whose usefulness is past; the desire to help customers who happen also to be friends by continuing their credit during depression; a genuine feeling of responsibility to serve the public. However, it is still probable that the most widely prevailing motive in modern business is the desire for profits. The following reading describes the profit motive and analyzes its services to the economy.

Beardsley Ruml (1894-1960) was Chairman of the Federal Reserve Bank of New York and Treasurer of R. H. Macy and Company, Inc. He was formerly on the staff of the University of Chicago. He was author of the Ruml Plan for the "pay-as-you-go" withholding tax. He was Chairman of the Business Committee of the National Planning Association; and he was a member of the Research Committee of the Committee for Economic Development. The reading is in Part 2, "Business as Private Government," Section 5, "Profits and Compensation," pp. 96-106, from *Tomorrow's Business*. Copyright, 1945, by Beardsley Ruml, and reprinted by permission of Holt, Rinehart, & Winston, Inc., Publishers.

Profit is the excess of selling price over cost. If a thing cannot be sold, there can be no profit. Nor will there be a profit unless the selling price is greater than the total cost of getting the article into the purchaser's hands.

This familiar relationship between selling price and costs, which results in profit, causes profit to serve two exceedingly important purposes. In the first place, profits are a test of whether the thing that is made is wanted, and whether enough people want it at the price at which it is offered more than they want something else at some other price. If they do not, there will be insufficient sales, and insufficient profits—or none at all.

In the second place, profits serve as a check on costs, and hence as a means of reducing wastes of all kinds. The costs must be brought below the price at which the thing will sell in adequate quantities, and the lower the cost the greater the profit and the greater the possibility of wider use.

The first purpose that profits serve is to make sure that the thing made is wanted by the people. The necessity of making things which must sell directs the energies of a company into the channels of making things which people want more than they want something else. It stops companies from trying to do things that get no public response and that meet no public need. And since most things compete with other things as objects of human desire, and since they compete both in desirability and in price, the managers of business are forced to seek a right price for the things they have to sell.

The fact that the thing made must be sold if there is to be a profit makes the managers of business attend to other matters than merely *making* things. They must give much attention to the *pricing* of the things they have made and to the *selling* of them. The selling activities of a business are informative services which help improve the standard of living, and the pricing process is a delicate and admirable device for letting people decide how much they want one thing as compared with something else.

The selling and pricing of things made by business for the use of people sometimes leads to business conduct of a character that the people, through their public government, have made illegal. Misrepresentation in advertising and false branding have been outlawed as a method of getting sales that will yield a profit. So also, most forms of collusion in the setting of prices are considered contrary to public interest and are made illegal as "conspiracy in restraint of trade." The beneficial influences of profit-making in the production and distribution of things for use must be protected by outlawing misrepresentation of the goods sold and collusion in fixing their price.

The second purpose which profits serve is to reduce the costs of production and distribution and, thereby, to eliminate waste of human effort and of natural resources and to make more things available to more people. The beneficial pressure of profit on cost reduction comes from giving an impulse to efficiency and ingenuity; it provides an incentive for the discovery of new processes and new machines for the elimination of waste motion and unneeded services. This kind of cost reduction results in the use of less human effort and less material in the producing and selling of a given article. Economy in the use of our resources of men and materials, while at the same time maintaining the same or a higher standard of living, serves a valuable social purpose, and the pressure for profits is the principal influence to this end.

Just as prices can be fixed and maintained in ways that are unwholesome, so also can the cost of things be cut in ways that are considered unfair and sometimes illegal. The setting of wage rates below minimum standards, pressure for output beyond the limits of health and sanity, adulteration and deterioration of product—these and other methods of cost reduction are at least on the shady side. Profit-making by such means must be checked by public regulation.

Profits, therefore, serve a double purpose: first, they direct the activities of business into channels which meet a public response; second, they provide a pressure for ingenuity and efficiency. Profits are needed for these two purposes, whether the profits, after they are made, are privately owned or not. The ownership of profits is a separate question from that of the usefulness of profits as a directive energizer of business power. An enterprise of the business type, producing goods and services for use, whether it be publicly, privately, or co-operatively owned, requires the profit motive and profit statement to make it work and work soundly.

How high can profits properly be? If the goods are sold squarely and priced competitively, if the costs of producing them are governed by intelligence and by the use of fair and legal methods, if there is no direct or indirect public subsidy that makes prices higher or costs lower than the managers of the business themselves could make them, then the higher the profits the better the interests of all are served. A special case exists in the exploitation of privately owned natural resources where the need of conservation for the benefit of future generations should be a reasonable limiting factor on present profits. But, even in this special case, given a public policy and law as regards conservation, the higher the profits the better.

Unfortunately, public opinion today is skeptical of accepting the highest obtainable profit as a desirable social standard. This skepticism is the result of the practices we have described, which have undermined the prestige of business.

These practices are: improper representation and misbranding in selling; controlled and noncompetitive pricing; exploitation of labor; adulteration of quality; the receipt of subsidies in the form of franchises, tariffs, tax exemptions, and grants of the public domain; and, finally, undue monopoly privileges in the use of patents, trademarks, and copyrights. When profits are made (1) within the law, (2) under competitive enterprise, (3) without public subsidy, or (4) without public protection of exclusivity, the higher the profits the greater the honor to the profit-maker. Under these circumstances there should be no limitation on the amount of profits which a business can make, because the greater the profits the greater the service.

In many cases, business receives direct or indirect public subsidy or public protection of exclusivity. These privileges are neither unusual nor are they undesirable. The American tradition of public co-operation with private enterprise is one of long standing and it takes many forms adapted to many special situations. These subsidies, protections, and immunities, although they have been legally granted, have been excessive in some cases, and they may have been continued over an unnecessarily long period of time. But such errors are errors in the application of principles that need have only pragmatic justification. We need only recognize that where there is public assistance and special privilege there is also the duty of public regulation and the right of public participation in the final resulting profit.

In addition to the two broad social purposes just discussed, profits serve in three necessary ways to safeguard and to promote the safety and welfare of any particular business. In the first place, they are a safeguard against errors in pricing; in the second place, they are the foundation on which additional capital can be raised as it is needed; and finally, they are the measuring standard against which the efficiency of the management is tested.

The first reason why profits are necessary for a business is to give a margin of protection against errors in pricing. Goods and services are offered for future delivery at an agreed price which is binding on the seller. The company making the sale estimates what its costs are likely to be. In the case of manufacturing, the selling price can be settled and the uncertainties will occur in the costs of the goods to be sold. In the retail business, commitments for the acquiring of merchandise to sell must be made far in advance of the time of sale, and an estimate must be made as to whether at this future date the merchandise will be desirable and whether it will be salable at a predetermined price. In distribution, the costs of goods and expenses can be estimated with fair accuracy, but the selling price and the quantities that can be sold are problematical. In any case, errors in judgment will occasionally be made and the margin of profit must be sufficient so that over a large number of transactions there is a plus and not a minus resulting from subtracting total costs from total sales.

It follows that the greater the uncertainty of the cost of goods, or of the price at which they can be sold, the larger the margin of profit which must be projected. Efficient management and shrewd forecasting of demand will make profits for some, and under the same circumstances losses will have to be taken by others. But unless the profit differential for the industry as a whole is wide enough to give to the industry as a whole a margin to cover normal human errors in estimating future selling prices and future costs, the position of the industry is untenable. Profits must be large enough to bring risk-taking in pricing and costing within the limits of ordinary business judgment.

The second reason why profits are necessary for a business is to provide a foundation for the raising of additional capital. As a justification for the investment of new capital, profits must be looked at differently, depending on whether the business is an old one with long operating history or whether it is a new one with its record yet to be made.

Let us consider first an old and established business. Such a business must have profits in order to have access to new capital; it must be able to attract the savings of the people to its operations, when additional capital funds are required. These savings can be brought into the company in any of three ways: (1) as the application of the earnings of the company not distributed to the stockholders; (2) as a loan to the company evidenced by bonds, mortgages, or other classes of indebtedness; or (3) by sale by the company of the company's preferred or common stock. In each case, a record of profits is necessary if the company is to get the capital it requires.

In the case of raising capital by the investment of undistributed earnings, the profits must have been made before they can be withheld. Further, no management is justified in withholding earnings which belong to the stockholders unless it believes that the withheld earnings can be used to make increased or surer profits.

If the company decides to raise its new capital by borrowing, the higher the profits have been and the longer and steadier the history of the earnings the lower will be the cost of capital. Unless a reasonable and satisfactory record of profit-making has been shown, new capital will not be available on any terms. And even when capital is available, the differences in the costs of capital will be significant, depending on the profit-making record of the company. These differences in the costs of new capital are matters of consequence to all parties at interest in the business.

The obtaining of new capital by the sale of stock to old stockholders or to the public nearly always means pricing the new stock somewhat below the existing market price of the stock already outstanding. This market price may be above or it may be below the book value of the stock; that is, of the historic investment which has already been made in the company. Unless the new stock can be sold at or above its book value, the existing stockholders are paying a premium for the new capital. So, unless the profits of a company are sufficient to support a market price that permits the sale of new stock at or above book value, the profits are insufficient to support equal treatment of old stockholders with new ones, and again the position of the company is untenable.

Profits are not the only factor which determines the market value of stock, and, therefore, the cost of new capital; but, over the long run, profits are the principal consideration. As a generalization, subject to exceptions in special cases, it may be said that for business as a whole profits as a whole must be considered insufficient unless common stocks as a whole are selling in the market at a price sufficiently above their book value to permit the sale of new stock at book value. If common stocks are selling at a price too low to permit the sale of new stock at book value, access to new capital is too restricted for the health of private business enterprise.

To induce new capital into new business or into an unseasoned business, the expectation of profit must be large indeed. How much return would have to be anticipated to induce the average person to take five thousand dollars out of his savings bank or out of government bonds for risk investment in a *new and untested* business? Would it be 6%, or 8%, or 10%? Obviously, such returns are much too low. Common stocks of standard companies should yield as much as this. Would it be 20%, or 25%? These rates of profit also are on the lean side. Even at 25% after corporate taxes, the business would have to go on earning at this rate for four years in order to return the investment, and at that, the return would be subject to income tax payable by the investor at the rate of his highest bracket. The plain fact is that new equity capital is ordinarily unavailable to new business on a business basis under present conditions. By and large, the possibilities of profits are too low, the tax rate is too high, the period for getting the stake back is too long, and the future is too uncertain. Under present conditions, therefore, new business cannot be started on a business basis. A going concern with a good profit record will find abundant capital at reasonable rates, but at reasonable rates it will be loan capital, not capital for the purchase of its common stock.

This is not only a problem for business, it is a problem for statesmanship. If we want new equity capital for new businesses —and even for most old businesses—profit must be higher, tax rates must be lower, and the future must be clearer than it has been in the recent past.

Finally, profits serve a necessary business purpose in providing the yardstick of management efficiency. The management of one company is compared with that of another company in terms of the profits it is able to earn in relation to its capital; the management of a company is compared with itself in terms of what it earned a year ago, or with its predecessor management in terms of the earnings of a previous decade; the several divisions and departments of a company are compared each with the other and with standard profit performances within the industry.

Profit as an evaluation of management efficiency is much more significant than mere money or purchasing power. Profit becomes numbers on a score board, the pay-off entry in a competitive game. The incentive to management is not the profit as profit, but the prestige that attaches to having made a good record, to being recognized as being more successful than the management of a competing firm in the same industry, or to having earned more than last year or more than a previous management was able to earn.

For management the profit motive is essentially a competitive motive, which drives where mere love of gain would never drive. The reward to the managers is not primarily the profit, but the prestige symbolized by the profit—success in a competitive game and status among friends and rivals who understand how the score is kept.

Profit as a directive energizer of business deserves more respect than it is sometimes accorded. It would be difficult indeed to find a substitute that would serve the public welfare so well.

READING 8

Industrialism

By "INDUSTRIALISM" IS MEANT that great revolution in economic life occurring from approximately the middle of the eighteenth century to the present by which the rise in importance of manufacturing brought about a vastly increased level of living to western civilization. The English Industrial Revolution (occurring roughly in the latter half of the eighteenth century) witnessed two great economic changes: first, a substitution of machines for men in manufacturing; second, a substitution of artificial power (steam) for natural power. These two central changes contributed to the emergence of the "factory system"; and an increased demand occurred for products, because lower prices resulted with "mass production" and the vast growth in size of manufacturing firms. Adam Smith, observing the changes occurring during the Industrial Revolution, erected the "classical" economic philosophy based upon laissez faire doctrines which in turn furnished a favorable political-economic climate for the flowering of "industrialism."

George Douglas Howard Cole (1889-1959) was an important English economist who has in the following reading delineated carefully and logically the changes occurring in "industrialism." He has written extensively on economic matters. The reading is from *Studies in World Economics* by G. D. H. Cole (London: Macmillan and Co., Limited, 1934, 285 pp.), Chapter IV, "Industrialism," pp. 60-69. Reprinted by permission of Mrs. Margaret Cole and Macmillan & Co., Ltd., London.

Industrialism is, fundamentally, an affair of productive technique. It is based upon the discovery and exploitation of improved methods of producing wealth, primarily in the processes of manufacture, but also to an increasing extent in agriculture and in the extractive industries yielding primary products. It is closely associated with an increase in the scale of production, with the development of capitalistic methods in both manufacture and marketing, and with the employment of wage-labour. Its secondary effects have included hitherto a concentration of the population in densely inhabited urban areas, a very rapid increase in the volume of international trade, much lending of capital for development by the more to the less advanced countries, and a very rapid increase in the number and social importance of the middle classes, including those engaged in the professions as well as in the administration and supervision of industry and commerce.

At the basis of industrialism is the machine. Both Capitalism and wage-employment are much older than industrialism, in the sense in which the term is used in this essay; and there were many factories before there was a factory system based on mechanical power. But industrialism can be said to have begun when machinery driven by a central supply of mechanical power became the typical method of manufacturing production. For from that point industry replaced commerce as the directing force of economic life, and the scale of production and the forms of business organisation came to be determined by the growth and character of mechanical power.

Thus, in England, where the Industrial Revolution proceeded a stage ahead of its development elsewhere, the industrial employer step by step ousted the merchant from his previous predominance. The typical rich men of the seventeenth and early eighteenth centuries were not industrial employers, but merchants and financiers, engaged in buying and selling goods gathered together from a host of small-scale producers. There were some big employers even then; but they were not typical. The rich clothier whose memory is kept alive by his monuments and benefactions in countless English churches was not primarily an employer of labour, but a merchant, though the position of the small producers who supplied him may often have differed little in effect from that of wage-workers. The *bourgeois* class, to which the aristocrats of England and France before the great changes of the eighteenth century were compelled to pay some attention, was above all a class of merchants.

The Industrial Revolution, based upon a great series of mechanical inventions and above all else on the economic utilisation of steam-power, radically changed the situation. For it substituted for a relatively static system of production and essentially self-expanding technique. The merchant of the seventeenth or eighteenth century had indeed an incentive to expand his sales, as a means to additional profits. But there was for him, as a rule, no economy in buying on a larger scale, or in larger total amount; for the small producers who supplied him could not produce more cheaply merely because they were asked to produce more. It is a commonplace among economists that handicraft production tends to obey a law of "constant cost", and indeed that, if additional workers have to be pressed rapidly into the service in order to meet an expansion of demand, costs will tend to increase on account both of the greater demand for labour and of the less skill of the new labour attracted into the trade. This was undoubtedly the position in handloom weaving in the eighteenth century, in that "golden age" of the handloom weaver that preceded the introduction of the power-loom. The desire of the eighteenth-century merchant to purchase more goods from the small producers was therefore conditional on his ability to sell more without reducing the price, or even while increasing it; and this, owing to the rapid expansion of trade with both America and the East, he was often able to do.

But as fast as machine-production based on mechanical power superseded handicraft, the situation was radically altered. Until then, the pace of production was set by the orders of the merchants, to whom the producers were for the most part merely subservient. But now the industrial employer, under the new factory system, had himself not only an incentive to get as large orders as he could, but also a means of stimulating the merchant's demand. For in most cases he could produce more cheaply by increasing his output; and he was therefore, unlike the handicraftsman, in a position to offer the merchant goods at low prices if only the merchant would increase his purchases.

This enabled the merchant in his turn to take new steps in stimulating demand, by offering goods at lower prices to the consumers, both at home and abroad; and the increased orders given by merchants under these conditions reacted upon industry. But the initiative in the system passed more and more into the hands of the industrial employers, whose offers of more goods at lower prices became the driving-force of material progress. From this point of view, the coming of industrialism meant in manufacturing industry the transition from a condition of constant to one of decreasing cost.

The industrial employer, who thus became the pivot of the new economic system, found himself urged on to new conquests by the pressure of the machine itself. He had to be abreast of his competitors in reducing prices; and this was a constant incentive to him both to increase his scale of production and to avail himself of the improved machines that were constantly being introduced. For, if he went on using obsolescent machines, there was no lack of rivals ready to supplant him; and, up to a certain point, his costs would fall as he was able to expand his scale of production.

There was, doubtless, even when the Industrial Revolution was at its height, an *optimum* size for any given business, beyond which it could not grow without loss of productive efficiency. But, as the *optimum* was growing larger with very great rapidity, the great majority of businesses were probably well below it, and racing to catch up. Accordingly, machine-technique gave the employer the greatest possible stimulus to increase his scale and quantity of production in order to cut his prices, and thus enabled the merchant to take full advantage of the elasticity of demand, especially in overseas markets.

I add this last qualification, because the strong competitive pressure on employers to reduce costs and prices, while it was a powerful stimulus to improved productive technique, reacted unfavourably upon the level of wages, and therefore upon the consuming power of the domestic market. The employer could cut his costs, not only by improving the efficiency of production, but also by reducing wages, or taking a firm stand against their increase; and this course appealed strongly to the less efficient employers, who were threatened otherwise with extinction. Relatively few employers could be brought to believe in Robert Owen's doctrine of the economy of good wages and conditions; and perhaps relatively few were efficient enough to make it true in their own case. The rapidly falling costs of the new industrialism were based on low wages as well as on a rapidly improving technique of production.

There was a second, and no less powerful, reason why wages and consuming power in the home market remained low in the period following the advent of industrialism. The new employers, under a constant necessity of improving their machinery and expanding their scale of production, were avid for fresh supplies of capital which they could apply to these purposes. But capital was hard to come by, in the days before the recognition of limited liability and the working out of the modern solution of joint stock companies and corporations based on widely diffused and easily transferable shares. The employer was therefore compelled, as far as possible, to expand his business out of his own resources, living frugally himself and putting back his profits as capital for the increase of future profits. Living thus, and under this pressure, he was disposed to resent increased wages as sheer waste, diverting to useless expenditure resources badly needed for the expansion of output.

It is true that money thus saved was spent on buildings and machinery. But the constructional trades, powerfully stimulated as they were by the new conditions, did not quickly respond to the new technique, or pass over from handicraft conditions of constant cost to conditions of decreasing cost. Building remained, and remains in part even to-day, a handicraft industry, in which prices tend to rise rather than fall with any quick expansion of demand. And machine-making continued for a long time to be a highly skilled job, needing the services of skilled craftsmen who were in short supply, and to be incapable of being reorganised on a basis of mass production. Not until the methods of producing iron and steel, and of forging and casting, had been revolutionised in the latter half of the nineteenth century did the engineering trades become at all largely subject to the conditions of decreasing cost which had come to prevail in the cotton trade more than fifty years earlier. Consequently, spending on buildings and machinery did not expand production in the same degree as spending on consumers' goods, which were on the whole more easily mass-produced. This helps to explain the intense concentration of the new industrialism on the development of exports, and the constant search for new markets abroad.

Industrialism grew, then, at first above all in the textile trades, making Manchester the effective capital of the new industrial world. It was no accident that the economists who based their doctrines upon industrialism in this first phase came to be called the "Manchester School", or that their outstanding dogma was a supreme faith in *laissez-faire*. For their own experience seemed plainly to demonstrate the self-expansive nature of the new industrial system, its capacity constantly to increase the supply of goods while lowering their cost, and the value of competition in weeding out the inefficient producers and compelling the survivors always to adopt the latest advances in technique on penalty of being left behind in the race. What could be better than a self-acting system which at once benefited the consumer by lowering prices, rewarded the efficient with the high profits of the pioneer, and weeded out the inefficient who misused the resources of production? It was not clearly seen at this stage how far these results depended on the superior efficiency of Great Britain over other countries, of whose markets she was therefore able to take her pick, or how low wages must retard the growth of consuming power in the home market. These difficulties came later; and before they had been fully realised the character of industrialism had been greatly changed.

For, by and by, the new technique was extended from industry to industry, until it came to embrace the industries producing capital goods as well as consumers' goods. The development of railways played a dominant part in this transformation, not only because the railways enabled the interior of countries and continents to be opened up for economic development, but also because the demand for railway material gave an enormous stimulus to the metal trades and compelled them to devise and resort to mass-production methods. The new steel-making processes of Bessemer, Siemens, and Gilchrist and Thomas gave the metal-using industries for the first time a reliable and durable raw material to which methods of standardised production could be applied, and thus made possible the development of large-scale enterprise in the engineering and kindred trades, as well as the translation of shipbuilding from wood into metal. The same causes revolutionised the coal industry, greatly expanded already in the earlier phases of industrialism, and created a new and powerful grouping of "heavy industries" to balance the older textile trades. With the coming of these new forces, the authority of Manchester began to wane; and industrialism, no longer so fully wedded to *laissez-faire* and competition, entered on a new phase, which led on before long to the growth of trusts and combines, the recrudescence of tariffs, and in general to a renewed attempt at regulating just those processes of production and sale which the Manchester School held should be left severely alone by the State.

The explanation of this difference is not hard to find. In the first phase of industrialism, the maximum expansion of wealth could be secured by concentrating as far as possible on those forms of production which most clearly showed their obedience to a law of decreasing cost—in other words, primarily upon textiles. This could be done as long as there was adequate scope for the expansion of the sales of industrialised countries in markets where native producers were well behind in efficiency. But in time it became clear that this expansion could not continue unabated unless steps were taken to develop the complementary powers of production of these less industrialised countries, so as to increase the supply of goods which they could give in exchange for the mass-produced manufactures of industrialism. The railway was the great instrument of this development, opening up in the less industrialised countries vast new sources for the supply of raw materials and foodstuffs. Incidentally, this expansion helped greatly to raise wages in the industrialised countries, both because it enabled export to go forward at a greater pace, and because it secured an abundant supply of cheap foodstuffs. In the fourth quarter of the nineteenth century, there was a rise both in money wages and in the purchasing power of money, with the result that a great stimulus was given to consumption in the home markets of the industrialised countries.

In building railways and supplying railway material, and later in the supply of machinery produced on a large scale, the industrialised countries advanced to a new type of export trade vitally different from the old. The sale of cotton textiles or woollen goods was essentially a cash transaction, to be balanced at once by an equivalent purchase of goods. But the sale of railway material and other classes of capital goods could not be conducted on these terms; for the purchase price could be paid by the buyers only if and when the railway or the factory became productive. Payment for such exports had to await the economic development of the countries to which they were sent, and then to be made in the products which their use had caused to be created. Consequently, this second phase of industrialism was marked by a great increase in the export of capital—that is, in the loan of capital in order to make possible the export of capital goods—from the industrialised to the less developed parts of the world. Great Britain especially exported huge masses of capital to all parts of the world, and above all to her own Dominions and India, to the United States, and to the South American Republics. She exported capital to Europe as well; but there it was as a rule more speedily repaid, as railways and factories built with British money were bought back by native investors.

It would take me far beyond the scope of this essay to describe the reactions of this growth of foreign investment on world politics and international rivalries, and on the development of Economic Imperialism. I am concerned here only with its effects on industrialism in a narrower sense. It made possible a very rapid growth of the industries producing capital goods, and speeded up in them the development of an intensified

technique of mass-production. Whereas in the first half of the
nineteenth century the typical instance of large-scale production
was a cotton mill, by its close the types of large-scale enterprise
were to be found above all in the heavy industries—in the great
steel-making plants of Bethlehem or Middlesbrough, the great
armament factories, the shipyards, and the great coal-mines already closely linked with steel. And, in the heavy industries,
there was already a growing tendency for combination to replace
competition, and for the size of the business unit far to transcend
that of the single manufacturing plant.

But before we come back to the vital point hinted at in the
last phrase, something must be said of the influence of technical
development upon business structure. As we have seen, the
earlier industrialists were sorely hampered by shortage of capital.
There was no investing public in the modern sense; and, broadly
speaking, no one could invest money in industrial development
unless he either lent it to a business man on his personal security,
or became a partner in the business without the protection of
limited liability, and therefore at the hazard of his entire fortune.
The gradually extended recognition by law of joint stock organisation and limited liability remedied this difficulty, and opened
the door to industrial investment by all who had savings or resources to spare.

Joint stock and limited liability not only increased immensely the total resources available for business expansion, but also
removed the limits upon the size of capitalist concerns. Before
their coming, the *entrepreneur's* difficulty lay in gathering together enough capital to equip and run a plant big enough to
take full advantage of the economics of large-scale production.
But now he was able not only to do this, but readily to expand
the scale of business organisation so as to bring a number of
separate plants under a unified control. The scale of business
organisation was still being continually expanded by the inherent
necessities of improving industrial technique; but it was now
able, not only to reach these limits, but also to pass beyond
them. Indeed, as the larger concerns were often at an advantage
both in raising fresh resources in the capital market, and in
getting credit from bankers and others, to some extent a premium
was put on a scale of business organisation considerably larger
than the technique of production in itself made necessary. In the
early days of the trust movement there was a marked tendency
for the increase in the size of the business unit to be dictated by
financial rather than technological considerations; and this ten-

dency was strongly manifested again in the troubled years after the war, in the gigantic mergers and concerns organised by Hugo Stinnes in Germany, and in the unwieldy aggregations of businesses gathered under one control by Messrs. Vickers or the late Lord Leverhulme in Great Britain.

There was, however, side by side with these megalomaniac financial aggregations, a new technological tendency leading towards an expansion of the business unit on a scale very much larger than that even of the largest single plant. Under the earlier conditions of industrialism, the plant was the essential technical unit, and each plant could face its own technical problems independently of the rest. But the modern development of industrial technology is making the separate plants growingly interdependent in a variety of ways. In the first place, it is often essential, if the maximum economy in production is to be secured, to group together in very close relation and under unified control plants engaged in complementary industrial processes—in order, for example, to save intermediate transport costs on bulky half-finished goods, or to utilise a waste product, such as blast-furnace gas, in a subsequent manufacturing process. Secondly, it is often an advantage from the standpoint of economical production to reduce and simplify the varieties of a particular commodity placed on the market, and therefore to secure at least as much unity of control as is necessary to ensure this. And thirdly, the maximum economy is likely to be realised in many trades if each plant, instead of producing a wide variety of goods in competition with the rest, is in some degree specialised to the manufacture of a limited range of products, and thus enabled to produce, within this range, upon a larger scale.

*   *   *

The first of these technological requirements leads to a growth of vertical combination, that is, the linking up of successive stages of production under a common control. The second leads to fairly loose horizontal agreements between the firms at the same stage of manufacture, but need not disturb the independence of each distinct business. The third leads to much closer horizontal integration, as it is found in such businesses as Imperial Chemical Industries, the English Steel Corporation, or the Steel Union in Germany.

READING 9

Communism

COMMUNISM IS THE EXTREME REACTION from the doctrines of "laissez faire." The "industrialism" which fared so well under the doctrines of laissez faire brought with it not only an increased level of living for most of the people, but also some deplorable conditions in Europe for masses of industrial workers. Communism purports to improve the general condition of mankind through the following process: The government, set up by the "proletariat" (working people) should closely manage and control the factors of *production* (land, labor, capital, enterprise) and it should also plan, organize, and control *consumption,* thereby effecting government direction of both *supply* and *demand.* The end aim of communism after a period of time in which such government control would succeed in eradicating all class barriers among men would be that government should become no longer necessary, for men free from class restraints would live in harmony forever.

Communism is considered a beautiful but impossible dream by some, and an unmitigated evil by others. The following reading is the classical central work, giving a concise statement of the origin, development, and projected results of communism.

Heinrich Karl Marx (1818-1883), along with Friederich Engels (1820-1895), is commonly recognized as the founder and leader of the communism of the nineteenth century to the present. He was not the first man to advocate communistic principles, for Plato's "Republic" is such a statement. Marx prepared himself as a university professor, but never taught. His chief activity was as the leader of the Communist Party. He made his living as a journalist. Engels, the coauthor of Marx, was trained by his father for a business career. He wrote extensively on the condition of the working classes and did much work in research and organization for the Communist Party. The following reading is from *Manifesto of the Communist Party* (Chicago: Charles H. Kerr & Company, 1902, 64 pp.), pp. 11-64.

A spectre is haunting Europe—the spectre of Communism. All the Powers of old Europe have entered into a holy alliance to exorcise this spectre; Pope and Czar, Metternich and Guizot, French Radicals and German police-spies.

Where is the party in opposition that has not been decried as communistic by its opponents in power? Where the Opposition that has not hurled back the branding reproach of Communism, against the more advanced opposition parties, as well as against its re-actionary adversaries?

Two things result from this fact.

I. Communism is already acknowledged by all European Powers to be itself a Power.

II. It is high time that Communists should openly, in the face of the whole world, publish their views, their aims, their tendencies, and meet this nursery tale of the Spectre of Communism with a Manifesto of the party itself.

To this end, Communists of various nationalities have assembled in London, and sketched the following manifesto, to be published in the English, French, German, Italian, Flemish and Danish languages.

I.

BOURGEOIS AND PROLETARIANS.[1]

The history of all hitherto existing society is the history of class struggles.

Freeman and slave, patrician and plebeian, lord and serf, guild-master and journeyman, in a word, oppressor and oppressed, stood in constant opposition to one another, carried on an uninterrupted, now hidden, now open fight, a fight that each time

---

[1] By bourgeoisie is meant the class of modern Capitalists, owners of the means of social production and employers of wage-labour. By proletariat, the class of modern wage-labourers who, having no means of production of their own, are reduced to selling their labour-power in order to live.

ended, either in a revolutionary re-constitution of society at large, or in the common ruin of the contending classes.

In the earlier epochs of history, we find almost everywhere a complicated arrangement of society into various orders, a manifold gradation of social rank. In ancient Rome we have patricians, knights, plebeians, slaves; in the middle ages, feudal lords, vassals, guild-masters, journeymen, apprentices, serfs; in almost all of these classes, again, subordinate gradations.

The modern bourgeois society that has sprouted from the ruins of feudal society, has not done away with class antagonisms. It has but established new classes, new conditions of oppression, new forms of struggle in place of the old ones.

Our epoch, the epoch of the bourgeoisie, possesses, however, this distinctive feature; it has simplified the class antagonisms. Society as a whole is more and more splitting up into two great hostile camps, into two great classes directly facing each other: Bourgeoisie and Proletariat.

From the serfs of the middle ages sprang the chartered burghers of the earliest towns. From these burgesses the first elements of the bourgeoisie were developed.

The discovery of America, the rounding of the Cape, opened up fresh ground for the rising bourgeoisie. The East-Indian and Chinese markets, the colonisation of America, trade with the colonies, the increase in the means of exchange and in commodities generally, gave to commerce, to navigation, to industry, an impulse never before known, and thereby, to the revolutionary element in the tottering feudal society, a rapid development.

The feudal system of industry, under which industrial production was monopolised by close [closed] guilds, now no longer sufficed for the growing wants of the new markets. The manufacturing system took its place. The guild-masters were pushed on one side by the manufacturing middle-class; division of labour between the different corporate guilds vanished in the face of division of labour in each single workshop.

Meantime the markets kept ever growing, the demand, ever rising. Even manufacture no longer sufficed. Thereupon, steam and machinery revolutionised industrial production. The place of manufacture was taken by the giant, Modern Industry, the place of the industrial middle-class, by industrial millionaires, the leaders of whole industrial armies, the modern bourgeois.

Modern industry has established the world-market, for which the discovery of America paved the way. This market has given an immense development to commerce, to navigation, to communication by land. This development has, in its turn, reacted on the extension of industry; and in proportion as industry, commerce, navigation, railways extended, in the same proportion the bourgeoisie developed, increased its capital, and pushed into the background every class handed down from the Middle Ages.

We see, therefore, how the modern bourgeoisie is itself the product of a long course of development, of a series of revolutions in the modes of production and of exchange.

Each step in the development of the bourgeoisie was accompanied by a corresponding political advance of that class. An oppressed class under the sway of the feudal nobility, an armed and self-governing association in the mediaeval commune, here independent urban republic (as in Italy and Germany), there taxable "third estate" of the monarchy (as in France), afterwards, in the period of manufacture proper, serving either the semifeudal or the absolute monarchy as a counterpoise against the nobility, and, in fact, corner stone of the great monarchies in general, the bourgeoisie has at last, since the establishment of Modern Industry and of the world-market, conquered for itself, in the modern representative State, exclusive political sway. The executive of the modern State is but a committee for managing the common affairs of the whole bourgeoisie.

The bourgeoisie, historically, has played a most revolutionary part.

The bourgeoisie, wherever it has got the upper hand, has put an end to all feudal, patriarchal, idyllic relations. It has pitilessly torn asunder the motley feudal ties that bound man to his "natural superiors," and has left remaining no other nexus between man and man than naked self-interest, than callous "cash payment." It has drowned the most heavenly ecstacies of religious fervour, of chivalrous enthusiasm, of philistine sentimentalism, in the icy water of egotistical calculation. It has resolved personal worth into exchange value, and in place of the numberless indefeasible chartered freedoms, has set up that single, unconscionable freedom—Free Trade. In one word, for exploitation, veiled by religious and political illusions, it has substituted naked, shameless, direct, brutal exploitation.

The bourgeoisie has stripped of its halo every occupation hitherto honoured and looked up to with reverent awe. It has converted the physician, the lawyer, the priest, the poet, the man of science, into its paid wage-labourers.

The bourgeoisie has torn away from the family its sentimental veil, and has reduced the family relation to a mere money relation.

The bourgeoisie has disclosed how it came to pass that the brutal display of vigour in the Middle Ages, which Reactionists so much admire, found its fitting complement in the most slothful indolence. It has been the first to shew what man's activity can bring about. It has accomplished wonders far surpassing Egyptian pyramids, Roman aqueducts, and Gothic cathedrals; it has conducted expeditions that put in the shade all former Exoduses of nations and crusades.

The bourgeoisie cannot exist without constantly revolutionising the instruments of production, and thereby the relations of production, and with them the whole relations of society. Conservation of the old modes of production in unaltered form, was, on the contrary, the first condition of existence for all earlier industrial classes. Constant revolutionising of production, uninterrupted disturbance of all social conditions, everlasting uncertainty and agitation distinguished the bourgeois epoch from all earlier ones. All fixed, fast-frozen relations, with their train of ancient and venerable prejudices and opinions, are swept away, all new-formed ones become antiquated before they can ossify. All that is solid melts into air, all that is holy is profaned, and man is at last compelled to face with sober senses, his real conditions of life, and his relations with his kind.

The need of a constantly expanding market for its products chases the bourgeoisie over the whole surface of the globe. It must nestle everywhere, settle everywhere, establish connexions everywhere.

The bourgeoisie has through its exploitation of the world-market given a cosmopolitan character to production and consumption in every country. To the great chagrin of Re-actionists, it has drawn from under the feet of industry the national ground on which it stood. All old-established national industries have been destroyed or are daily being destroyed. They are dislodged by new industries, whose introduction becomes a life and death question for all civilised nations, by industries that no longer work up indigenous raw material, but raw material drawn from the remotest zones; industries whose products are consumed, not only at home, but in every quarter of the globe. In place of the old wants, satisfied by the productions of the country, we find new wants, requiring for their satisfaction the products of distant lands and climes. In place of the old local and national seclusion and self-sufficiency, we have intercourse in every direction, universal inter-dependence of nations. And as in material, so also in intellectual production. The intellectual creations of individual nations become common property. National one-sidedness and narrow-mindedness become more and more impossible, and from the numerous national and local literatures there arises a world-literature.

The bourgeoisie, by the rapid improvement of all instruments of production, by the immensely facilitated means of communication, draws all, even the most barbarian, nations into civilisation. The cheap prices of its commodities are the heavy artillery with which it batters down all Chinese walls, with which it forces the barbarians' intensely obstinate hatred of foreigners to capitulate. It compels all nations, on pain of extinction, to adopt the bourgeois mode of production; it compels them to introduce what it calls civilisation into their midst, i.e., to become bourgeois themselves. In a word, it creates a world after its own image.

The bourgeoisie has subjected the country to the rule of the towns. It has created enormous cities, has greatly increased the urban population as compared with the rural, and has thus rescued a considerable part of the population from the idiocy of rural life. Just as it has made the country dependent on the towns, so it has made barbarian and semi-barbarian countries dependent on the civilised ones, nations of peasants on nations of bourgeois, the East on the West.

The bourgeoisie keeps more and more doing away with the scattered state of the population, of the means of production, and of property. It has agglomerated population, centralised means of production, and has concentrated property in a few hands. The necessary consequences of this was political centralisation. Independent, or but loosely connected provinces, with separate interests, laws, governments and systems of taxation, became lumped together in one nation, with one government, one code of laws, one national class-interest, one frontier and one customs-tariff.

The bourgeoisie, during its rule of scarce one hundred years, has created more massive and more colossal productive forces than have all preceding generations together. Subjection of Nature's forces to man, machinery, application of chemistry to industry and agriculture, steam-navigation, railways, electric telegraphs, clearing of whole continents for cultivation, canalization of rivers, whole populations conjured out of the ground—what earlier century had even a presentiment that such productive forces slumbered in the lap of social labour?

We see then: the means of production and of exchange on whose foundation the bourgeoisie built itself up, were generated in feudal society. At a certain stage in the development of these means of production and of exchange, the conditions under which feudal society produced and exchanged, the feudal organisation of agriculture and manufacturing industry, in one word, the feudal relations of property became no longer compatible with the already developed productive forces; they became so many fetters. They had to burst asunder; they were burst asunder.

Into their places stepped free competition, accompanied by a social and political constitution adapted to it, and by the economical and political sway of the bourgeois class.

A similar movement is going on before our own eyes. Modern bourgeois society with its relations of production, of exchange and of property, a society that has conjured up such gigantic means of production and of exchange, is like the sorcerer, who is no longer able to control the powers of the nether world whom he has called up by his spells. For many a decade past the history of industry and commerce is but the history of the revolt of modern productive forces against modern conditions of production, against the property relations that are the conditions for the existence of the bourgeoisie and of its rule. It is enough to mention the commercial crises that by their periodical return put on its trial, each time more threateningly, the existence of the entire bourgeois society. In these crises a great part not only of the existing products, but also of the previously created productive forces, are periodically destroyed. In these crises there breaks out an epidemic that, in all earlier epochs, would have seemed an absurdity—the epidemic of over-production. Society suddenly finds itself put back into a state of momentary barbarism; it appears as if a famine, a universal war of devastation had cut off the supply of every means of subsistence; industry and commerce seem to be destroyed; and why? Because there is too much civilisation, too much means of subsistence, too much industry, too much commerce. The productive forces at the disposal of society no longer tend to further the development of the conditions of bourgeois property; on the contrary, they have become too powerful for these conditions, by which they are fettered, and so soon as they overcome these fetters, they bring disorder into the whole of bourgeois society, endanger the existence of bourgeois property. The conditions of bourgeois society are too narrow to comprise the wealth created by them. And how does the bourgeoisie get over these crises? On the one hand by enforced destruction of a mass of productive forces; on the other, by the conquest of new markets, and by the more thorough exploitation of the old ones. That is to say, by paving the way for more extensive and more destructive crises, and by diminishing the means whereby crises are prevented.

The weapons with which the bourgeoisie felled feudalism to the ground are now turned against the bourgeoisie itself.

But not only has the bourgeoisie forged the weapons that bring death to itself; it has also called into existence the men who are to wield those weapons—the modern working-class— the proletarians.

In proportion as the bourgeoisie, i.e., capital, is developed, in the same proportion is the proletariat, the modern working-class, developed, a class of labourers, who live only so long as they find work, and who find work only so long as their labour increases capital. These labourers, who must sell themselves piecemeal, are a commodity, like every other article of commerce, and are consequently exposed to all the vicissitudes of competition, to all the fluctuations of the market.

Owing to the extensive use of machinery and to division of labour, the work of the proletarians has lost all individual character, and, consequently, all charm for the workman. He becomes an appendage of the machine, and it is only the most simple, most monotonous, and most easily acquired knack that is required of him. Hence, the cost of production of a workman is restricted, almost entirely, to the means of subsistence that he requires for his maintenance, and for the propagation of his race. But the price of a commodity, and also of labour, is equal to its cost of production. In proportion, therefore, as the repulsiveness of the work increases, the wage decreases. Nay more, in proportion as the use of machinery and division of labour increases, in the same proportion the burden of toil also increases, whether by prolongation of the working hours, by increase of the work enacted in a given time, or by increased speed of the machinery, etc.

Modern industry has converted the little workshop of the patriarchal master into the great factory of the industrial capitalist. Masses of labourers, crowded into the factory, are organised like soldiers. As privates of the industrial army they are placed under the command of a perfect hierarchy of officers and sergeants. Not only are they the slaves of the bourgeois class, and of the bourgeois State, they are daily and hourly enslaved by the machine, by the over-looker, and, above all, by the individual bourgeois manufacturer himself. The more openly this despotism proclaims gain to be its end and aim, the more petty, the more hateful and the more embittering it is.

The less the skill and exertion or strength implied in manual labour, in other words, the more modern industry becomes developed, the more is the labour of men superseded by that of women. Differences of age and sex have no longer any distinctive social validity for the working class. All are instruments of labour, more or less expensive to use, according to their age and sex.

No sooner is the exploitation of the labourer by the manufacturer, so far, at an end, that he receives his wages in cash, than he is set upon by the other portions of the bourgeoisie, the landlord, the shopkeeper, the pawnbroker, etc.

The lower strata of the Middle class—the small tradespeople, shopkeepers, and retired tradesmen generally, the handicraftsmen and peasants—all these sink gradually into the proletariat, partly because their diminutive capital does not suffice for the scale on which Modern Industry is carried on, and is swamped in the competition with the large capitalists, partly because their specialised skill is rendered worthless by new methods of production. Thus the proletariat is recruited from all classes of the population.

The proletariat goes through various stages of development. With its birth begins its struggle with the bourgeoisie. At first the contest is carried on by individual labourers, then by the workpeople of a factory, then by the operatives of one trade, in one locality, against the individual bourgeois who directly exploits them. They direct their attacks not against the bourgeois conditions of production, but against the instruments of production themselves; they destroy imported wares that compete with their labour, they smash to pieces machinery, they set factories ablaze, they seek to restore by force the vanished status of the workman of the Middle Ages.

At this stage the labourers still form an incoherent mass scattered over the whole country, and broken up by their mutual competition. If anywhere they unite to form more compact bodies, this is not yet the consequence of their own active union, but of the union of the bourgeoisie, which class, in order to attain its own political ends, is compelled to set the whole proletariat in motion, and is moreover yet, for a time, able to do so. At this stage, therefore, the proletarians do not fight their enemies, but the enemies of their enemies, the remnants of absolute monarchy, the landowners, the nonindustrial bourgeois, the petty bourgeoisie. Thus the whole historical movement is concentrated in the hands of the bourgeoisie; every victory so obtained is a victory for the bourgeoisie.

But with the development of industry the proletariat not only increases in number; it becomes concentrated in greater masses, its strength grows, and it feels that strength more. The various interests and conditions of life within the ranks of the proletariat are more and more equalised, in proportion as machinery obliterates all distinctions of labour, and nearly everywhere reduces wages to the same low level. The growing competition among the bourgeois, and the resulting commercial crises, make the wages of the workers ever more fluctuating. The unceasing improvement of machinery, ever more rapidly developing, makes their livelihood more and more precarious; the collisions between individual workmen and individual bourgeois take more and more the character of collisions between two classes. Thereupon the workers begin to form combinations (Trades' Unions) against the bourgeois; they club together in order to keep up the rate of wages; they found permanent associations in order to make provision beforehand for these occasional revolts. Here and there the contest breaks out into riots.

Now and then the workers are victorious, but only for a time. The real fruit of their battles lies, not in the immediate result, but in the ever expanding union of the workers. This union is helped on by the improved means of communication that are created by modern industry, and that place the workers of different localities in contact with one another. It was just this contact that was needed to centralise the numerous local struggles, all of the same character, into one national struggle between classes. But every class struggle is a political struggle. And that union, to attain which the burghers of the Middle Ages, with their miserable highways, required centuries, the modern proletarians [sic], thanks to railways, achieve in a few years.

This organisation of the proletarians into a class, and consequently into a political party, is continually being upset again by the competition between the workers themselves. But it ever rises up again, stronger, firmer, mightier. It compels legislative recognition of particular interests of the workers, by taking advantage of the divisions among the bourgeoisie itself. Thus the ten-hours'-bill in England was carried.

Altogether collisions between the classes of the old society further, in many ways, the course of development of the proletariat. The bourgeoisie finds itself involved in a constant battle. At first with the aristocracy; later on, with those portions of the bourgeoisie itself, whose interests have become antagonistic to the progress of industry; at all times, with the bourgeoisie of foreign countries. In all these battles it sees itself compelled to appeal to the proletariat, to ask for its help, and thus, to drag it into the political arena. The bourgeoisie itself, therefore, supplies the proletariat with its own elements of political and general education, in other words, it furnishes the proletariat with weapons for fighting the bourgeoisie.

Further, as we have already seen, entire sections of the ruling classes are, by the advance of industry, precipitated into the proletariat, or are at least threatened in their conditions of existence. These also supply the proletariat with fresh elements of enlightenment and progress.

Finally, in times when the class-struggle nears the decisive hour, the process of dissolution going on within the ruling class, in fact within the whole range of old society, assumes such a violent, glaring character, that a small section of the ruling class cuts itself adrift, and joins the revolutionary class, the class that holds the future in its hands. Just as, therefore, at an earlier period, a section of the nobility went over to the bourgeoisie, so now a portion of the bourgeoisie goes over to the proletariat, and in particular, a portion of the bourgeois ideologists, who have raised themselves to the level of comprehending theoretically the historical movements as a whole.

Of all the classes that stand face to face with the bourgeoisie to-day, the proletariat alone is a really revolutionary class. The other classes decay and finally disappear in the face of modern industry; the proletariat is its special and essential product.

The lower middle-class, the small manufacturer, the shopkeeper, the artisan, the peasant, all these fight against the bourgeoisie, to save from extinction their existence as fractions of the middle class. They are therefore not revolutionary, but conservative. Nay more, they are reactionary, for they try to roll back the wheel of history. If by chance they are revolutionary, they are so, only in view of their impending transfer into the proletariat, they thus defend not their present, but their future interests, they desert their own standpoint to place themselves at that of the proletariat.

The "dangerous class," the social scum, that passively rotting mass thrown off by the lowest layers of old society, may, here and there, be swept into the movement by a proletarian revolution; its conditions of life, however, prepare it far more for the part of a bribed tool of reactionary intrigue.

In the conditions of the proletariat, those of old society at large are already virtually swamped. The proletarian is without property; his relation to his wife and children has no longer anything in common with the bourgeois family-relations; modern industrial labour, modern subjection to capital, the same in England as in France, in America as in Germany, has stripped him of every trace of national character. Law, morality, religion, are to him so many bourgeois prejudices, behind which lurk in ambush just as many bourgeois interests.

All the preceding classes that got the upper hand, sought to fortify their already acquired status by subjecting society at large to their conditions of appropriation. The proletarians cannot become masters of the productive forces of society, except by abolishing their own previous mode of appropriation, and thereby also every other previous mode of appropriation. They have nothing of their own to secure and to fortify; their mission is to destroy all previous securities for, and insurances of, individual property.

All previous historical movements were movements of minorities, or in the interest of minorities. The proletarian movement is the self-conscious, independent movement of the immense majority, in the interest of the immense majority. The proletariat, the lowest stratum of our present society, cannot stir, cannot raise itself up, without the whole superincumbent strata of official society being sprung into the air.

Though not in substance, yet in form, the struggle of the proletariat with the bourgeoisie is at first a national struggle. The proletariat of each country must, of course, first of all settle matters with its own bourgeoisie.

In depicting the most general phases of the development of the proletariat, we traced the more or less veiled civil war, raging within existing society, up to the point where that war breaks out into open revolution, and where the violent overthrow of the bourgeoisie, lays the foundation for the sway of the proletariat.

Hitherto, every form of society has been based, as we have already seen, on the antagonism of oppressing and oppressed classes. But in order to oppress a class, certain conditions must be assured to it under which it can, at least, continue its slavish existence. The serf, in the period of serfdom, raised himself to membership in the commune, just as the petty bourgeois, under the yoke of feudal absolutism, managed to develop into a bourgeois. The modern labourer, on the contrary, instead of rising with the progress of industry, sinks deeper and deeper below the conditions of existence of his own class. He becomes a pauper, and pauperism develops more rapidly than population and wealth. And here it becomes evident, that the bourgeoisie is unfit any longer to be the ruling class in society, and to impose its conditions of existence upon society as an over-riding law. It is unfit to rule, because it is incompetent to assure an existence to its slave within his slavery, because it cannot help letting him sink into such a state, that it has to feed him, insead [instead] of being fed by him. Society can no longer live under this bourgeoisie, in other words, its existence is no longer compatible with society.

The essential condition for the existence, and for the sway of the bourgeois class, is the formation and augmentation of capital; the condition for capital is wage-labour. Wage-labour rests exclusively on competition between the labourers. The advance of industry, whose involuntary promoter is the bourgeoisie, replaces the isolation of the labourers, due to competition, by their involuntary combination, due to association. The development of Modern Industry, therefore, cuts from under its feet the very foundation on which the bourgeoisie produces and appropriates products. What the bourgeoisie therefore produces, above all, are its own grave-diggers. Its fall and the victory of the proletariat are equally inevitable.

II.

PROLETARIANS AND COMMUNISTS.

In what relation do the Communists stand to the proletarians as a whole?

The Communists do not form a separate party opposed to other working-class parties.

They have no interests separate and apart from those of the proletariat as a whole.

They do not set up any sectarian principles of their own, by which to shape and mould the proletarian movement.

The Communists are distinguished from the other working class parties by this only: 1. In the national struggles of the proletarians of the different countries, they point out and bring to the front the common interests of the entire proletariat, inde-pendently of all nationality. 2. In the various stages of develop-ment which the struggle of the working class against the bour-geoisie has to pass through, they always and everywhere represent the interests of the movement as a whole.

The Communists, therefore, are on the one hand, practically, the most advanced and resolute section of the working class parties of every country, that section which pushes forward all others; on the other hand, theoretically, they have over the great mass of the proletariat the advantage of clearly understanding the line of march, the conditions, and the ultimate general results of the proletarian movement.

The immediate aim of the Communists is the same as that of all the other proletarian parties: formation of the proletariat into a class, overthrow of the bourgeois supremacy, conquest of political power by the proletariat.

The theoretical conclusions of the Communists are in no way based on ideas or principles that have been invented, or dis-covered, by this or that would-be universal reformer.

They merely express, in general terms, actual relations springing from an existing class struggle, from a historical move-ment going on under our very eyes. The abolition of existing property-relations is not at all a distinctive feature of Communism.

All property relations in the past have continually been subject to historical change consequent upon the change in his-torical conditions.

The French Revolution, for example, abolished feudal property in favour of bourgeois property.

The distinguishing feature of Communism is not the aboli-tion of property generally, but the abolition of bourgeois prop-erty. But modern bourgeois private property is the final and most complete expression of the system of producing and appropriating products, that is based on class antagonism, on the exploitation of the many by the few.

In this sense, the theory of the Communists may be summed up in the single sentence: Abolition of private property.

We Communists have been reproached with the desire of abolishing the right of personally acquiring property as the fruit of a man's own labour, which property is alleged to be the ground work of all personal freedom, activity and independence.

Hard-won, self-acquired, self-earned property! Do you mean the property of the petty artizan and of the small peasant, a form of property that preceded the bourgeois form? There is no need to abolish that; the development of industry has to a great extent already destroyed it, and is still destroying it daily.

Or do you mean modern bourgeois private property?

But does wage-labour create any property for the labourer? Not a bit. It creates capital, i.e., that kind of property which exploits wage-labour, and which cannot increase except upon condition of getting a new supply of wage-labour for fresh exploitation. Property, in its present form, is based on the antagonism of capital and wage-labour. Let us examine both sides of this antagonism.

To be a capitalist, is to have not only a purely personal, but a social status in production. Capital is a collective product, and only by the united action of many members, nay, in the last resort, only by the united action of all members of society, can it be set in motion.

Capital is therefore not a personal, it is a social power.

When, therefore, capital is converted into common property, into the property of all members of society, personal property is not thereby transformed into social property. It is only the social character of the property that is changed. It loses its class-character.

Let us now take wage-labour.

The average price of wage-labour is the minimum wage, i.e., that quantum of the means of subsistence, which is absolutely requisite to keep the labourer in bare existence as a labourer. What, therefore, the wage-labourer appropriates by means of his labour, merely suffices to prolong and reproduce a bare existence. We by no means intend to abolish this personal appropriation of the products of labour, an appropriation that is made for the maintenance and reproduction of human life, and that leaves no surplus wherewith to command the labour of others. All that we want to do away with is the miserable character of this appropriation, under which the labourer lives merely to increase capital, and is allowed to live only in so far as the interest of the ruling class requires it.

In bourgeois society, living labour is but a means to increase accumulated labour. In Communist society, accumulated labour is but a means to widen, to enrich, to promote the existence of the labourer.

In bourgeois society, therefore, the past dominates the present; in communist society, the present dominates the past. In bourgeois society capital is independent and has individuality, while the living person is dependent and has no individuality.

And the abolition of this state of things is called by the bourgeois, abolition of individuality and freedom! And rightly so. The abolition of bourgeois individuality, bourgeois independence, and bourgeois freedom is undoubtedly aimed at.

By freedom is meant, under the present bourgeois conditions of production, free trade, free selling and buying.

But if selling and buying disappears, free selling and buying disappears also. This talk about free selling and buying, and all the other "brave words" of our bourgeoisie about freedom in general, have a meaning, if any, only in contrast with restricted selling and buying, with the fettered traders of the Middle Ages, but have no meaning when opposed to the Communistic abolition of buying and selling, of the bourgeois conditions of production, and of the bourgeoisie itself.

You are horrified at our intending to do away with private property. But in your existing society, private property is already done away with for nine-tenths of the population; its existence for the few is solely due to its non-existence in the hands of those nine-tenths. You reproach us, therefore, with intending to do away with a form of property, the necessary condition for whose existence is, the non-existence of any property for the immense majority of society.

In one word, you reproach us with intending to do away with your property. Precisely so: that is just what we intend.

From the moment when labour can no longer be converted into capital, money, or rent, into a social power capable of being monopolised, i.e., from the moment when individual property can no longer be transformed into bourgeois property, into capital, from that moment, you say, individuality vanishes.

You must, therefore, confess that by "individual" you mean no other person than the bourgeois, than the middle-class owner of property. This person must, indeed, be swept out of the way, and made impossible.

Communism deprives no man of the power to appropriate the products of society: all that it does is to deprive him of the power to subjugate the labour of others by means of such appropriation.

It has been objected, that upon the abolition of private property all work will cease, and universal laziness will overtake us.

According to this, bourgeois society ought long ago to have gone to the dogs through sheer idleness; for those of its members who work, acquire nothing, and those who acquire anything, do not work. The whole of this objection is but another expression of the tautology: that there can no longer be any wage-labour when there is no longer any capital.

All objections urged against the Communistic mode of producing and appropriating material products, have, in the same way, been urged against the Communistic modes of producing and appropriating intellectual products. Just as, to the bourgeois, the disappearance of class property is the disappearance of production itself, so the disappearance of class culture is to him identical with the disappearance of all culture.

That culture, the loss of which he laments, is, for the enormous majority, a mere training to act as a machine.

But don't wrangle with us so long as you apply, to our intended abolition of bourgeois property, the standard of your bourgeois notions of freedom, culture, law, etc. Your very ideas are but the outgrowth of the conditions of your bourgeois production and bourgeois property, just as your jurisprudence is but the will of your class made into a law for all, a will, whose essential character and direction are determined by the economical conditions of existence of your class.

The selfish misconception that induces you to transform into eternal laws of nature and of reason, the social forms springing from your present mode of production and form of property—historical relations that rise and disappear in the progress of production—this misconception you share with every ruling class that has preceded you. What you see clearly in the case of ancient property, what you admit in the case of feudal property, you are of course forbidden to admit in the case of your own bourgeois form of property.

Abolition of the family! Even the most radical flare up at this infamous proposal of the Communists.

On what foundation is the present family, the bourgeois family based? On capital, on private gain. In its completely developed form this family exists only among the bourgeoisie. But this state of things finds its complement in the practical absence of the family among the proletarians, and in public prostitution.

The bourgeois family will vanish as a matter of course when its complement vanishes, and both will vanish with the vanishing of capital.

Do you charge us with wanting to stop the exploitation of children by their parents? To this crime we plead guilty.

But, you will say, we destroy the most hallowed of relations, when we replace home education by social.

And your education! Is not that also social, and determined by the social conditions under which you educate, by the intervention, direct or indirect, of society by means of schools, &c.? The Communists have not invented the intervention of society in education; they do but seek to alter the character of that intervention, and to rescue education from the influence of the ruling class.

The bourgeois clap-trap about the family and education, about the hallowed co-relation of parent and child, become all the more disgusting, the more, by the action of Modern Industry, all family ties among the proletarians are torn asunder, and their children transformed into simple articles of commerce and instruments of labour.

But you Communists would introduce community of women, screams the whole bourgeoisie in chorus.

The bourgeois sees in his wife a mere instrument of production. He hears that the instruments of production are to be exploited in common, and, naturally, can come to no other conclusion, than that the lot of being common to all will likewise fall to the women.

He has not even a suspicion that the real point aimed at is to do away with the status of women as mere instruments of production.

For the rest, nothing is more ridiculous than the virtuous indignation of our bourgeois at the community of women which, they pretend, is to be openly and officially established by the Communists. The Communists have no need to introduce community of women; it has existed almost from time immemorial.

Our bourgeois, not content with having the wives and daughters of their proletarians at their disposal, not to speak of common prostitutes, take the greatest pleasure in seducing each others' wives.

Bourgeois marriage is in reality a system of wives in common and thus, at the most, what the Communists might possibly be reproached with, is that they desire to introduce, in substitution for a hypocritically concealed, an openly legalised community of women. For the rest, it is self-evident, that the abolition of the present system of production must bring with it the obolition [abolition] of the community of women springing from that system, i.e., of prostitution both public and private.

The Communists are further reproached with desiring to abolish countries and nationalities.

The working men have no country. We cannot take from

them what they have not got. Since the proletariat must first of all acquire political supremacy, must rise to be the leading class of the nation, must constitute itself the nation, it is, so far, itself national, though not in the bourgeois sense of the word.

National differences, and antagonisms between peoples, are daily more and more vanishing, owing to the development of the bourgeoisie, to freedom of commerce, to the world-market, to uniformity in the mode of production and in the conditions of life corresponding thereto.

The supremacy of the proletariat will cause them to vanish still faster. United action, of the leading civilised countries at least, is one of the first conditions for the emancipation of the proletariat.

In proportion as the exploitation of one individual by another is put an end to, the exploitation of one nation by another will also be put an end to. In proportion as the antagonism between classes within the nation vanishes, the hostility of one nation to another will come to an end.

The charges against Communism made from a religious, a philosophical, and generally, from an ideological standpoint, are not deserving of serious examination.

Does it require deep intuition to comprehend that man's ideas, views, and conceptions, in one word, man's consciousness, changes with every change in the conditions of his material existence, in his social relations and in his social life?

What else does the history of ideas prove, than that intellectual production changes in character in proportion as material production is changed? The ruling ideas of each age have ever been the ideas of its ruling class.

When people speak of ideas that revolutionize society, they do but express the fact, that within the old society, the elements of a new one have been created, and that the dissolution of the old ideas keeps even pace with the dissolution of the old conditions of existence.

When the ancient world was in its last throes, the ancient religions were overcome by Christianity. When Christian ideas succumbed in the 18th century to rationalist ideas, feudal society fought its death-battle with the then revolutionary bourgeoisie. The ideas of religious liberty and freedom of conscience, merely gave expression to the sway of free competition within the domain of knowledge.

"Undoubtedly," it will be said, "religious, moral, philosophical and juridical ideas have been modified in the course of historical development. But religion, morality, philosophy, political science, and law, constantly survived this change."

"There are, besides, eternal truths, such as Freedom, Justice, etc., that are common to all states of society. But Communism abolishes eternal truths, it abolishes all religion, and all morality, instead of constituting them on a new basis; it therefore acts in contradiction to all past historical experience."

What does this accusation reduce itself to? The history of all past society has consisted in the development of class antagonisms, antagonisms that assumed different forms at different epochs.

But whatever form they may have taken, one fact is common to all past ages, viz., the exploitation of one part of society by the other. No wonder, then, that the social consciousness of past ages, despite all the multiplicity and variety it displays, moves within certain common forms, or general ideas, which cannot completely vanish except with the total disappearance of class antagonisms.

The Communist revolution is the most radical rupture with traditional property-relations; no wonder that its development involves the most radical rupture with traditional ideas.

But let us have done with the bourgeois objections to Communism.

We have seen above, that the first step in the revolution by the working class, is to raise the proletariat to the position of ruling class, to win the battle of democracy.

The proletariat will use its political supremacy, to wrest, by degrees, all capital from the bourgeoisie, to centralise all instruments of production in the hands of the State, i.e., of the proletariat organised as the ruling class; and to increase the total of productive forces as rapidly as possible.

Of course, in the beginning, this cannot be effected except by means of despotic inroads on the rights of property, and on the conditions of bourgeois production; by means of measures, therefore, which appear economically insufficient and untenable, but which, in the course of the movement, outstrip themselves, necessitate further inroads upon the old social order, and are unavoidable as a means of entirely revolutionising the mode of production.

These measures will of course be different in different countries.

Nevertheless in the most advanced countries the following will be pretty generally applicable:

1. Abolition of property in land and application of all rents of land to public purposes.

2. A heavy progressive or graduated income tax.

3. Abolition of all right of inheritance.

4. Confiscation of the property of all emigrants and rebels.

5. Centralisation of credit in the hands of the State, by means of a national bank with State capital and an exclusive monopoly.

6. Centralisation of the means of communication and transport in the hands of the State.

7. Extension of factories and instruments of production owned by the State; the bringing into cultivation of waste lands, and the improvement of the soil generally in accordance with a common plan.

8. Equal liability of all to labour. Establishment of industrial armies, especially for agriculture.

9. Combination of agriculture with manufacturing industries; gradual abolition of the distinction between town and country, by a more equable distribution of the population over the country.

10. Free education for all children in public schools. Abolition of children's factory labour in it's present form. Combination of education with industrial production, etc., etc.

When, in the course of development, class distinctions have disappeared, and all production has been concentrated in the hands of a vast association of the whole nation, the public power will lose its political character. Political power, properly so called, is merely the organised power of one class for oppressing another. If the proletariat during its contest with the bourgeoisie is compelled, by the force of circumstances, to organise itself as a class, if, by means of a revolution, it makes itself the ruling class, and, as such, sweeps away by force the old conditions of production, then it will, along with these conditions, have swept away the conditions for the existence of class antagonisms, and of classes generally, and will thereby have abolished its own supremacy as a class.

In place of the old bourgeois society, with its classes and class antagonisms, we shall have an association, in which the free development of each is the condition for the free development of all.

IV.

POSITION OF THE COMMUNISTS IN RELATION TO THE VARIOUS EXISTING OPPOSITION PARTIES.

Section II. has made clear the relations of the Communists to the existing working class parties, such as the Chartists in England and the Agrarian Reformers in America.

The Communists fight for the attainment of the immediate aims, for the enforcement of the momentary interests of the working class; but in the movement of the present, they also represent and take care of the future of that movement. In France the Communists ally themselves with the Social-Democrats, against the conservative and radical bourgeoisie, reserving, however, the right to take up a critical position in regard to phrases and illusions traditionally handed down from the great Revolution.

In Switzerland they support the Radicals, without losing sight of the fact that this party consists of antagonistic elements, partly of Democratic Socialists, in the French sense, partly of radical bourgeois.

In Poland they support the party that insists on an agrarian revolution, as the prime condition for national emancipation, that party which formented the insurrection of Cracow in 1846.

In Germany they fight with the bourgeoisie whenever it acts in a revolutionary way, against the absolute monarchy, the feudal squirearchy, and the petty bourgeoisie.

But they never cease, for a single instant, to instill into the working class the clearest possible recognition of the hostile antagonism between bourgeoisie and proletariat, in order that the German workers may straightway use, as so many weapons against the bourgeoisie, the social and political conditions that the bourgeoisie must necessarily introduce along with its supremacy, and in order that, after the fall of the reactionary classes in Germany, the fight against the bourgeoisie itself may immediately begin.

The Communists turn their attention chiefly to Germany, because that country is on the eve of a bourgeois revolution, that is bound to be carried out under more advanced conditions of European civilisation, and with a more developed proletariat, than that of England was in the seventeenth, and of France in the eighteenth century, and because the bourgeois revolution in

Germany will be but the prelude to an immediately following proletarian revolution.

In short, the Communists everywhere support every revolutionary movement against the existing social and political order of things.

In all these movements they bring to the front, as the leading question in each, the property question, no matter what its degree of development at the time.

Finally, they labour everywhere for the union and agreement of the democratic parties of all countries.

The Communists disdain to conceal their views and aims. They openly declare that their ends can be attained only by the forcible overthrow of all existing social conditions. Let the ruling classes tremble at a Communistic revolution. The proletarians have nothing to lose but their chains. They have a world to win.

Working men of all countries unite!

READING 10

*

A Utopia

SIR THOMAS MORE wrote the first *Utopia* in 1516. Since that time other books on "utopias," meaning ideal societies in which all men live the best life, have appeared; for example, Edward Bellamy's *Looking Backward 2000-1887,* published in 1888, and William Morris's *News From Nowhere,* published in 1891. Of these dreamers of a new and ideal society, Robert Owen, an English economist, was an important figure. The following reading lists the constitution, or code of laws, for the new society of which he dreamed.

The "utopias" have usually been founded, if not upon a communistic or socialistic idea of society, at least upon one of a highly "collectivist" nature. The "collectivist" nature of Owen's ideal society may be discerned in the laws he formulated: All children shall be reared by the group (society) rather than by individual families; private property shall not exist; public provision shall be made for the sustenance of life. We may criticize such a society because it would be barren of leadership, since each man would be "leveled" to a common denominator. A great degree of "regimentation" would exist and this "regimentation" would substitute for individual liberty a so-called "collective" liberty.

Robert Owen (1771-1858) began his career as an industrialist. He became proprietor of the New Lanark Mills in Scotland, where his social reforms and improvements in manufacturing drew widespread interest. In later years he founded the colony of New Harmony in Indiana in the United States, which was relatively unsuccessful in establishing a communistic society. The reading is from *The Book of the New Moral World* (New York: G. Vale, 84 Roosevelt Street, 1845, 264 pp.), pp. 227, 228-230.

UNIVERSAL LAWS.

1. All shall have liberty to express their opinions upon all subjects, as nature compels them to be received by the strongest impressions made upon the mind.

2. No one shall have any other power, than by fair argument, to control the opinions or belief of another.

3. No praise or blame, no merit or demerit, no reward or punishment, shall be awarded for any opinions or belief.

4. But as the human race has been made to become variously superstitious over the world, all shall have equal right to express their opinions respecting the incomprehensible power which moves the atom and controls the universe, and to worship that power under any name or form, or in any manner agreeable to their consciences; not interfering with the equal rights of others.

5. All shall be equally provided, through life, with the best of everything for human nature, by public arrangements; which arrangements shall give the best known direction to the industry and talents of every one.

6. All shall be educated, from infancy to maturity, in the best manner known at the time.

7. All shall pass through the same general routine of education, domestic teaching, and employment.

8. All children, from their birth, shall be under the especial care of the community of families in which they are born; but their parents shall have free access to them at all proper times, so as not to interfere in the formation of a superior character for them.

9. All children in the same community, shall be trained and educated together, as children of the same family, without partiality; and shall be early taught the fundamental principles of their nature, and how to apply them, on all occasions, consistently to practice.

10. All shall be encouraged from birth to express their feelings and convictions only; or, in other words, to speak the truth solely on all occasions.

11. All, of both sexes, to have equal education, rights, privileges, and personal liberty; the union or marriage of the sexes to arise from the general sympathies and natural feelings of affection, uninfluenced by artificial distinctions.

12. Under the Rational System of society—after the children have been trained to acquire new habits and new feelings, derived from the laws of human nature—there shall be no useless private property.

13. As soon as the members of these families shall have been educated from infancy in a knowledge of the laws of their nature, and to apply them rationally to practice, and surrounded by circumstances in unison with those laws, there shall be no other individual punishment or reward than the wise and benevolent punishments and rewards of nature.

14. Society to be formed of a union of single families into communities, or associations of men, women, and children, in the usual proportions, with not less than about five hundred, nor more than from two thousand to three thousand.

15. As these family unions increase in number, unions of them shall be formed for local and general purposes, in tens, hundreds, thousands, &c., according to the less or more extended objects and interests which shall require their consideration and direction.

16. Each of these associated families shall possess in perpetuity around it land sufficient for the support, for ever, of all its members, even when it shall contain the maximum in number.

17. These communities shall be so arranged as to give to all

the members of each of them, as nearly as possible, the same advantages, and to afford the most easy communication with other.

18. Each community shall be governed in its *home* department by a general council, composed of all its members between the ages of thirty and forty; and each department shall be under the immediate direction of a committee formed of members of the general council, chosen by the latter, in the order to be determined upon; and in its external or foreign affairs, by all its members from forty to sixty years of age.

19. After all the members of the community shall have been rendered capable of taking their full share of the duties in the general council of government, there shall be no selection or election of any individuals to the governing councils, either in the home or foreign department.

20. All the members, at thirty years of age, who shall have been trained from infancy in the communities, shall be officially called upon to undertake their full share of the duties of management in the *home* department; and at forty they will be officially called upon to undertake the duties of the external or foreign department; and at sixty they will be excused from officially attending to them.

21. The duties of the general council of the home department shall be, to govern all the circumstances within the boundaries of its community—to organize the various departments of production, distribution, and formation of character—to remove all those circumstances the least favorable to happiness, and to replace them with the best that can be devised among themselves, or of which they can obtain a knowledge from other communities. The duties of the general council of the external or foreign department will be, to receive visiters [sic] or delegates from other associations or communities—to communicate with other similar associations—to visit and arrange with them the best means of forming roads and conveying surplus produce to each other—to travel, to give and receive information of inventions, improvements, and discoveries, and of every other kind useful to promote the happiness of society; and also to regulate and assist in the establishment of new associations, composed of the surplus population of the community from among themselves, and to send delegates to the circle of communities to which their community shall be attached.

22. The general councils, home and foreign, shall have full

power of government in all things under their direction, as long as they shall act in unison with the laws of human nature, which laws shall be their sole guidance on all occasions.

23. All individuals, trained, educated, and placed in conformity with the laws of their nature, must, of necessity, at all times think and act rationally, except they shall become physically, mentally, or morally diseased; in which case the council shall remove them into the hospital for bodily or mental or moral invalids, where they shall remain until they shall be recovered by the mildest treatment that can effect their cure.

24. The council, whenever it shall be necessary, shall call to its aid the practical abilities and advice of any of the members not in the council.

25. If the general council should ever attempt to contravene the laws of human nature, which is scarcely possible, the elders of the family who have passed the councils, shall call a general meeting of all the members of the community between sixteen and thirty years of age who have been trained within it. This meeting shall calmly and patiently investigate the conduct of the general council, and if a majority of the young and old shall determine that they have acted, or attempted to act, in opposition to these laws, the general government shall devolve upon the members of the community who have passed the councils, and are above sixty years of age, united with those who have not entered the council, and are between twenty and thirty years of age. It is scarcely possible to conceive, that men and women trained to be rational beings from their birth, should render it necessary to resort to the application of this clause; but if required, it can only be for a short period of temporary application.

All other differences of every description, if, indeed, it be possible for any to exist in these families, shall be immediately determined, and amicably adjusted between the parties, by the decision of a majority of the three senior members of the foreign council: except when the difference shall exist between members of the councils; when it shall be, in like manner, determined by the three members who have last passed the councils.

When the human race shall be trained from birth in strict consistency with the . . . fundamental laws of human nature; shall be placed within external circumstances in accordance with those laws, and shall be classified and employed according to age, there will be no necessity for any other laws than the twenty-five now enumerated and explained. During the transition state from irrationality to rationality, regulations in conformity with these laws will be required; but when all shall be educated from birth to be rational beings, they will under every change of circumstances, and on all occasions, without additional laws, act rationally.

READING 11

Free Private Enterprise

FEW DESCRIPTIONS OF THE private enterprise system are as cogent as the following reading by Sumner Slichter. The reading defines free enterprise and describes how the system organizes production, how it determines distribution, and how it regulates consumption. Then Professor Slichter proceeds to examine the claims for free enterprise, the assumptions, and the role of competition. He gives a penetrating critique of the status of the free enterprise system in the modern economy.

Sumner H. Slichter (1892-1959) was an outstanding American economist, late Lamont University Professor at Harvard University. Slichter was a prolific writer of stimulating articles and books, writing as well for the layman as for the professional economist. The reading is from *Modern Economic Society*, Chapter III, "Free Private Enterprise," pp. 35-48. Reprinted by permission from *Modern Economic Society*, by Sumner H. Slichter. Holt, Rinehart & Winston, Inc., New York. 1931.

I. *Possible Forms of Economic Organization*

We have seen that every economic system must provide some way of doing three fundamental things: (1) getting goods produced; (2) determining what share each person shall have in the total product; and (3) regulating the consumption of goods, that is, determining who shall consume this good and who that. The manner in which these three basic economic processes are performed stamps the economic system with its most essential characteristics. How does the existing economic order organize and regulate the production, distribution, and consumption of goods?

There are several ways in which these activities *might* be organized and regulated:

1. On the basis of family autonomy. Each family might produce everything which it uses, relying upon others for nothing. In such a society there would be no trade.

2. On a communistic basis. What is produced and what each person does might be determined by the group as a whole and the product might be the property of the group, to be divided in accordance with socially determined rules.

3. On a despotic basis. The things produced and the tasks of each person might be decided by a despot or a despotic class, the product in all or in part being the property of the despot to be shared with the others as he saw fit.

4. On the basis of custom and heredity. Instead of choosing his own work or having it selected for him by the group or a despot, each person might be born into his occupation. He might be expected to do the thing which his father did, and other occupations might be closed to him. Likewise the share of each person in the product and the things which he is permitted or forbidden to consume might also be determined by custom.

All of these methods of organizing and controlling economic activities have been more or less prevalent in the past and, indeed, instances of them still exist. They are not, however, the methods which prevail today in the United States. It may seem a strange way of doing, but we organize industry by, in effect, saying to each individual, "Choose your own occupation. Produce what you like. What you do, to whom you sell, what or from whom you buy, the prices you get or give, are all your own concern. You are free, subject to a few restrictions, to produce whatever you wish regardless of whether or not it is needed, regardless of whether or not too much of it already exists. You are likewise free to refrain from engaging in any occupation no matter how acute may be the shortage of goods or how pressing the need for your help. You are free to buy from whoever is willing to sell and to sell to whoever is willing to buy. You are equally free to refuse to buy or sell whenever you please and for any reason or no reason."

This is what we mean by *free private enterprise*. Under it the government confines itself in the main to the suppression of fraud and violence and to the enforcement of contracts. It does not itself engage in or attempt to guide the course of industry. It pursues a "let alone" or "hands off" policy. Let us now see how, under free enterprise, the three fundamental economic processes of production, distribution, and consumption take place.

II. *How Free Enterprise Organizes Production*

Why does not a system of freedom, in which each person is at liberty to pursue whatever occupation he pleases and to produce whatever he wishes, result in hopeless chaos? Why do not many essential articles fail to get made and why does not the output of many things far exceed the demand for them? How can we get along without a central directing body to discover how much different things are in demand and to tell each of us what to produce?

To put the problem concretely and specifically, how does New York City each day obtain about the quantity of milk that it demands? The city's daily consumption in 1922 was approximately 2,000,000 quarts. This was supplied by 450,000 cows and came from 1,150 creameries and 40,000 farms in New York, New Jersey, Connecticut, Massachusetts, Pennsylvania, New Hampshire, and Canada. Of the thousands of people engaged in supplying New York with milk, almost none knows either how much the city consumes or how much is being produced. And yet, despite this ignorance, New York each day receives about the amount of milk that it demands. There is neither a great surplus nor a shortage. Milk does not spoil because there is no one to consume it, and babies do not go without it because too small a supply reaches the city on some days. At the same time, other cities in the neighborhood are also receiving their daily supply from the same territory. Each uses a different quantity, yet each receives about the amount that it demands.

This comparatively simple case illustrates our problem. What determines the relative quantities of each and everything produced—how much cotton, corn, oats, wheat, or oranges we raise, how much steel, lumber, coal, or cloth we produce? What tells us when to make more and when less of each commodity?

The guide upon which we rely is the profit in making different goods, which, of course, depends upon the prices which they command and the cost of producing them. Suppose, for example, that New York failed to receive enough milk to satisfy the demand. Rather than go without milk or drink less, many people would be willing to pay more. Consequently the price would promptly rise. This would tend to end the shortage. More milk would be shipped to New York and less to other places. This would continue until there was no greater profit in selling milk in New York than elsewhere.

Just as price regulates the distribution of milk between cities, so it also determines the total amount produced in the country as a whole. Failure of the supply to keep pace with the demand would cause the price to rise. The greater profit to be had from the sale of milk would cause farmers to produce more of it. Some farmers, who had been separating their milk and selling the cream to be made into butter, might turn to the sale of whole milk. Others might abandon raising grain, stock, or fruit and enter dairy farming. As the output of milk increased, the price, of course, would drop. This would continue until producing milk was no more attractive than alternative branches of farming. If, furthermore, the demand for milk were to fall off or the supply to increase faster than the demand, farmers, in order to dispose of their supply, would be compelled to lower the price. Milk production would become a less profitable occupation, men would be deterred from entering it, and some of those already engaged in it might be led to abandon it or at least to reduce their output. And this would continue until the price rose and milk production became no less attractive than alternative occupations.

Innumerable illustrations could be given of the guidance of production by prices. A striking instance is supplied by the effect of changes in the price of wheat upon wheat acreage. During the fifteen years immediately preceding the war [World War I], the acreage planted to wheat in the United States remained substantially stationary. The European war caused the price of wheat to rise rapidly. On December 1, 1914, the average farm price in the United States was 98.6 cents a bushel, the highest in over forty years. In consequence, the area planted increased from 53,541,000 acres in 1914 to 60,169,000 in 1915, the largest in the history of the country. The weather in 1915 was so favorable that the yield per acre was the largest on record. The result of the record-breaking acreage and the record-breaking yield was a crop of over a billion bushels—the first in the country's history

—and a drop in the average farm price by December 1, 1915, to 91.9 cents, causing the acreage for 1916 to decline to 52,316,000. But in 1916 the weather was so unfavorable that the yield per acre was the lowest since 1900. The small crop led to a pronounced advance in price. On December 1, 1916, the farm value was $1.60 per bushel. In August, 1917, after the United States had entered the war, Congress passed the wheat guarantee bill. The President fixed the price for the 1917 crop at $2.20 for No. 1 spring wheat or its equivalent. Stimulated by the high guarantee, acreage increased in 1918 to 59,181,000 and in 1919 to 75,694,000, an unprecedented amount. In 1920, the guarantee expired and a general business depression set in. The result was a rapid fall in both price and acreage. The average farm value, which was $2.15 on December 1, 1919, was $1.44 a year later, and the acreage for 1920 was 61,143,000, or over fourteen and a half millions less than in the previous year.

Price also determines in large measure where and how goods are made. Because living in New York City is expensive, it might seem a poor place in which to locate a factory. But the great stream of immigrants who for many years entered the country at New York and who were reluctant to undertake a long journey through a strange country provided the city with a bountiful supply of cheap labor. To take advantage of this, many industries, such as the needle trades, grew up in or near the East Side. At one time, the Genesee valley in western New York was an important wheat region and Rochester, at the falls of the Genesee, was a great milling center. As the urban population in the East has grown, the greater profits in dairying and in fruit and truck raising have driven wheat raising to the west. The same is true of sheep raising. At one time, New York State contained nearly 5,000,000 sheep; now it has less than one-tenth that number. The growth of urban population has made dairying so profitable that most farmers cannot afford to raise sheep in New York.

Whether goods shall be made by hand or by machinery is often a question of money costs. Shall houses be built of wood or brick? As long as our immense forests were far from exhaustion, wooden houses were the almost universal rule. In Europe, where timber is less plentiful, frame dwellings are the exception. We still use timber to a greater extent than do most countries, but the cost of certain woods, such as white pine, has caused us to use cheaper varieties—Norway pine, hemlock, spruce, Douglas fir. Shall land be farmed intensively or extensively? The English obtain about twice as many bushels of wheat per acre as do the Americans, but we obtain about twice as many bushels per man. The reason is that in England, where land is relatively expensive, it is economized by the use of more labor and less land. Here, where labor is expensive in comparison with land, labor is economized by the use of more land and less labor.

III. *How Shares in the Output of Industry Are Determined*

In our highly specialized society, each of us, at the best, contributes to industry's output very few things. One man may produce wheat, another wool, another milk, another cattle, another corn. In fact, most men do not contribute even one complete product. Hundreds of workers combine their efforts to make a suit of clothes, a pair of shoes, an automobile, or a telephone.

Although each individual makes a very specialized contribution to the product of society, each wishes to obtain from that output hundreds of articles. The man who produces only wheat desires flour, butter, sugar, clothing, shoes, hats, magazines, furniture, services of doctors, dentists, lawyers, and much else. If he contributes 2,000 bushels of wheat to society's stock of goods, how much is he entitled to withdraw?

Just as prices determine what things are produced, in what proportions, and by what methods, so, under free enterprise, they also determine the share of each person in the output of industry. If our imaginary wheat grower, who has produced a crop of 2,000 bushels, obtains $1.25 for each bushel, he is thereby enabled to purchase articles valued at $2,500. Just how much this is, will depend upon the price of shoes, hats, sugar, and the various other things which he desires. The next year he may work harder and produce 2,400 bushels. In the meantime, however, the price of wheat may drop to 75 cents a bushel. Hence, despite the fact that he has worked harder and raised more wheat, he has only $1,800 to spend for goods. And if, perchance, prices in general have risen, each of his dollars will buy him less than the year before. In a word, what share a man receives in the product of industry is determined by the prices of what he has to sell quite as much as by how industriously and efficiently he labors.

IV. *How Consumption Is Regulated Under Free Enterprise*

There are many ways in which we might determine what goods each person shall consume. We might undertake to ascertain the peculiar needs of each and see that he was afforded some special opportunity to obtain the things which would satisfy them. Or we might study the ability of different persons to use goods to the advantage of the rest of us and arrange for men of outstanding ability to receive the things which they require in order to be of greatest service to the community.

To a limited extent, we do regulate consumption upon the basis of either needs or ability to use goods advantageously. Schooling is considered so important that many governments supply a certain amount of it free or below cost. Police and fire protection, parks, playgrounds, and, to some extent, transportation, communication, and insurance are also considered so essential that they are provided by the government. Fellowships and scholarships, awarded to students of special promise, are among the few attempts which we make to place goods within reach of those who can use them to special advantage.

Under a system of free enterprise, however, which permits men to buy whatever they can get on the best terms that they can obtain, neither need nor ability to use goods for the benefit of others necessarily has much to do with determining how goods are consumed. Of far greater importance are the prices of different commodities and the ability of different persons to pay these prices. Goods go to those who are able and willing to pay the most for them—not to those who have the greatest need for them or who will do the greatest good with them.

In some respects, the control of consumption by price and ability to pay works out very satisfactorily. Suppose, for example, that unfavorable weather or blight made it likely that the potato crop would be exceptionally small. It is obvious that we should need to consume potatoes sparingly, making more than customary use of substitutes. If, on the other hand, the outlook were for a large crop, it would be to our interest to use more potatoes than usual. In each case, price produces the desired effect. If the prospects are for a small crop, the higher price induces sparing consumption; if a large crop seems probable, the low price encourages larger consumption. Because skilled labor is scarce, it is desirable that we economize it by using its products sparingly. The high wages of skilled craftsmen make their products expensive and encourage consumers to avoid wasting them. Commodities which can be made only at great risk of accident or industrial disease should also be used sparingly. In so far as these hazards cause workmen to demand higher wages, they increase the price of the products and limit their consumption.

Although the regulation of consumption by prices usually encourages the economizing of scarce goods, it does so in a manner not altogether satisfactory. If consumption must be reduced, this should perhaps be accomplished by those using less who can do so with the smallest inconvenience and sacrifice. As a matter of fact, the well-to-do, who are best supplied, are least induced by higher prices to curtail their purchases. It is the poor, who can least afford to reduce their consumption, who get along with less when the supply falls short. In periods of severe food shortage, such as often occur during war time, the regulation of consumption by ability to pay works such hardship that it is sometimes superseded by a system of rationing.

V. *Some Claims on Behalf of Free Enterprise*

Since free enterprise is the principal method by which our economic activities are organized and controlled, our study of modern industrial society must very largely consist of an inquiry into how freedom works under present-day conditions—such as machine industry, huge corporations, and science applied to business. But before we proceed further with our analysis, it will be helpful to become familiar in a general way with some of the claims which have been made in behalf of free enterprise. The "obvious and simple system of natural liberty," as Adam Smith called freedom of enterprise,[1] has been regarded as the one and only way in which men might attain the maximum satisfaction of their desires with a minimum outlay of sacrifice. It is true that this extreme view has been accepted by few economists of repute and that since the middle of the last century it has been increasingly under attack. Nevertheless it has had and still does have wide acceptance by the general public and by certain schools of politicians, and it is appealed to frequently in political controversies. And even though we no longer spend much time discussing whether or not we can *always* trust free enterprise to regulate economic activity better than any other method, we are frequently compelled to decide whether or not it is the best way of controlling a specific economic activity under specific circumstances. Consequently the claims which have been made on its behalf are still very live issues.

The reasoning in support of the belief that freedom of enterprise results in the maximum of satisfaction at the minimum

---

[1] *Wealth of Nations,* Bk. IV, Ch. IX.

of cost is very simple. Each individual, it is said, is better able than any one else to judge his own interests. If men are at liberty to spend their money as they choose, they will naturally purchase those things that will yield them the most satisfaction. Consequently the very commodities which give consumers the greatest pleasure are the most profitable for business enterprises to produce. Likewise, if men are free to use such methods of production as they wish, they will select those which involve the least cost per unit of output. With the goods which give the greatest gratification being made by the methods which are least costly, it follows, according to the theory, that there will be the maximum surplus of satisfaction over sacrifice.

VI. *Some Assumptions of the Theory of Free Enterprise*

But if this result is to follow, two things would appear to be necessary: (1) goods must go to the consumers who will derive the greatest pleasure from them, and (2) the tasks of making goods must be assigned to the workers who can perform them with the least sacrifice for each unit of product. Does freedom of enterprise cause either goods or jobs to be distributed in this manner?

We have already seen that under a system of free enterprise goods tend to get into the hands of those who offer the best prices for them. But how then can they be consumed so as to yield the maximum of satisfaction? Are the people who are willing and able to pay most for goods also those who will derive the most satisfaction from using them? If they are not, it would appear possible to increase the surplus of satisfaction over sacrifice by causing goods to be distributed more in accordance with needs and less in accordance with ability to pay. We have no way of comparing the amount of pleasure which two persons derive from consuming an article. And yet it seems ridiculous to assert that ability to derive satisfaction from goods is proportionate to ability to pay for them. Assume that A and B each wish a pair of shoes. A, who is well-to-do, is willing to pay $12; B, who is poor, will offer only $7. Obviously A will get the shoes. But because he is rich and well supplied with shoes, an additional pair is only a slight convenience to him. B, poor and scantily supplied, has urgent need for another pair. It seems clear that the sum total of satisfaction would be greater if B obtained the shoes, and yet it seems equally clear that under freedom of enterprise they will go to A.

We are no better able to compare the pains suffered by different persons than we are the pleasures which they enjoy. Nevertheless it does not appear probable that freedom of enterprise necessarily causes jobs to be distributed so as to result in a minimum sacrifice for each unit of output—so that, for example, persons who can do heavy work with least fatigue will be given heavy work. Rather jobs tend to go to those who are willing to do the most work for the least money. Now the fact that X is willing to do a job for a dollar a day less than Y does not necessarily mean that X finds the task less onerous or unpleasant than Y. It may simply mean that he needs the money more and is willing to work at a lower rate in order to get it.

In face of the fact that ability to derive pleasure from goods does not appear to correspond to capacity to pay for them and that jobs are not necessarily given to the men who can do them with the least sacrifice for each unit of product, how can it be asserted that industrial liberty results in a maximum of satisfaction over sacrifice? But the exponents of free enterprise are not without a reply. To interfere with liberty in order to bring about a distribution of goods upon the basis of needs rather than ability to pay, or in order to cause jobs to be assigned to those who could perform them with least sacrifice, might have the *immediate* effect of increasing the surplus of satisfaction over sacrifice. But this result, it is said, would be short lived. Men have the greatest incentive to improve their efficiency when they are free to compete for any jobs which they desire and to spend their income as they see fit. Were this incentive diminished by distributing jobs to those who could perform them with the least sacrifice and goods to those who would derive the most pleasure from them, output would inevitably decline. What would be gained by a different distribution of goods and jobs would be lost through smaller production.

VII. *The Significance of Competition*

But how is it possible for us to trust business enterprises with so much freedom? In other branches of human relations, laws to regulate conduct seem to be quite essential. Why should industry be an exception to this general rule? If we leave business concerns free to make anything they like by any methods which they see fit, what is to prevent them from supplying the public with poorly made or adulterated goods or from using methods that are cheap in terms of dollars but expensive in terms of human sacrifice? Might not the sum total of pleasure be greater and of pain be less if the state enforced certain standards of quality or prohibited the use of certain methods of production?

The theory of free enterprise does not, it is important to emphasize, assert that restraints upon human selfishness are not needed. It simply assumes that they are provided by *competition*. This, according to the theory, is the great regulative force which establishes effective control over economic activities and gives each of us an incentive to observe the interests of others. Thus business establishments are deterred from furnishing adulterated or poorly made goods by the fear that customers may shift their patronage to rivals. Likewise the enterprises which fail to protect their men against accidents or industrial disease or which work them unusually hard, are penalized by the refusal of laborers to work for them except at a higher wage than other employers pay.

The mere existence of competition, however, is not enough. For it to perform satisfactorily the protective function attributed to it, certain very definite conditions must be present.

To begin with, an appreciable proportion of buyers and sellers must be willing to discriminate against those sellers or buyers who ignore, and in favor of those who take account of, the welfare of others. Otherwise, of course, no one has an economic incentive to pay attention to the wellbeing of his fellows. Assume, for example, that an enterprise pollutes a stream by dumping refuse and chemicals into it. From the standpoint of the firm, this may be an economical method of production. But from the standpoint of the community it is an expensive one, because it kills the fish, spoils the stream for bathing, and makes it foul and ill-smelling. But competition will not stop the pollution unless an appreciable number of consumers, wage earners, or investors refuse to deal with the firm which is responsible—that is, unless a substantial number of consumers refuse to buy from it, or wage earners to work for it, or investors to put money into it. But if the enterprise charges no more than its rivals for goods of equal grade, offers equally attractive conditions of employment, and pays as high dividends, who has an interest in discriminating against it? Perhaps the very fact that the enterprise pollutes the stream enables it to offer better terms than its rivals. Or take the case of child labor—another method of production cheap in dollars and cents but expensive in terms of human cost. If the firms which employ children are able, *because of that very fact,* to sell for less or to pay higher wages to adults or higher profits to investors, who is going to discriminate against them?

Under these circumstances, does not competition positively encourage the employment of children?

But willingness to discriminate between those who consider the interests of others and those who do not is insufficient. Competition protects consumers against inferior ware only when they know good quality from bad; it protects laborers from unguarded machines only when they know which employers have and which have not guarded their machines. In other words, competition is an efficient protective agency only when buyers or sellers have the information necessary to make intelligent choices. It fails, for example, to protect consumers against milk from tubercular cattle because the ordinary buyer of milk has no way of distinguishing the milk of healthy cows from that of diseased.

The information needed for intelligent choices may be available, and yet many buyers or sellers may be too ignorant, too careless, too neglectful of their own interests to use it. If, for example, workmen show no disposition to shun plants which are notoriously dangerous or unsanitary, what incentive have employers to improve conditions?

Discrimination can have an effect only when those who are its objects realize that it is being practiced. For years, wage earners, by quitting and seeking work elsewhere, have discriminated against employers who gave poor treatment. But all of this produced little effect upon working conditions and labor policies because employers were not aware how many men were quitting. As soon, however, as enterprises began to keep track of the number of resignations, great improvements occurred in the treatment of labor.

Finally, competition works well as a protective force only when there is not great disparity in bargaining power between buyers and sellers. If workmen are so numerous and jobs so scarce that competition among laborers for jobs is more intense than competition among employers for men, conditions of employment are bound to be unsatisfactory. Likewise in boom times, when goods are scarce and deliveries are slow, competition fails to protect consumers against poor ware. In the clothing industry, for example, it is notorious that in busy years the quality of garments goes down.

PART II

NATIONAL INCOME
AND WEALTH

READING 12

Wealth

WEALTH CONSISTS OF THOSE ARTICLES which have utility, scarcity, and transferability. Nowhere is this made more clear than in the work of Nassau William Senior. Since an article to be wealth must possess the ability to be transferred, which is the same thing as being "exchanged," wealth may be measured and therefore has *value*. Value has been defined most aptly by Alfred Marshall as "the worth of a thing in exchange." Further, value arises from a commodity having the constituents of utility and scarcity. We see, then, that the two concepts "wealth" and "value" are closely intertwined. Value is an expression of a measurement of wealth. Of these three constituents of wealth, Senior is at considerable pains to point out the extraordinary importance of scarcity, or, as he calls it, "limitation in supply."

On one count in particular we criticize Senior's attitude: He believed, like Adam Smith and the other great "classical" economic scholars, that the total of national or public wealth could be measured by adding up all of the private wealth in the economy. However, the Earl of Lauderdale in his work on scarcity, quoted in Reading 5 of this volume, points out that artificial scarcity may be manufactured by an individual which is to the detriment of the whole society; this artificial scarcity would make for a great value being placed upon this scarce object and a nation with little of this particular item would be worse off than if it had so much of this item that the item possessed no value whatsoever.

Nassau William Senior (1790-1864) was an English economist, Professor of Political Economy at Oxford University. He also held various government posts; he was a member of the Royal Commission of 1832 which investigated the English "poor laws." His principal work in economics was his *Political Economy*, first published as a long article in Samuel Taylor Coleridge's *Encyclopedia Metropolitana*. He has given us one of the clearest and most comprehensive statements defining wealth. The reading is from *Political Economy* (London and Glasgow: Richard Griffin and Company, 4th ed., 1858, 231 pp.), "Nature of Wealth," pp. 6-13.

Wealth Defined.—Having stated that the science which we propose to consider, and to which we apply the term Political Economy, is the science which treats of the Nature, the Production, and the Distribution of Wealth, our first business is to explain the meaning in which we use the word Wealth.

Under that term we comprehend all those things, and those things only, which are transferable, are limited in supply, and are directly or indirectly productive of pleasure or preventive of pain; or, to use an equivalent expression, which are susceptible of *exchange* (using the word exchange to denote hiring as well as absolute purchase); or, to use a third equivalent expression, which have *Value*; a word which, in a subsequent portion of this treatise, we shall explain at some length, merely premising at present that we use it in its popular sense, as denoting the capacity of being given and received in exchange.

Constituents of Wealth.

I. Utility.—Of the three qualities which render anything an article of Wealth, or, in other words, give it value, the most striking is the power, direct or indirect, of producing pleasure, including under that term gratification of every kind, or of preventing pain, including under that term every species of discomfort. Unfortunately, we have no word which precisely expresses this power; *utility*, which comes nearest to it, being generally used to express the quality of preventing pain or of indirectly producing pleasure, as a means. We shall venture to extend the signification of that word, and consider it as also including all those things which produce pleasure directly. We must admit that this is a considerable innovation in English language. It is, however, sanctioned by Mr. Malthus (*Definitions,* p. 234), and has been ventured by M. Say in French, a language less patient of innovation than our own. Feeling the same difficulty, he has solved it in the same way by using the term *utilité* as comprehending every quality that renders anything an object of desire. Attractiveness and desirableness have both been suggested to us as substitutes, but on the whole they appear to us more objectionable than *utility*, objectionable as we must admit that word to be.

Utility, thus explained, is a necessary constituent of value; no man would give anything possessing the slightest utility for a thing possessing none; and even an exchange of two useless things would be, on the part of each party to the exchange, an act without a motive. Utility, however, denotes no intrinsic quality in the things which we call useful; it merely expresses their relations to the pains and pleasures of mankind. And, as the susceptibility of pain and pleasure from particular objects is created and modified by causes innumerable, and constantly varying, we find an endless diversity in the relative utility of different objects to different persons, a diversity which is the motive of all exchanges.

II. Limitation in Supply.—The next constituent of value is *limitation in supply*.—It may appear inaccurate to apply this expression to any class of things, as it, in fact, belongs to all; there being nothing which, strictly speaking, is unlimited in supply. But, for the purposes of Political Economy, everything may be considered as unlimited in supply *in its existing state*, of which a man may have as much as he pleases for the mere trouble of taking it into his possession. Thus the water of the open sea is, in our use of the term, unlimited in supply; any man who chooses to go for it may have as much of it as he pleases: that portion of it which has been brought to London is limited in supply, and is to be obtained not merely by going to the reservoir and taking possession of it, but by giving for it an equivalent. The copper ores which Sir John Franklin discovered on the shores of the Arctic Seas may be considered, *in their existing state*, as unlimited in supply; any man may have as much of them as he has strength and patience to extract. The extracted portion would be limited in supply, and therefore susceptible of value. Many things are unlimited in supply for some purposes, and limited for others. The water in a river is in general more than sufficient for all the domestic purposes for which it can be required; nobody pays, therefore, for permission to take a bucketful: but it is seldom sufficient for all those who may wish to turn their mills with it; they pay, therefore, for that privilege.

It must be further observed that, for economical purposes, the term *limitation in supply* always involves the consideration of the causes by which the existing supply is limited. The supply of some articles of Wealth is limited by insurmountable obstacles. The number of Raphael's pictures, or of Canova's statues, may be diminished, but cannot possibly be increased. There are others of which the supply may be increased to an indefinite extent. Such things may be considered as comparatively limited in supply, in proportion, not to the existing supply of each, but to the force of the obstacles opposed to their respective increase. It is supposed that there is now about forty-five times as much of silver extracted from the mines, and current in Europe, as there is of gold. Human exertion is the only means by which the supply of either can be increased, and they may both be increased by human exertion to an amount of which we do not know the limit. The obstacle, therefore, by which they are each limited in supply is, the amount of human exertion necessary to their respective increase. About sixteen times more exertion is necessary to produce an ounce of gold than an ounce of silver. The obstacle, therefore, which limits the supply of gold is sixteen times more powerful than that which limits the supply of silver. In our sense of the term, therefore, gold is only sixteen times more limited in supply than silver, though the actual weight of silver in Europe is forty-five times as great as that of gold. To take a more familiar example, the number of coats and waistcoats in England is perhaps about equal. The supply of each may be increased by human exertion to an indefinite extent; but it requires about three times as much exertion to produce a coat as to produce a waistcoat. As the obstacle, therefore, which limits the supply of coats is three times as forcible as that which limits the supply of waistcoats, we consider coats three times more limited in supply than waistcoats, though the existing supply of each may perhaps be equal. Whenever, therefore, we apply the words *limited in supply*, as a comparative expression, to those commodities of which the quantity can be increased, we refer to the comparative force of the obstacles which limit the respective supplies of the objects compared.

III. Transferableness.—The third and last quality which a thing must possess to constitute it an article of Wealth, or, in other words, to give it value, is *Transferableness*, by which term (we are sorry to say, an unusual one) we mean to express that all or some portion of its powers of giving pleasure, or preventing pain, are capable of being transferred, either absolutely, or for a period. For this purpose it is obvious that it must be capable of appropriation; since no man can give what he cannot refuse.

The sources of pleasure and preventives of pain which are absolutely incapable of appropriation are very few. We almost doubt whether there are any, and we are sure that the instances which are usually given are incorrect. "The earth," observes M. Say (*Econ. Pol.*, liv. ii, ch. ix.), "is not the only material agent with productive power, but it is the only one, or nearly so, that can be appropriated. The water of rivers and of the sea, which supplies us with fish, gives motion to our mills, and supports our vessels, has productive powers. The wind gives us force, and the sun heat, but happily no man can say, 'The wind and the sun belong to me, and I will be paid for their services.'" Now, in fact, air and sunshine are local. This is so obvious that it would be absurd to prove, by serious induction, that some situations have too much wind, and others too little, or that the sun's rays are more powerful productive agents in England than in Melville Island, or in the tropics than in England. And as the land is everywhere capable of appropriation, the qualities of climate, which are attributes of that land, must be so too. What gives their principal value to the vineyards of the Côte Rotie, but the warmth of their sun? or to the houses which overlook Hyde Park, but the purity of their air? Rivers and the sea are equally unfortunate illustrations. Many of the rivers of England are not less strictly appropriated, and are far greater sources of wealth, than any equal superficies of land. When M. Say visited Lancashire, he must have found every inch of fall in every stream the subject of lease and purchase. And so far are the services of the sea from being incapable of appropriation, that, during the late war, £60,000 was sometimes paid for a license to make use of it for a single voyage; and the privilege of fishing in particular parts of it has been the subject of wars and treaties.

The things of which the utility is imperfectly transferable may be divided into two great classes. The first comprises all those material objects which are affected by the peculiar mental associations, or adapted to the peculiar wants, of individuals. A mansion may flatter the pride of its owner as having been the residence of his ancestors, or be endeared to him as the scene of his childhood; or he may have built it in a form which pleases no eye, or laid it out in apartments that suit no habits but his own. Still his substantial powers of affording warmth and shelter will obtain him purchasers or tenants, though they may demand a reduction from the price, in consequence of those very qualities which, with him, formed its principal merits. The palace of St. James's is full of comfort and convenience, and would supply a man of large fortune with an excellent residence; but the long suite of apartments within apartments, which is admirably adapted to holding a Court, would be a mere incumbrance to any but a royal personage. Any individual might hire Alnwick or Blenheim, and enjoy their mere beauty and magnificence, perhaps, more than their owners who have been long familiarized to them; but he could never feel the peculiar pleasure which they seem fitted to give to a Percy and a Churchhill. There are many things, such as clothes and furniture, which sink in utility in the estimation of every one but their purchaser, from the mere fact of having changed hands. A hat or a table which has been just sent home does not appear to the purchaser less useful than when he saw it in the shop; but if he attempt to resell either, he will find that with the rest of the world it has sunk into the degraded rank of second-hand.

The second class of things imperfectly transferable includes the greater part, perhaps all, of our personal qualities. This classification, which places talents and accomplishments among the articles of Wealth, may appear at first sight strange and inconvenient; it certainly is different from that of most Economists. We will therefore venture to illustrate it more fully.

Health, strength, and knowledge, and the other natural and acquired powers of body and mind, appear to us to be articles of Wealth, precisely analogous to a residence having some qualities that are universally useful, and others peculiarly adapted to the tastes of its owner. They are limited in supply, and are causes of pleasure and preventives of pain far more effectual than the possession of Alnwick or of Blenheim. A portion of the advantages which arise from them are inseparably annexed to their possessor, like the associations of an hereditary property: another portion, and often a very large one, is as transferable as the palpable convenience of the mansion, or beauty of the gardens. What cannot be transferred are the temporary pleasure which generally accompanies the exercise of any accomplishment, and the habitual satisfaction arising from the consciousness of possessing it. What can be transferred are the beneficial results which follow from its having been employed during the period for which its services have been hired. If an Erskine or a Sugden undertakes my cause, he transfers to me, for that occasion, the use of all his natural and acquired ability. My defence is as well conducted as if I had myself the knowledge and the eloquence of an accomplished advocate. What he cannot transfer is the pleasure which he feels in the exercise of his dexterity; but how small is his pleasure compared to mine, if he succeeds for me! A passenger may envy the activity and intrepidity of the crew; they cannot actually implant in him their strength, or their insensibility to danger; but so far as these qualities are means towards an end, so far as they enable him to perform his voyage with quickness and safety, he enjoys the use of them as fully as if they belonged to himself. A hunter [horse] probably feels somewhat the same sort of pleasure in the chase which Erskine felt in court; and this pleasure cannot be transferred any more than his muscles or his lungs; but, so far as his strength, speed, and bottom are means towards the end of enabling his rider to keep up with the hounds, they can be purchased or hired as effectually as his bridle or saddle. In the greater part of the world a man is as purchasable as a horse. In such countries the only difference in value between a slave and a brute consists in the degree in which they respectively possess the saleable qualities that we have been considering . . . The only difference in this respect between a freeman and a slave are, first, that the freeman sells *himself,* and only for a period, and to a certain extent: the slave may be sold by others, and absolutely; and, secondly, that the personal qualities of the slave are a portion of the wealth of his master; those of the freeman, so far as they can be made the subject of exchange, are a part of his own wealth. They perish indeed by his death, and may be impaired or destroyed by disease, or rendered valueless by any changes in the customs of the country which shall destroy the demand for his services; but, subject to these contingencies, they are wealth, and wealth of the most valuable kind. The amount of revenue derived from their exercise in England far exceeds the rental of all the lands in Great Britain.

Limitation in Supply the most Important.—Of the three conditions of value, utility, transferableness, and limitation in supply, the last is by far the most important. The chief sources of its influence on value are two of the most powerful principles of human nature, the love of variety, and the love of distinction. The mere necessaries of life are few and simple. Potatoes, water, and salt, simple raiment, a blanket, a hut, an iron pot, and the materials of firing, are sufficient to support mere animal existence in this climate: they do, in fact, support the existence of the greater part of the inhabitants of Ireland; and in warmer countries much less will suffice. But no man is satisfied with so limited a range of enjoyment. His first object is to vary his food; but this desire, though urgent at first, is more easily satisfied than any other, except perhaps that of dress. Our ancestors, long after they had indulged in considerable luxury in other respects, seem to have been contented with a very uniform though grossly abundant diet. And even now, notwithstanding the common declamation on the luxury of the table, we shall find that most persons, including even those whose appetites are not controlled by frugality, confine their principal solid food but to a few articles, and their liquids to still fewer.

The next desire is variety of dress; a taste which has this peculiarity, that, though it is one of the first symptoms that a people is emerging from the brutishness of the lowest savage life, it quickly reaches its highest point, and, in the subsequent progress of refinement, in one sex at least, diminishes until even the highest ranks assume an almost quaker-like simplicity.

Last comes the desire to build, to ornament, and to furnish; tastes which are absolutely insatiable where they exist, and seem to increase with every improvement in civilization. The comforts and conveniences which we now expect in an ordinary lodging, are more than were enjoyed by people of opulence a century ago; and even a century ago a respectable tradesman would have been dissatisfied if his bedroom had been no better furnished than that of Henry VIII., which contained, we are told, only a bed, a cupboard of plate, a joint-stool, a pair of andirons, and a small mirror. And yet Henry was among the richest and the most magnificent sovereigns of his times. Our great grandchildren perhaps will despise the accommodations of the present age, and their poverty may, in turn, be pitied by their successors.

It is obvious, however, that our desires do not aim so much at quantity as at diversity. Not only are there limits to the pleasure which commodities of any given class can afford, but the pleasure diminishes in a rapidly increasing ratio long before those limits are reached. Two articles of the same kind will seldom afford twice the pleasure of one, and still less will ten give five times the pleasure of two. In proportion, therefore, as any article is abundant, the number of those who are provided with it, and do not wish, or wish but little, to increase their provision, is likely to be great; and, so far as they are concerned, the additional supply loses all, or nearly all, its utility. And in proportion to its scarcity the number of those who are in want of it, and the degree in which they want it, are likely to be increased; and its utility, or, in other words, the pleasure which the possession of a given quantity of it will afford, increases proportionally.

But strong as is the desire for variety, it is weak compared with the desire for distinction: a feeling which, if we consider its universality and its constancy, that it affects all men and at all times, that it comes with us from the cradle, and never leaves us till we go into the grave, may be pronounced to be the most powerful of human passions.

The most obvious source of distinction is the possession of superior wealth. It is the one which excites most the admiration of the bulk of mankind, and the only one which they feel capable of attaining. To seem more rich, or, to use a common expression, to keep up a better appearance, than those within their own sphere of comparison, is, with almost all men who are placed beyond the fear of actual want, the ruling principle of conduct. For this object they undergo toil which no pain or pleasure addressed to the senses would lead them to encounter; into which no slave could be lashed or bribed. But this object is obtained by appearances, and, indeed, cannot be attained by anything else. All the gold in the Pactolus, even if the Pactolus were as rich as when Midas had just washed in it, would obviously confer no distinction on the man who was unable to exhibit it. The only mode by which wealth can be exhibited, is by the apparent possession of some object of desire which is limited in supply. Mere limitation of supply, indeed, unless there be some other circumstance constituting the article in question an object of desire, or, in other words, giving it utility, is insufficient. This circumstance must be its having some quality to which some person beside the owner annexes the notion of utility. The original manuscript of every schoolboy's exercise is as limited in supply as anything can be, but there is nothing to make it an object of desire after it has served its purpose in school. It is merely a blotted manuscript, unique certainly, but valueless. But if the original manuscript of the *Wealth of Nations* could be discovered, it would excite an interest throughout Europe. Curiosity would be eager to trace the first workings of a mind whose influence will be felt as long as civilized society endures. It might, perhaps, be purchased by some ignorant collector only for the purposes of ostentation, but it could not serve even those purposes unless recommended by some circumstance beyond mere singularity.

It is impossible, however, to conceive anything more trifling or more capricious than the circumstances which may make a thing an object of desire, and therefore, in our extended use of that word, give to it utility when its supply is narrowly limited.

The substance which at present is the greatest object of desire, and of which, therefore, a given quantity will exchange for the greatest quantity of all other things, is the diamond. A bracelet belonging to the king of Persia, the stones in which do not weigh two ounces, is said to be worth a million sterling. Now, a million sterling would command the whole labour of about thirty thousand English families for a year. If that labour were employed in producing and reproducing commodities for the purpose of sale, it would probably give for ever a clear annual income equal to the labour of three thousand families, or twelve thousand individuals. It would place at the disposal of its owner all the commodities that could be produced by all the labour of all the inhabitants of a considerable town. And a few pieces of mineral, not weighing two ounces, capable of gratifying no sense but the sight, and which any eye would be tired of looking at for a minute, is invested by our caprice with a value equal to that of the commodities which would give comfortable support to thousands of human beings in an advanced state of civilization. Hardness and brightness must have been the qualities which first attracted notice to the diamond. They enabled it to please the eye and adorn the person, and thus associated with it the union of utility. But a diamond weighing an ounce is not found once in a century; there are not five such known to exist. The possession of an object of desire so limited in supply soon became one of the most unequivocal proofs of wealth. And, as to appear rich is the ruling passion of the bulk of mankind, diamonds will probably continue the objects of eager competition while the obstacles that limit their supply are undiminished. If a Sinbad should discover a valley of diamonds, or we should succeed in manufacturing them from charcoal, they will probably be used only as ornaments for savages, playthings for children, and as affording tools and raw materials for some of the arts; and we may send cargoes of diamonds to the coast of Guinea to be bartered for equal quantities of ivory or gum.

READING 13

Prosperity and Depression

THE PHASES OF BUSINESS ACTIVITY called prosperity and depression, or the business cycle, are often considered manifestations of the highly industrialized modern economy. There is some merit, therefore, in reading Daniel Defoe's description of the business cycle, written in 1728. His direct and graphic description has few peers in modern literature. In this reading, Defoe would seem to lay the foundation for the "overproduction" theory of the causes of the business cycle; and there are certainly evidences of a psychological explanation also.

While Defoe intimated an overproduction-psychological explanation of the business cycle, he attributed the immediate cause of each excess of prosperity (which leads into the following depression) to what he called "Accidents of Trade": the plague in France (1720), the Treaty of Utrecht (1713), and such causes. Historians in America have attributed our depressions at least in part to such immediate factors: the depression of 1837 to an excess of canal and road-building speculation and destruction of the second United States Bank; the depression of 1873 to an excess of railroad-building speculation; the depression of the 1930s to financial overspeculation and resulting panic. Defoe's description of prosperity and depression, written more than 225 years ago, shows us that the prosperity-depression problem is a fundamental problem of economies in any stage of development.

Daniel Defoe (1660-1731) is best known as the author of *Robinson Crusoe*. Possibly if he had not been such a prolific and popular narrative writer, he would have been better known as an economist. A mercantilist, he acted on many economic commissions for the King and wrote relatively widely on economic matters. The reading is from *A Plan of the English Commerce* (Oxford: Basil Blackwell, 1928 [first published in 1728], 277 pp.), Part II, "Containing an Answer to that great and important Question now depending, Whether our *Trade,* and

Especially our *Manufactures,* are in a declining Condition, or
no?" Chapter I, "A Solid Enquiry into that important Question,
whether our Trade in general, and our Woollen Manufacture
in particular, are sunk and declined, or not," pp. 191-196. Reprinted by permission of Basil Blackwell, Publisher, Oxford.

Upon the whole then it does not appear, that our Manufactures are lessen'd, or that the Consumption of them is abated
either Abroad or at Home, but rather the contrary; and that our
Trade in general, and even our Woollen Manufacture in particular, is greatly encreas'd, and is at this Time arriv'd to such a
Magnitude, as it was never at before. And here it occurs to notice
a particular Thing, which may be of Use to us in its Kind, on
several Occasions, *viz.* That the Magnitude of the Manufacture
is really at present its only Grievance, being encreased to such a
Degree, by the Ignorance and Wealth of the Manufacturers, that
it is too great for its self; the Quantity too great for the Consumption, or at least too great for the Market, tho' the Market
was intirely open, and uninterrupted by any Rival Manufacture,
or any Prohibition whatsoever. And here I ask to be spared a
Word or two of the present imprudent Encrease of the Woollen
Manufacture of *England,* by the ill Conduct of the Manufacturers
in particular Cases; and how unjustly a Check of that Encrease
is called a Decay of the Trade.

As the Veins may be too full of Blood, so a Nation may be
too full of Trade; the fine fresh Rivers, when they run with a
full and gentle Stream, are the Beauty and Glory of a Country;
they water the Meadows, moisten the Earth, drive our Mills, fill
our Moats and Canals, carry our Vessels, and enrich the whole
Nation; but when swell'd by sudden and hasty Showers, they
turn rapid in their Course, overflow their Banks, and rise to an
undue Height; then they turn frightful and dangerous, drown
the Country, and sometimes the People; carry away Cattle,
Stacks of Corn, Bridges, Buildings, and whatever stands in their
Way, leaving Mud, and Sand, and Stones among the Grass, and
rather starve the Land, than assist to make it fruitful, and thus
they become a Grievance, not a Blessing to the Publick; on the
other Hand, when by long Drought their Sources are withheld,
the Streams fail, the Rivers are dry, the Mills stand still, the
Boats lye a Ground, the Lands are parch'd up, and the whole
Country suffers.

Our Manufactures of Wool in this Nation, bear a just Analogy with this Case, like a Stream, they are in their prosperous Course the Wealth and Glory of the Country: While the Trade flourishes Abroad and at Home, and the Consumption makes a moderate current Demand, the Manufacture goes on at a steady, chearful, even Pace, the Wool is consum'd and wrought up, the Poor are employ'd, the Master Manufacturer thrives, the Merchant and the Shop-keepers go on with their usual Strength, and all the Trade flourishes.

1. Upon some sudden Accident in Trade here comes a great unusual Demand for Goods, the Merchants from Abroad have sudden and unusual Commissions, the Call for Goods this Way or that Way encreases, this makes the Factors send large Orders into the Country; and the Price of Goods always rises according to the Demand: The Country Manufacturer looks out sharp, hires more Looms, get more Spinners, gives more Wages, and animated by the advanc'd Price, is not content to answer his new Orders only, but he continues the Excursion he had made into the Country for Spinners, &c. runs on to an Extremity in Quantity, as far, or perhaps farther, than his Stock will allow: and in a Word, gluts the Market with the Goods.

2. The Accident of Trade, which from Abroad fill'd the Merchants Commissions, and the Factor's Orders being over, those Demands are also over, and the Trade returns to its usual Channel; but the Manufacturer in the Country, who had run out to an unusual Excess in his Business, without Regard to the Circumstances of it, having not stopt his Hand as his Orders stopt, falls into the Mire; his Goods lye on Hand, the Poor which he call'd from the Plow and the Dary to spin and weave, are cast off again, and not finding their Way presently back to their old Drudgery, lye and starve for Want of Work, and then they cry out Trade is decay'd, the Manufactures are lost, Foreigners encroach upon us, the Poor are starv'd, and the like.

Whereas the Sum of the Matter is, the Manufacturer went mad, his Stream run over into a Flood, he run himself imprudently out of Breath; and upon a little Start of the Trade, willing to furnish the Orders all himself, and loth to let a Neighbour come in with him, run himself out, drag'd the Poor into his Business, nay perhaps robb'd his poorer Neighbour of his Workmen, by giving high Wages; and when the Trade stops a little, he runs a-ground; so the Poor are starving, and ready to mutiny for Want of Work: And this we call a Decay of Trade, whereas the contrary is manifest several Ways.

Trade must certainly decay, if we will run it up to such a Length, as to make more Goods than the World can consume: But it is not to be justly call'd a Decay of Trade, 'tis only abating of the Flood; the Waters were out, and now they are down again, and reduced to their old Channel.

Let us examine a little such Accidents as may raise or sink our Manufacture as above, or as perhaps have done so at this Time, and see if it does not hit exactly with this Account.

1st, The late Accident of a Plague in *France.* Upon that sad Occasion, the Commerce being entirely stop'd between *France* and *Spain,* and indeed all other Parts of the World, the Manufactures of the City of *Marseilles* in particular, and the Country adjacent, being wholly interrupted, occasion'd a very great Addition to the Trade of *Great Britain*; particularly for such Manufactures as the *French* used to send to *Turkey,* to *Spain,* and to *Italy*; and the Merchants Commissions from Abroad were visibly enlarged hither for near Two Years, upon that particular Occasion: It was plain they cou'd have no Goods from *France.*

The like Occasion added to the Encrease of our Trade, upon the concluding of the Treaty of *Utrecht,* after the Confusions in *Spain* had put a Check to the Trade between *England* and that Country, for several Years; as likewise again upon the Accommodation with *Spain,* after the Surrender of *Sicily,* when Trade breaking out like the Sun after an Eclipse, the Demand for our *English* Manufactures, Bayes, Says, Perpetts, broad Cloaths, Serges, &c. was such, that the Manufacturers thought they could never make too many.

These Excursions are not to be cast up in any View of the real Magnitude of the Trade, or of the Manufacture, any more than the true Channel of a River is to be judged of, or its Waters measured by the overflowing of a Winter's Rain, as above.

Nor on the contrary is the Stop of those sudden high Demands, by any extraordinary Check of the Call on like Accidents, to be esteemed a Decay of the Trade, any more than the dry Bottom of a large River, when the Stream withheld by a Summer's Drought leaves the Channel empty, can describe the usual Dimensions of that River, or Quantity of its Waters.

Should we ever see here such a fatal Time as that was in *France,* when Heaven sent the Infection among them at *Marseilles,* or as was here in 1665, *God preserve us from it,* what a general Stop would it make to all our Trade? who would send any Commissions hither for *English* Manufactures, when they did not know but every Bale would have a Plague pack'd up with the Goods, as certainly as the Bales of Wool or Hair brought it from *Cyprus* to *Marseilles*?

Yet this would not justly be call'd a Decay of our Commerce; it would indeed be a Wound, and a very desperate Blow to it for the Time; but as it was an Accident to the Trade, so the Cause being removed, the Trade would revive, return to its former Channel, and be the same as before.

If now (*to return to the Case before us*) the Manufacturers of *Britain,* upon any such hasty Demand from Abroad, shall run rashly out into Extremes in their Business, seek out of their usual Bounds for Spinners and Weavers, and other working People, and draw them by Thousands, and Hundreds of Thousands, as was lately the Case, from their other Imployments, shall they call the Stop of these hasty Demands a Decay of Trade? 'tis a Mistake, it is no Decay, it is no more but a Return of the Stream to its usual stated Bounds, bringing Trade into its right Channel again, and to run as it did before: And this I take to be the State of our Manufacture at this Time.

READING 14

Underconsumption

NEARLY ALL THEORIES of the causes of "business cycles," meaning the prosperity-depression phases of economic activity, can be divided into two categories: "underconsumption" and "underinvestment." The theory that depression is caused by "underconsumption" really means that it is caused by a lack of demand. The theory implies that *during* depression there is both a lack of demand and a lack of supply, but states explicitly that the cause of low consumption and low production during depression is that demand has fallen off. Instead of using the term "underconsumption," we might substitute the term "overproduction." This would merely mean that we had produced too much goods relative to the existing demand for the goods. When we witness the tremendous overproduction that existed at the beginning of the last depression, namely, warehouses stocked with grains and other foods and excessively heavy stocks of inventories on merchant's shelves, we can well believe in the validity of the theory. The following reading is a statement of the case for "underconsumption" as an explanation of why depressions occur.

The case for those economists advocating "underinvestment" as an explanation for business depression is made in the reading immediately following this one, by Gustave Cassel. This theory holds essentially that depressions are caused by insufficient investment to continue the economy at the high level of activity which existed when the depression began.

John A. Hobson (1858-1940) was an English economist and social reformer. He was one of the founders of university extension teaching, an effort to foster adult education. He is famous in economics for his early and succinct statement of "underconsumption" as the cause of business depression. The reading is from *The Economics of Unemployment* (London: George Allen & Unwin Ltd., 1931, 152 pp.), Chapter II, "The Failure of Consumption," pp. 30-42. Reprinted by permission of the publisher.

During the war [World War I], and for some time after, trade was prosperous and employment full, because there was an assured effective demand for all that could be produced. In other words, consumption kept pace with production, taking off without delay all that was produced. The full pace of this artificially stimulated production could not, indeed, have been maintained indefinitely. But, if this war-economy could have been converted into a peace economy operating at, say, four-fifths the full war pace, the fighters, absorbed into the working classes on a shorter working day, producing the housing, railway developments and other work of capital repair and extension, while public expenditure was maintained on a high-tax basis without further borrowing or inflation, there seems no economic reason (apart from political and social considerations) why effective demand for British products should have failed and depression supervened. The high level of wages and full employment for our workers would have enabled the size of the effective demand to compensate for the slack demand of foreign customers, as during the war itself. This policy could not, indeed, have continued indefinitely for this or any other highly peopled country. For a considerable export trade is indispensable for a people who must buy half of their food and much of their materials abroad. But this signifies that a world-depression, or any other world-problem, cannot finally be solved for any single country on its separate national policy. Cyclical depressions are the gravest of international diseases, and demand an agreed diagnosis and a common line of treatment—industrial, commercial and financial.

The general shrinkage of effective demand which constitutes a cyclical depression implies a failure of consumption to keep pace with production in the industrial world taken as a whole. There may be areas, whole countries, where production is active, as during the present depression. But their very activity is aggravating the depression elsewhere.

A period of depression is marked by under-consumption and under-production. But it is not a matter of indifference through which of these two gates of explanation we enter. The business world, employers and workers alike, is, as we have seen, strongly and variously committed to the belief that at any given time there is a limited market, in the sense of an effective demand insufficient to take all the goods it can produce, on terms enabling production to continue. In other words, the limited market signifies a normal tendency for consumption to fall below production. Everyone knows that in ordinary times it is easier to buy than to sell, and that more and more economic activity is given to pushing wares and the arts of salesmanship, while an ever-increasing proportion of the retail prices paid for most goods is swallowed up in costs of distribution.

But in focussing our attention upon under-consumption, or the chronic failure of consumption to keep pace with production, it is necessary to define our meaning of consumption. The term is applied in the business world not only to the withdrawal of final commodities for purposes of personal consumption, but to the use of raw materials, fuel and other capital goods which are said to be consumed when they are worked up into other products. Although in periods of general depression both sorts of consumption are reduced, the latter sort is not properly regarded as part of the problem of under-consumption. In this analysis we shall confine the terms consumption and under-consumption to the effective demand of final consumers for finished commodities.

For only thus can we challenge sharply and clearly the accepted economic dogma, which renders it impossible to get a comprehension of the real social economic significance of unemployment. The orthodox economist regards all the opinions and practices, to which we have appealed in support of a belief in a limited market, as based on fallacious thinking. He is convinced that general over-production is impossible, though it stares him in the face at the outbreak of each cyclical depression. Under-consumption is for him equally absurd. For does not everything that is produced belong to its producers, who must either want to consume it, or to consume something else against which they can exchange it, or to use it for producing more things which they will consume later on? The wants of man being expansible without limit, how is it possible that too much can be produced? If he is confronted with the progress of a trade cycle, the full activity in boom years evoking an output which presently becomes so large that it can only be marketed at lower prices—this fall of prices proceeding until a level is reached at which costs of production are no longer covered and surplus stocks of goods are accumulated, which, if thrown upon the market, could only be sold by driving down prices to a still lower level—this economist refuses to recognise this condition as over-production, and confines his attention to the resulting stoppage of industry which he rightly diagnoses as under-production. Now a trade depression manifestly is a state of under-poduction, but this state is the product of an excessive activity preceding it. Over-production, congestion, stoppage, is the visible order of events. Theoretically, no doubt, it ought not to be possible. Every increase of output ought to find its outlet in consumption without reducing prices below the level at which it pays to produce.

But since it does not work this way, it is well to inquire why it does not. Why does consumption fail to keep pace with increased powers of production? Or, conversely, why do the powers of production increase faster than the rate of consumption?

The answer is found in two related phenomena: first, the conservative character of the arts of consumption, or standards of living, as compared with the modern arts of production; second, the ways in which the current distribution of income confirms this conservation of consumption.

In primitive societies the standards or methods of work are almost as conservative as those of consumption. Of civilised societies, and especially of modern industrial nations, this is no longer true. Invention and business initiative, enlisted in the cause of quick profiteering, transform with great rapidity the arts of industry, raising this productivity by leaps and bounds. Though modern man, in his capacity of consumer, is far more progressive than his ancestors, his power of taking on new economic needs and of raising rapidly the quantity, variety and quality of his consumption, is limited by a narrowness of imagination and a servitude to habit which are far less dominant in production. There is in modern business a strong stimulus to progress in the great pain which comes to the man of inventive and initiative power, while, on the other hand, there is a strong stimulus to the early imitation and adoption of new superior methods by the whole body of members of a trade, who are otherwise out-competed and ruined by their conservatism. Now a large part of consumption is carried on in the privacy of separate homes, under the bonds of custom, and withdrawn from any strong continual stimulus to imitation and competition; and though changes are quicker and more numerous in those factors of consumption, such as dress, travel and recreation, which are sub-ject to publicity and imitation and carry personal prestige, the capacity of assimilating easily and quickly large new personal expenditure is comparatively rare. Indeed, it is needless to set out in detail the evidence for the comparative conservatism of con-sumption. For, if everyone was driven by a natural impulse to raise his consumption immediately, so as to absorb the whole of any enlargement in the output of industry which came to him as income, there could be no increase in the provision of capital, and all further progress in the arts of production, so far as they demanded capital, would be inhibited.

Indeed, it must be admitted that upon this natural con-servatism of present consumption, strengthened and directed by reasonable regard for future consumption, the economic progress of mankind depends. It is this conservatism that is expressed in saving. The real economic function of saving must be clearly kept in mind. It does not consist in not spending, i.e. in putting money income in a bank, or even in making an investment. It consists in paying producers to make more non-consumable goods for use as capital, instead of paying them to make more con-sumable goods and consuming them. This is the vital distinction between spending and saving, so often obscured by dwelling upon the merely monetary aspect.

Now, if we hold, as seems to be the case, that a depression is due to, or testifies to, the existence of an excess of producing power and a corresponding deficiency of consuming power, we can only mean that somehow or other there has been over-saving or under-spending on the part of industrial society, in the sense that more non-consumable, i.e. capital, goods have been created than have been capable of being properly utilised for the supply of future consumption. This is not a theory or an explanation, but rather a description of the actual facts. At a time of depression large bodies of capital stand idle, together with the labour and business ability that could operate them. They simply represent a surplus or excess of former savings, which cannot get used without delay and waste for the productive end for which they were designed.

I am aware that long before this many readers will be bursting with impatience, because they think I am ignoring what seems to them other and truer explanations of depression, resting upon the play of psychological-financial forces. Now, without denying the important part taken by these forces in exaggerating the fluctuations of concrete industry and commerce, I propose to show that they are secondary and not primary causes, and have no initiatory and independent influence. Having this intention, I must first complete the chain of reasoning by which I trace the under-production and under-consumption, which are the chief factors of a depression, to the normal tendency to save a larger proportion of income than can effectively and continuously function as capital.

I have referred to a natural conservatism in the arts of consumption in part explanation of the failure of consumption to keep full pace with the moral progressive arts of production. But this natural tendency is strongly reinforced by inequalities in the distribution of income, which place a larger proportion of the aggregate incomes in the possession of comparatively small classes, who, after satisfying all their economic desires, have large surpluses for automatic saving and investment. The great bulk of the saving, normally applied to capital purposes in this and other industrially developed countries, belongs to this almost automatic accumulation of the surplus incomes of the well-to-do. I speak of it as 'almost automatic,' meaning that its provision involves no appreciable sacrifice in current satisfaction from consumption on the part of its possessors, and very little thought, excepting as regards its application for investment.

That the large incomes resulting from the inequality of wealth distribution enlarge the volume of savings, available for the increase and improvement of the capital structure of industry, is the accepted view of most economists.

* * *

There is nothing unreasonable in the conclusion, . . . that any approximation towards equality of incomes would reduce the proportion of income saved to income spent. At a time like the present [1931], when the aggregate amount of saving is greatly reduced, it is natural that qualms should be felt as to the effect of any movements making for a greater equalisation of incomes, and a consequent reduction of the automatic savings from high incomes. Under such circumstances my thesis, that under-consumption due to over-saving arising from maldistribution of income, is the normal cause of cyclical depression, is liable to grave misunderstanding.

I hasten, therefore, to explain that the over-saving of which I speak refers solely to the proportion of saving to spending, and does not imply any fixed limit to the amount that can be serviceably saved. This thesis may be presented in the following form:

Just as waste of productive power admittedly occurs by misapplication of capital, skill and labour, as between one trade and another, or one area of investment and another (too much applied here, too little there), so income as a whole may be wastefully applied as between purchase of commodities and purchase of new capital goods.

For just as it is clear that waste ensues unless some accurate proportion is kept between the amounts of capital, skill and labour placed in the several productive processes required for converting raw materials into finished goods, so there is waste if these finished goods are not effectively demanded and consumed as fast as the productive processes enable them to pass into the form of finished goods. In other words, consumption is simply the final link in a chain of economic processes, each of which should be kept in accurate proportion to the preceding ones, unless stoppage and waste are to occur. This is quite evident if the series of processes comprising the production, sale and consumption, of any single commodity such as bread or boots, is taken under survey. Having regard to the current condition of the arts of industry, there will be a just balance both between the productive power applied at the respective stages of production on the one hand, and between the quantity of purchasing power applied to buy the bread or boots, and the quantity applied to maintain and improve the productive processes as a whole, upon the other hand. And what applies to any kind of commodity applies to commodities in general. In the use of the current income there must exist, at any time, an economically right proportion between expenditure in withdrawing commodities from the retail shops for consumption, and expenditure in maintaining and enlarging the plant and materials functioning in each stage of production. Or, putting it otherwise, saving and investment for enlargement of production are only economically valid on condition that the enlarged production is accompanied or soon followed by a proportionately enlarged consumption. In the last resort the rate of saving (in this sense) must bear an accurate proportion to rate of spending. This proportion of saving may be exceeded by any person or group, or even (within limits) any nation, but it must be kept by industrial society as a whole. Any attempt on the part of the whole society to live beyond its income is soon frustrated, for it is impossible to continue taking out more consumables than are passed through the productive processes. A nation may let down its productive plant, and stocks of materials or semi-manufactured articles, in order to over-consume for a brief spurt, as we did in the emergency of war; but even this national over-consumption was only rendered possible by the belligerent nations drawing upon the surplus accumulations of the neutral world. The world as a whole would be pulled up very soon in any collective refusal of its inhabitants to make the necessary provision for future production.

There might, indeed, be under-saving, in the sense of a refusal to save enough to realise the enlargements and improvements of the machinery of production that are required to furnish a larger output of commodities for a higher standard or a growing population.

Such a society might be said to over-spend and under-save, though it would not strictly speaking live beyond its income. Such under-saving on the part of society would mean a retardation or even a paralysis of economic progress.

This, indeed, presumably is what our economists consider would be the natural result of a process of equalisation of incomes. As under this condition the proportion of savings to consumption would be reduced, the growth of capital, and therefore the progress of production, would be checked. And this seems true on one assumption, vis. that the total income to be spent or saved is not directly affected in its dimensions by the process of 'equalisation.' Suppose, however, that this equalisation, with its increased pressure of demand for consumables, kept the machinery of production more fully and more quickly working to supply the increased outflow of consumables, this would constitute an actual increase of real income, by reason of the higher productivity of the capital and labour continuously under full employment. Under such circumstances, although a smaller proportion of the larger income might be saved, and a larger proportion consumed, the actual amount of saving might be as large as or even larger than before, and, being more fully utilised as capital, might maintain as high a rate of economic progress as before.

This is the thesis which I here maintain.

The waste of production actually experienced in our normal operation of industry, by slowing down and stoppages, represents an attempt to save and employ as capital a larger proportion of income than *can* function in supplying the reduced consumption. This is to be attributed to a maldistribution of income, which upsets the true balance between present and future consumption that would obtain in a well-constituted society.

A self-sustaining individual (were such possible) would balance as exactly as he could present labour against future enjoyment. So would any group whose earnings were strictly proportionate to efforts. Such group-economy would apply a certain proportion of its present toil to making more or better tools, so as to lighten future toil and make it more productive of consumables. But there would be no tendency to sacrifice so large a proportion of possible present enjoyment as to provide more tools than were wanted, and more than could possibly be put continuously to full use in the production of future goods. But if in any society you get considerable groups of men whose incomes come to them by others' toil instead of their own, and if these incomes are so large as to afford little or no additional satisfaction by any considerable increase of their expenditure, this natural balancing of present against future enjoyment is upset. It becomes too easy for a rich man, living on unearned income, to cause an excessive proportion of the labour which he commands, but does not himself perform, to be directed to the production of future goods which he, or someone else, may or may not consume. In other words, the 'surplus' nature of much of the income which results from inequality of distribution disturbs the true balance of productive activities, and disturbs it normally in the direction of the postponed consumption of articles which, if consumed now by those into whose hands they would fall, would satisfy no felt want but would spell repletion.

READING 15

Underinvestment

"UNDERINVESTMENT" as the cause of business depression is explained in the following reading by Gustav Cassel. Cassel points out that depressions are characterized by low production and says that this low production must be the result of a low investment in the *means* of production. He specifically attempts to negate the case for "overproduction" as the cause of business depression.

When one observes the extra heavy inventories and bulging warehouses preceding a depression, one can certainly wonder if overproduction does not give a more satisfactory explanation of the cause of depression. On one other count Cassel might be criticized: He regards the interest rate as having a *causal* nature; whereas most economists consider the interest rate as a *symptom* of an economic condition rather than the *cause* of an economic condition. There is some doubt that the interest rate plays such an important part in the economy as Cassel assigns it.

Gustav Cassel (1866-1945) was an outstanding Swedish economist. Possibly the work that he is most famous for was in connection with monetary theory, and particularly with the application of the quantity theory of money to the economy. He is also famous for his work in value theory, business cycles, and foreign trade. The reading is from *The Theory of Social Economy,* Volume II (London: T. Fisher Unwin, Ltd., 1923, 654 pp.), Book IV, "The Theory of Conjuncture-Movements," Chapter XIX, "The Determining Factors of Conjuncture-Movements," pp. 614-617, 624-628. Reprinted by permission of Ernest Benn Limited, London.

The Principle of Action and Reaction.

In our studies of conjunctures [prosperity and depression cycles] we have so far confined ourselves to the concrete processes and their direct connections. Now let us look more closely at the forces which determine the movement as impelling or restricting factors.

Of these forces the interest on capital occupies the central place. The low rate of interest that rules in the depression clearly acts as a powerful impulse to the further production of fixed capital. With a given return the value of fixed capital is so much higher the lower the rate of interest is. Hence the low rate of interest is equivalent to high prices for the already produced capital. At a time, therefore, of long-maintained low interest employers see a prospect of considerable profit if they are engaged in building, railway-construction, or in other works which represent a large amount of fixed capital. The profit can be realised by selling the houses or shares of the undertakings to members of the public in search of investments.

We have already seen . . . that there are always latent possible enterprises which require a good deal of fixed capital, and are therefore not remunerative when the rate of interest is high. But as soon as the rate falls, a certain proportion of these enterprises become remunerative. It will then not be long before the possibilities begin to be turned into realities. If, for instance, a railway from which we estimate a net annual revenue of £400,000 requires an outlay of £10,000,000, it cannot be constructed as long as the rate of interest is 5 per cent. But if the rate falls to 3 per cent. the enterprise becomes profitable, and will, in all probability, be carried out. Hence to a great extent the rate of interest is the decisive factor as to the economic possibility of providing permanent capital objects. In regard to the current production of consumers' goods the rate of interest has, as we know, nothing like the same importance. Hence a protracted low rate of interest is bound to accelerate the production of fixed capital much more than any other kind of production, and so bring about in the course of time that diversion of social production to the advantage of the production of fixed capital which we described as an essential symptom of the high conjuncture [prosperity].

On the other hand, a high rate of interest must lower the value of fixed capital and cause loss to employers who are engaged in creating such capital. Many enterprises can scarcely be completed as long as the rate is high. The economic possibilities of the further production of fixed capital are greatly restricted. Only enterprises which promise an exceptionally high profit can be persisted in. If they prove less remunerative than had been expected, and unable to bear the high interest that is asked for the use of capital, this must have a depressing effect upon any inclination to take up new plans for the production of fixed capital.

This explains why a protracted high rate of interest brings about a decline in the production of fixed capital. But the production of consumers' goods does not suffer to anything like the same extent from a high rate of interest. This production may evince some abatement together with the decline in the production of fixed capital, but this is not to be regarded as a direct consequence of the high rate of interest during a high conjuncture; it is a secondary phenomenon. However, the direct effect of the high rate of interest on the production of fixed capital is enough to convert the high conjuncture into a depression.

Hence the rate of interest has a quite definite effect upon the conjuncture-movement, and an effect always in a contrary direction to that movement. In the depression there is a low rate of interest, and this has a restorative effect upon enterprise; in the high conjuncture there is a high rate of interest, and this acts as a brake. On the other hand, the rate of interest is itself affected by the conjunctures. The depression itself causes the low rate of interest which helps to make an end of it; the high conjuncture forces the rate up to a point where it becomes intolerable, and the high conjuncture itself is bound to collapse. There is thus a reciprocal action of rate of interest and conjuncture-movement.

This reciprocal action is only an instance of the general principle of action and reaction. If there is to be any stability at all, all action must, in the economic as well as the physical world, provoke a reaction. The fluctuations of the rate of interest are, however, not the only reactions which serve to check the conjuncture-movements. Other restricting forces are, first, the rise in the prices of the materials of fixed capital, which may, as we have seen, be very considerable, and must naturally greatly hamper the further production of such capital. A second factor checking the high conjuncture is the advance of wages. Both these elements tend to make the production of fixed capital dearer; houses, railways, factories, etc., will cost a great deal more to build than was allowed for in the plans. This phenomenon, which is a rule almost without exception during a high conjuncture, has naturally a very disturbing effect upon the possibilities of profit, even upon the economic vitality of many enterprises, and it clearly gives little encouragement to further enterprise. When the value of the already produced fixed capital is reduced in addition, on account of the low rate of interest, we quite understand how the rise of prices and wages, together with the higher rate of interest, must act as a powerful brake upon the high conjuncture. We are not surprised that these restricting forces bring to an end the abnormally swollen production of fixed capital, and consequently the whole high conjuncture.

It might rather have been asked how it is possible that in the high conjuncture proper, when the prices of the accumulated fixed capital have already begun to yield, the high prices of the materials and labour required for the creation of fixed capital can be maintained for some time. It is due to the fact that the equipment, buildings, etc., which are here in question, for the most part promise an exceptionally high profit and so leave a certain margin for advance of cost; also to the fact that the enterprises in question must, if they have been begun, be carried through even at a sacrifice.

The depression also brings out corresponding forces in opposition to itself: low prices of all materials of fixed capital and low wages. These factors cheapen the production of fixed capital, at the same time as the low rate of interest, itself a result of the depression, raises the value of the completed capital objects. The co-operation of these forces puts an end to the depression and brings on a new advance.

The rate of interest has, of course, a certain significance in connection with production itself, just as have the prices of materials. But we may leave this element out of consideration in order to bring out more clearly the essential effect of changes in the rate of interest.

The fluctuations of conjunctures are, as a rule, somewhat accentuated by the action of the banks, which we mentioned previously. If the banks keep the rate of interest too low at the beginning of a period of advance, this acts as a special encouragement to the production of capital, and helps to raise the high conjuncture still higher. The rise in the general level of prices which is caused by the unduly low rate ought at first to have the same effect.

* * *

Crises.

Why cannot a high conjuncture, when the conditions for its continuance exist no longer, not pass gradually into the depression, much as it itself gradually developed out of the depression? Experience teaches us that this is not the case: that the high conjuncture suddenly breaks, and often ends in a catastrophe. This catastrophe, which we call an economic crisis, is mainly characterised by a general incapacity to meet existing liabilities. The well-known accompaniments of it are great losses, compulsory sales, abnormal increase in the number and extent of bankruptcies, and a general want of confidence.

This situation shows that the employers must have gone astray on some point; they must have made calculations which have proved unsound. What is this point?

According to a very widely accepted view, the crisis must be regarded as a result of overproduction. It would therefore be due to a wrong estimate of the demand, an overestimate of the real needs of the community. It cannot be denied that wrong estimates and overestimates of this sort do commonly play a part in every high conjuncture and intensify the crisis. This was especially the case with the older forms of crisis. But in modern crises it is not primarily a question of overproduction in this sense. As the high conjuncture is characterised by an extraordinarily increased production of fixed capital, we should have to look to this sphere above all for the overproduction. But, as we proved previously, it appears that the services of fixed capital, which are the object of the demand of the consuming public, are, as a rule, not in excess even in the last part of a high conjuncture; that, on the contrary, the fixed capital has to be used to the utmost to meet the demand. Even the materials of fixed capital are not produced to excess during the high conjuncture. On the contrary, it commonly shows an unmistakable scarcity of these materials—a scarcity which makes itself felt especially in the extraordinarily high prices of such commodities. The iron output, for instance, is often sold up to the crisis, and sometimes even beyond. There can, therefore, be no question of an overproduction of the materials of fixed capital to such an extent as to serve as a general explanation of crises.

It seems, then, that no link is missing in the chain that normally connects the producers with the consumers. How is it, in that case, that the chain breaks? The answer is: *The typical modern high conjuncture does not mean overproduction or an overestimate of the demands of consumers or the needs of the community for the services of fixed capital, but an overestimate of the supply of capital, or of the amount of savings available for taking over the real capital produced.* What is overestimated is the capacity of the capitalists to provide savings in sufficient quantity. We must bear in mind that this capacity has to be estimated several years in advance, since, on the average, there are several years between the time when the work is planned and the time when it makes its full demand upon the community's savings. The individual employer has no other means of judging the condition of the capital-market except the rate of interest. During the depression and the first part of the high conjuncture however, the rate is low, or at least moderate. The demands for capital-disposal which result from the increased activity of employers in the sphere of the production of fixed capital do not yet make themselves fully felt. It is, therefore, quite possible that enterprises, such as the construction of houses, railways, etc., will be planned, and even begun, in such quantities that, when their need of capital afterwards makes itself felt, it cannot be satisfied.

The high conjuncture must thus be pressed onward, but at last there will come a time when it is clear that the market cannot find savings for the purchase of the real capital produced in sufficient amounts. There must then be a sudden fall in the value of the real capital, and employers must find it extraordinarily difficult to get the capital they need, either by loan or selling. On this they have not calculated in incurring the current liabilities they did in the course of their productive undertakings. When it becomes clear that they have gone astray on this point, the consequence is bound to be a general incapacity to meet liabilities incurred. This spreads wider and wider, as the whole business world depends to a great extent on the punctual discharge of obligations that fall due. There is bound to be an economic crisis.

This wrong estimate of the future condition of the capital market would not lead to such a catastrophe if the individual employer secured in advance the whole of the capital he needs to carry out his plans. Under present conditions this can rarely be done. Share-capital, which is subscribed for the purpose of realising a large undertaking, represents, as a rule, only a part, sometimes only a very small part, of the whole of the capital needed. People generally persuade themselves that in the future it will be possible to get the requisite capital by the issue of debentures, by bank-credits, and so on. Moreover, share-capital is, as a rule, not paid up at once. The payments are often deferred for fairly long periods. Here again, therefore, calculations are based upon the capital market of the future. In addition, the share subscribers usually go beyond their own means, and require capital that they must get by loans, often only for a short period. It is clear that subscriptions of this sort do not, from the economic point of view, represent a real actual command of capital on the part of employers. But even in the case where the individual enterprise has secured capital in advance, this capital will be temporarily put out at interest before it is used in the enterprise and will be placed at the disposal of the community through the banks or in some other way. It will be used in other enterprises, and will, from the economic point of view, be no longer available. In these complicated circumstances we can easily understand how the demands which actual enterprise makes upon the capital market of the future are not in their totality clearly realised, and how the capacities of this future market, to meet the demands, are overestimated. The individual who would put his business on solid foundations has always the alternative of securing the whole of his capital from the start. If the deepest cause of the crisis is a wrong estimate of the possibilities of obtaining on the future market the capital that is required for carrying out an enterprise that has been begun, the best means of meeting the danger of a crisis is in this policy. Obviously, however, it can only be done in practice to a limited extent. Calculation in advance of the future capital-requirements of an enterprise is up against the difficulty that the rise of prices and wages during a high conjuncture often adds considerably to the cost, and thus the future requirements of capital, both of the individual enterprise and the whole business world, will be greater than was calculated. To avoid unpleasant surprises of this kind it would be necessary to take account of the coming rise of prices at the beginning of a high conjuncture.

However, the question of the provision of capital during a high conjuncture cannot be fully considered from this private economic point of view. From the general economic point of view there can be no such thing as a securing of capital in advance: the capital that is used to-day must always be taken from the social income of to-day. Actually, therefore, there can only be question in any case of a correct estimate of the whole of the demands for capital which will arise simultaneously during the high conjuncture; and it is not easy to make such an estimate.

That the crisis really consists in an acute scarcity of capital—that is to say, of savings—to purchase the real capital produced is partly shown by the great difficulty of selling the ready-made fixed capital or getting means to pay the costs of its production, and partly by the very general inability to complete undertakings that have been begun. In either case the lack of capital must mean heavy losses. They are bound to be especially severe when enterprises that have been begun and cannot be completed must suffer damage, or even be destroyed and entirely abandoned. Instances of both effects of the lack of capital may be seen in every severe crisis.

The increasing stringency of the supply of capital during a high conjuncture is hidden in a confusing way from the business world by the usual considerable increase of bank media of payment at such a time, as the individual employer naturally regards these as capital. When the banks afterwards find it necessary in their own interest to cut down this excessive supply of media of payment, the real scarcity of capital is suddenly and acutely felt. It is obvious that this may accelerate and greatly aggravate the crisis.

READING 16

The Principle of Acceleration

IT IS CHIEFLY IN CONNECTION with the study of "business cycles" that the principle of acceleration is discussed. This principle, along with the "multiplier" of John Maynard Keynes, is generally credited with giving the dynamic force to the upward and downward movements of business enterprise which we call "prosperity" and "depression." In the following reading, the importance of the acceleration principle is explained and its nature investigated. The acceleration principle arises, of course, from the implications of the "law of derived demand." Thus, its chief influence would seem to be found in the manufacturing of tools and machines to be used in the further production of finished goods. However, the principle of acceleration has implications in wholesaling and retailing as well. This is clearly explained in the following reading. In the reading immediately following this one, *The Business Cycle* by Alvin H. Hansen, the principle of acceleration, as well as the multiplier, is tied into a theory of the business cycle.

John Maurice Clark (1884-   ) is an outstanding contemporary American economist. He was formerly Professor of Economics at Columbia University, succeeding his father, the late John Bates Clark, famous for his work on "marginal productivity." J. Maurice Clark has worked chiefly in the theory of production, in costs, and in social control; probably he is most famous for his *Economics of Overhead Costs*. The reading is from "Business Acceleration and the Law of Demand: A Technical Factor in Economic Cycles" (*The Journal of Political Economy*, Volume 25, No. 3, March 1917; copyright 1917 by The University of Chicago), pp. 217-235. Reprinted by permission of The University of Chicago.

I. *Introduction*

The publication of W. C. Mitchell's book, *Business Cycles*, has rendered obsolete all attempts to explain crises in terms of any one fact or any one narrow chain of causes and effects. The central problem, however, is as clearly defined throughout his remarkably comprehensive study of the details of the actual process as in more abstract treatments of single phases of it. It is the question why business adjustments do not stop at a point of equilibrium, but go on to a point from which a more or less violent reaction is inevitable, and so on without apparent end. And it seems probable that of all the many circumstances which at every stage of the cycle lead to the next stage, the greater part can hardly be held primarily responsible for this primary fact; certainly not all are responsible in equal measure.

Disturbances originating outside the business world, so to speak, such as wars and crop fluctuations, can scarcely be held primarily responsible. Some such disturbances there are bound to be, and our system seems capable of manufacturing its crises out of any raw material that comes to hand, when the crisis is due, and of rising superior to serious provocation at other times. Some forces act to spread the effect of prosperity or adversity from one industry to another, thus insuring that a boom or sharp crisis will effect industry in general, but they cannot be held responsible for the condition which they merely transmit. Nor can the familiar "forces of equilibrium" be held responsible, though they are acting at all stages of the process.

There is one circumstance whose natural effect is different from all of these in that (1) it acts as an intensifier of the disturbances it transmits and (2) without any diminution of demand to start with it can produce a diminution. It can convert a slackening of the rate of growth in one industry into an absolute decline in another. This circumstance is not psychological, nor does it depend upon the nature of our credit system, nor upon the distribution of income, but rather upon the elementary technical necessities of the case. It is concerned with the way in which the demand for finished products is handed on in the form of a demand for machines, tools, construction materials, and unfinished goods in general. This circumstance is not to be erected into a "theory of crises," but it is put forward as indicating that the purely technical side of this phenomenon is of prime importance, though it has been somewhat overshadowed by the more spectacular features of credit inflation, speculation, capitalization, and mob psychology, while its details have been blurred in the more general theories of "overproduction" or "maladjusted production."

II. *Chief Data to be Interpreted*

There are certain outstanding facts in the behavior of crimes which point in one direction and can be linked together by one explanation. It appears, first, that raw materials and producers' goods in general vary more sharply both in price and in the physical volume of business done than do consumers' goods, while wholesale prices fluctuate more than retail.

The work of constructing industrial equipment appears to fluctuate more intensely than other types of production. Its revival coincides, naturally, with a sudden and very great increase of investments. The failures which precipitate a panic are likely to be among producers of industrial equipment, although as to this "there is no general rule." Another fact closely connected with those already mentioned is the shrinkage of merchants' stocks of goods in hard times and their expansion in times of prosperity. Raw materials for manufacture are also carried in larger quantities at times when production is more active. In point of time, also, it appears that raw materials take the lead, beginning to fall in price before the finished products, while "technical journals usually report that the factories and wholesale houses are restricting their orders some weeks, if not months, before they report that retail sales are flagging." Mr. Babson notes in one of his reports that "the production of pig iron forecasts the condition of the whole building industry and construction of all kinds," and that "the turning point of the statistics on new building has been from two years to six months earlier than the general crisis." In 1907 a comparison of prices indicates that certain goods bought by producers reached their highest point and began their decline earlier than the goods sold by the same producers. These latter were in some cases goods for consumption and in some cases tools, etc., to be used in further production. Manufactured producers' goods are not shown to be especially quick in feeling the upward trend of prices, though they rise farther than other types of goods. The demand for consumers' goods fluctuates quite decidedly, but the greater part of its fluctuations appears to be the result of the changes in the amount of unemployment which result from the business cycle itself. Some changes in consumption are independent of this cause, and these may well be among the independent causes of business cycles, but it would seem that only a comparatively minor part of the total fluctuations in consumption can be of this character.

III. *Industrial Expansion and Derived Demands*

These data suggest a unified explanation, and group themselves about one industrial fact: the production of capital goods. Its importance has long been recognized, and several theories of crises have turned upon it. The aim of the present study is to present the underlying technical facts in a definite quantitative formulation.

Every producer of things to be sold to producers has two demands to meet. He must maintain the industrial equipment already in use and the stocks of materials and goods on their way to the final consumer, and he must also furnish any new equipment that is wanted for new construction, enlargements, or betterments, and any increase in the stocks of materials and unsold goods. Both these demands come ultimately from the consumer, but they follow different laws. The demand for maintenance and replacement of existing capital varies with the amount of the demand for finished products, while the demand for new construction or enlargement of stocks depends upon whether or not the sales of the finished product are growing. Normally, over a long period of years, there is a certain demand for new construction on which producers can rely, and hence the demand for new construction is a normal part of any demand schedule for this kind of goods. But it does not come regularly.

The nature of the mechanical law at work can be emphasized by imagining the industry reduced to a mere machine. Price, for the time being, is to be disregarded. Finished goods are turned out as fast as wanted, and materials and means of production are instantly supplied as fast as the process of finishing requires them. On this simplified basis we can predict accurately how the speed of the different parts of the machine must needs vary, and the results will furnish an index of the varying strains that are put on the much less mechanical system that does these things in real life.

The demand for a certain product, let us say, begins to increase steadily, each year seeing an increment equal to 10 per cent of the original demand. At the end of five years the increase stops and the demand remains stationary. If the productive equipment has kept pace with the need, it is now enlarged by 50 per cent and calls for 50 per cent more expenditure for maintenance and replacements. Meanwhile there has been an added demand for new constructions equal in five years to half the entire original equipment. If renewals are at the rate of 5 per cent a year, the first effect of an increase in demand at the rate of 10 per cent in a year is to treble the demand for the means of production, since a demand for new construction has arisen twice as large as the previous demand for maintenance. At the end of a year the demand for maintenance has been increased because of the fact that there is now 10 per cent more capital to be maintained. Under practical conditions the increase in maintenance would probably be considerably less than 10 per cent, as it takes some time for the new machinery to be installed, and after that it is some time before it reaches its average condition of wear and tear. Until then the repair bills are comparatively light. However, this consideration does not affect the main feature of our problem, which is the suddenness of the increased demand for the means of production and the fact that it is far greater as a percentage change than the disturbance of demand that causes it.

What happens at the end of the five years when the demand stops growing? By this time the requirements for maintenance are 50 per cent greater than they were, while new construction has been going on at a rate equal to twice the original maintenance account. The total output has grown to three and one-half times its former volume. But the demand for new construction now ceases abruptly. This means that if the producers engaged in construction work had enough capacity to meet the demand of the fifth year, the sixth year would see them running with four-sevenths of their capacity idle.

This is a serious condition for any industry in the real world.

It might well be serious enough to produce a panic if any considerable number of industries were in the same condition at the same time. And yet something like it is a normal effect, an inevitable effect, of changes in consumers' demands in a highly capitalistic industrial system.

Thus the law of demand for intermediate products states that the demand depends, not only on the demand for the final product, but on the manner in which that demand is fluctuating. A change from one year to the next in the rate of consumption has a temporary effect on the demand for the intermediate product which is greater than its permanent effect, in just about the proportion by which the total amount of investment in the intermediate product exceeds the amount annually spent for maintenance. In order to bring about an absolute shrinkage in the demand for the intermediate product, all that may be needed is that the final demand should slacken its rate of growth. Making all due allowances for mitigating factors in translating the illustration back into real life, it is still difficult to see how the building and machine-making industries can possibly avoid the disagreeable experience of outgrowing themselves in time of prosperity. For demand can never be expected to grow at an absolutely steady rate, and the slightest fluctuation seems destined to put the producer of capital goods in a situation comparable to that of a passenger forcibly carried by his station.

This principle may be illustrated by a town which grows rapidly up to the size at which its industrial advantages are fully utilized and beyond which its normal production can expand but slowly. When the point of transition is reached from rapid to slow expansion, the town may find that it has outgrown itself by the number of people engaged in the extra construction work involved in the process of growing. Houses to take them in, stores to feed and clothe them, trucks to haul the materials they work with, offices, etc., all will be demanded, and thus a boom may be created which is none the less temporary for being based on tangible economic needs. The experience of the boom town has been common enough in the growth of our western country, and the blame need not be laid entirely upon the vagaries of mob psychology. In a similar way the great work of rebuilding which must follow the present war will give rise to a huge temporary addition to the demand made upon the industries engaged in reconstruction, and as this special work is accomplished and a state of slower and more natural growth takes its place, these industries will have to count on a corresponding shrinkage, not merely relative, but absolute. This will almost inevitably lead to a depression, and, if unforeseen, it may lead to a crisis.

VI. *What Governs the Size of Stocks*

So far the assumption has been made that the need for productive instruments and materials varies with the output. It may be that this assumption will be challenged in some cases, however well it tallies with common experience in most situations. Where the rate of turnover can be easily increased, it may seem natural that producers should take their gains partly in this way rather than bear the burden of an increased investment. However, this could only happen if the producers had previously been either careless enough to let the turnover become unduly slow, or else had been unable to speed up the turnover in slack times by carrying a decreased stock. In production of a technical sort such as that of factories, machine-shops, railroads, etc., the length of the process cannot be reduced at will. It is the business of the staff, from president to foremen, to keep the work moving at all times as fast as is reasonably possible, for waste time is waste time always. It is only in mercantile production that the rate of turnover can be increased more or less at will, and even here it is natural to increase the investment when the output increases.

The size of merchants' stocks is governed by many considerations, some psychological, some commercial, and some speculative. If a dealer knew beforehand just what goods would be demanded and just when, what kind and brand and quality and quantity, he would really have no need of keeping any stocks at all, save to serve as samples. If the static state means absolute steadiness in the demand for everything—if there were absolutely no change and hence no uncertainty in the matter of consumers' wants—dealers would be able to predict demand exactly. Even stock for sample purposes would hardly be needed, and the necessity for the investment of capital in large reserve stores of goods would virtually disappear. This need is the child of uncertainty, and uncertainty is a dynamic fact. Goods held against future demand are the playthings of chance and change.

The chief reasons for keeping a stock are, first, to give the customer a wide selection of goods which he can actually inspect and, secondly, to give assurance of being able to fill large orders without delay. What is the effect of expanding demand on the amount of stock needed to fulfil these functions? Obviously, the larger the orders, the greater the danger of being sold out, unless the stock is increased in a corresponding proportion, or something not too far short of it. The increase in demand would not seem to make it necessary to keep any wider range of goods in stock. But if we are thinking, not of what is necessary, but of what is profitable, we have a different situation. The range of goods a merchant carries is limited largely by a process of natural economic selection, by weeding out the "stockers," whose turnover is too slow to pay for keeping them in stock. With a quickened demand there are fewer "stickers." Some goods which were just below the line of toleration will become profitable to handle on the basis of the increased rate at which they can be sold, and the natural result is the carrying of a greater variety of goods as well as of more goods of each kind. If the dealer is in doubt whether or not to keep a certain line in stock at all, a brisk state of demand will be likely to decide him to keep it.

When we begin considering what is profitable, rather than merely what is physically necessary, we open up a wide range of considerations. The size of the stock is one element in the quality of service rendered by any dealer, which means that it is something in which he is likely to economize when business is poor, and to be liberal when he can afford it. When demand is expanding, merchants are in general prosperous enough to be able to afford to spend money for the purpose of improving the quality of their service. If the increase in demand is part of a general growth of business activity, the customers themselves will be in just such a prosperous state of mind as would put petty economics at a discount. They would be less influenced by a slight saving in price, which can only be made sure of after close study of the qualities of the goods, than by an obvious superiority in quality of service and range of selection. When the buyer's mind swings in this direction the merchant is invited to respond in kind if he wishes to attract his share of the increase in business, rather than to attempt to do it merely by keeping prices down and seeing that the quality of the goods themselves is maintained. A time of general activity in business is a time when large stocks are good tactics commercially.

One other fact which may make merchants more willing to invest in considerable stocks is that a time of growing demand for some one commodity, or a time of general increase in activity, are both times of rising prices for the intermediate products called for in the business affected. This makes these commodities a profitable investment so long as credit can be had on easy terms

These are but a few of the dynamic laws of demand. Two others may be mentioned which have been brought incidentally into the current of the argument and which have been discussed by other writers. We have seen that the demand for durable goods depends, not merely on the price, but on the direction in which the price is expected to move in the near future, as judged chiefly by the direction in which it has been moving in the immediate past. As this has been worked out by other writers, it need not be elaborated here, but may be listed as one of the dynamic laws of demand. Another fact clearly brought out by Mitchell's study is that the demand for materials is sometimes hindered from reacting promptly to a change in the demand for the finished product by the existence of standing contracts, which divide the market into open and closed sections. The result may be under certain conditions to accentuate the suddenness of changes.

READING 17

The Business Cycle

THE NATURE AND CAUSES of the business cycle have been subject to great discussion since the depression of the 1930s. Of our modern economists, Alvin H. Hansen has written about it extensively. The reading that follows explains methods of combating the extreme fluctuations we characterize as prosperity and depression. It includes an explanation of those two important principles: the "acceleration principle" and the "multiplier." The reading ends with a statement of conclusions which summarize the interaction of these two principles in the business cycle.

Alvin H. Hansen (1887-   ) is Professor of Political Economy at Harvard University. He is one of the outstanding American economists. He is best known for his work in business cycles and the accompanying fiscal policy to be applied in combating the fluctuations. The reading is in Chapter XII, "Pump-Priming and Compensatory Fiscal Policy," pp. 261-268; 274-276; 283-288, reprinted from *Fiscal Policy and Business Cycles* by Alvin H. Han-

Monetary policy is an important weapon which we cannot afford to dispense with in cyclical compensatory policy. But it has severe limitations and must be supplemented with other methods. This statement must not be interpreted to mean, however, that even a complete arsenal, involving all the known weapons of attack upon the cycle, is really adequate to stabilize a private enterprise economy. While a program of positive action is necessary, and to a degree effective, complete stability is, nevertheless, unattainable.

Cyclical fiscal policy may be discussed under two headings: first, a cyclically adjusted public spending program; second, a cyclically administered tax policy.

The policy of public spending with respect to the business cycle involves a consideration of "pump-priming," in the strict sense in which that term should be used, in contrast with a policy of public compensatory spending as an offset to fluctuations in private investment. It involves, moreover, theoretical consideration of the Multiplier Principle and the Principle of Acceleration. It involves, in addition, a consideration of the types of expenditure most effective in view of the Multiplier and Acceleration principles as instruments to lift the national income, whether through pump-priming or through compensation.

It is important to make a sharp distinction between the pump-priming concept and the concept of compensation. Pump-priming is not to be confused with compensatory spending.

The term "pump-priming" carries with it the implication that a certain volume of public spending, varying under different conditions, will have the effect of setting the economy going on the way toward full utilization of resources on its own power without further aid from governmental spending. It is not true, as has sometimes been suggested, that the pump-priming concept implies that only a very small amount of public spending will set the economy operating at full capacity. A pump may require much or little priming, depending upon a variety of conditions; and, similarly, the pump-priming concept carries with it no implication as to the amount of spending necessary, but only the implication that, whatever the amount required, sooner or later the economy can operate on its own motive power.

The Multiplier Principle has no necessary connection with pump-priming. It carries with it no connotation with respect to whether the economy can function at full capacity sooner or later without the aid of government spending. It involves, strictly speaking, only the notion that a given amount of public spending will have an effect upon the national income in excess of the volume of expenditures made. It involves the notion of a "multiplier," but not the notion of a self-perpetuating mechanism which under normal conditions has the capacity of operating under its own "steam."

Pump-priming, using the term in the strict sense indicated above, is intended to be a remedy for a temporary maladjustment which prevents the society from functioning in a normal manner so as to recover from depression. The economy needs to be shoved off dead center, so to speak, in order to resume the normal movement from crisis and depression to revival and recovery. It may be that the missing spark is a maladjustment in the cost-price structure, which rigidities in the system make it difficult to overcome without the application of a special remedy. In this case, public expenditures may have the effect of temporarily increasing income and output in the depressed areas, thereby facilitating a readjustment of the price structure toward a more normal relationship. It may be that the missing spark is lack of confidence on the part of business entrepreneurs, owing to the depressing effects of contraction. A given volume of public expenditures may, however, start activity in an upward direction and encourage people to a less pessimistic and truer view of future prospects. It may be that the accumulation of replacement needs owing to depreciation and absolescence has reached a point very favorable to larger capital expenditures, or that the accumulation of innovations with respect to new products and new techniques has reached a point favorable to new investment. But these investment possibilities may await a determined and vigorous leadership behind which a host of timid entrepreneurs are ready to follow. Such leadership, however, may for many reasons not be forthcoming from private entrepreneurs, but may require government action. Under these conditions, pump-priming may prove very effective.

Question may be raised how far the situations just cited are realistic descriptions of actual conditions. Such situations doubtless do more or less prevail in different depressions, varying from country to country and from one cycle to another, but their importance is difficult to appraise.

The concept of "pump-priming" is different from "compensation" in that the latter connotes no implications with respect to setting the system going on its own momentum. The latter concept, strictly conceived, implies merely that public expenditures may be used to compensate for the decline in private investment. What is the order of magnitude of the effectiveness of the compensation is not in question. A policy of compensation may be said to accomplish its purpose even though the public expenditures do not succeed in bringing the economy to full recovery. It may be said to be successful even though it succeeds in achieving a rise in the national income no greater than the volume of expenditures made. It accomplishes the purpose intended, at least in a measure, in so far as it succeeds, whether applied in the period of depression and contraction or in the period of upswing, in lifting the income higher than would have been the case had these expenditures not been made. The expenditures are intended to compensate in some measure for the inadequate volume of private investment.

The Leverage Coefficient

Expenditures made, whether with the intent of priming the pump or the intent of compensating for low private investment, *may,* however, operate with magnified effect. The force of each dollar spent may turn out to have a considerable leverage. This leverage may operate in one of two directions. An expenditure may have secondary effects (a) upon consumption expenditures and (b) upon private investment expenditures. The secondary effects of a given volume of public expenditures upon consumption are in the current literature usually discussed under the term "Multiplier Principle," while the secondary effects upon private investment are referred to under the term "Acceleration Principle." This terminology is, of course, quite arbitrary, since the initial expenditures may be regarded as having raised the national income by a "multiplier" or may be thought of as having an "accelerated effect" on the income. To avoid confusion, the coefficient which must be attached to the initial increment of expenditure in order to raise this increment to the incremental increase in the national income may be termed the "leverage." The leverage coefficient, therefore, in itself indicates nothing with respect to whether the secondary effects operate through consumption or through investment. It may measure the effect of the Multiplier Principle, or the effect of the Acceleration Principle, or a combination of both. Where it is desired to segregate the two, the terms "multiplier leverage" and "acceleration leverage" may be used.

The leverage coefficient may, of course, apply to both pump-priming expenditures and compensation expenditures. If a leverage coefficient is, in fact, applicable to pump-priming expenditures, it is clear that the volume of necessary expenditures is thereby less than would otherwise be the case. Similarly, if a leverage coefficient is applicable to compensation expenditures, it is clear that the desired increase in the national income can be achieved by a smaller volume of initial expenditures. It is, of course, clear that the distinction between pump-priming expenditures and compensation expenditures is simply a matter of the intent with respect to what it is sought to achieve; or after the event one may conclude what, in fact, was the effect of a given volume of expenditure—whether, in fact, the pump was primed or the effect was merely to compensate for the time being for current low private expenditures. Looking back over the experience after the event, it may, of course, turn out that neither effect was achieved. The expenditures might (a) fail to have any effect on the national income; (b) have an exclusively compensatory effect upon the national income; or (c) have a compensatory effect plus a pump-priming effect.

This brings us to a more detailed consideration of the Multiplier and Acceleration Principles. The Multiplier Principle, as we have just indicated, has to do with the secondary effects of the governmental expenditures upon consumption expenditures and, therefore, upon income and employment, while the Acceleration Principle has to do with the induced effects of the governmental expenditures upon private investment and, therefore, upon income and employment.

The Multiplier

The Multiplier Principle, applied to fiscal policy, relates an increment of governmental expenditures to a consequent increment of consumption expenditures. Let us assume that a billion dollars is expended on public works. The billion dollars of new funds poured out into the community is received by the contractors, who, in turn, pay out a part in wages and salaries, a part in dividends, a part in the purchase of materials from manufacturers, and a part in the purchase of materials from raw material producers. These, in turn, similarly pay out a part in wages and salaries, a part in dividends, and a part in finished, semifinished, and raw materials. The Multiplier Principle is, however, concerned exclusively with the effect of the initial expenditure on *consumption,* and is, therefore, peculiarly concerned with the effect of such expenditures upon the receipt of wages, salaries, and dividends. It is clear that it is highly improbable that the full billion dollars spent by the government will materialize down through the various stages in a billion dollars of wages, salaries, or dividends. The reason for this is that many entrepreneurs in the various links in the productive chain will supply the goods sold from stock, will convert inventories into idle cash balances, or pay off bank loans and other debt obligations. Moreover, even though they supply their sales from current production, they will use a part of their profits not to pay dividends, but to accumulate cash or to pay off debts. Thus, it is clear that the billion dollars spent by the government on public works does not all materialize in income for individuals, whether wage earners, salaried employees, or stockholders. A part of the funds is diverted from becoming a part of the income stream by being drained off into idle balances or debt cancellation.

In a similar manner, the enlarged income of individuals flowing from the governmental expenditure and public works—the increased income in wages, salaries, and dividends—is not all used for consumption expenditures. The part that is not expended on consumption goods is saved. Such savings may be used either to pay off debt, held in idle balances, or used for financial investment in mortgages, securities, life insurance policies, and the like. It may, of course, be true that in certain cases the individual will directly expend his savings on real investment in a house, farm equipment, or other investment goods. In this latter case it will be seen that such an individual is performing a dual function. On the one side, he is saving a part of the income and, on the other side, he is simultaneously making a purchase of real investment goods. As far as the Multiplier Principle is involved, we are concerned only with the saving function, and we shall regard his real investment purchases as quite independent, just as though they were performed by another individual.

To repeat, the initial billion dollars of private investment or government outlays on public works does not all eventuate in consumption expenditures. A part is drained off directly by the entrepreneurial units engaged in the productive process in debt payments and in idle balances, and a part of that paid out to wage earners, salaried employees, and dividend recipients is saved. Thus leakages, whether in the form of debt cancellation, the hoarding of idle balances, or financial investment, occur down the entire line of business units and individuals engaged in the private investment or public works project. The magnitude of these leakages determines, in the final analysis, what the secondary effects of the initial expenditures will be upon the volume of consumption expenditures.

The ultimate effects of the initial billion-dollar investment or public works expenditures upon consumption, of course, do not stop at the stage we have reached in our analysis. The individuals participating in the private investment or public works project decide to spend a portion of the new income they have received in consumption purchases. Thus, we have reached the first stage in tracing out the secondary consequences of investment or public works expenditure upon consumption. The expenditures made on consumption goods now set in motion a new productive process necessary to supply these consumption goods. The funds thus expended again seep down through an entire productive process. Again, a part is not paid to wage and salary earners or dividend recipients, but is side-tracked in the form of debt cancellation and idle balances; and, again, a part of the income received by wage and salary earners and dividend recipients is shunted off into savings and utilized for repayment of debt, held in idle balances, or used for financial investment.

* * *

The Acceleration Principle

Thus, the Multiplier Principle concerns exclusively the effect of private investment expenditure or governmental expenditure, as the case may be, upon subsequent net additions to consumption expenditure. The Acceleration Principle, to which we now turn, concerns exclusively the effect of a net increase in consumption expenditures upon induced investment expenditures. If we are to measure the full effect of private investment expenditures or governmental expenditures, as the case may be, on income, we must take account of both the Multiplier and the Acceleration Principle; we must measure not only the effect of these initial expenditures upon subsequent consumption, but also the effect of the subsequent increases in consumption upon investment induced by increase in consumption expenditures.

The volume of replacement investment expenditures is

determined by the volume of consumption expenditures. In the event that consumption expenditures remain constant, no *new* investment expenditures are induced, but only a given volume of replacement. In the event, however, that consumption expenditures rise, the net increment of consumption may induce a given volume of additional investment. This will occur even before existing equipment is fully utilized. If we start from the bottom of a depression, a rise in consumption expenditures is likely to induce a larger volume of replacement expenditures in the old, established industries. This follows from the fact that during depression depreciation allowances are not fully expended, and recovery tends to restore replacement to a normal level. If the increases in consumption expenditures occur in new lines, a given volume of new investment will occur, even though industry in general is still depressed. Thus, it is by no means easy to determine precisely in what degree a rise of consumption expenditures from the bottom of the depression affects, on the one side, replacement investment expenditures, and, on the other side, new investment expenditures. Statistical inquiry (see Kuznets) does, however, reveal that a rise in consumption expenditures from the bottom of the depression brings about a very smooth rise in gross investment, and there appears to be no point in the upswing at which one can clearly demarcate replacement investment expenditures from new investment expenditures; nor is there any sharp break in the gross investment expenditure curve, such as might be implied from an overemphasis on the effect of reasonably full utilization of existing equipment upon new investment, as consumption expenditures continue to rise.

The magnitude of the "Acceleration leverage"—we are here precluded by the current terminology from using the term "multiplier," since that is reserved, as we have seen, for a special case—will depend upon the concrete character of the new consumption. Certain types of consumption goods involve in their production virtually no capital equipment, while others require a very high ratio of capital to each unit of output. Thus, the "Acceleration leverage" cannot be determined on a priori grounds, but must be determined by investigation of the actual character of the new consumption. In general, we know that the average ratio of manufacturing capital to value added is about two to one. It by no means follows, however, that the marginal increments of income will require this ratio of capital to output. This ratio would vary with the different phases of the cycle and with the character of the new consumption purchases.

* * *

Conclusions

Certain extremely important conclusions follow from an examination of the operation of the Multiplier Principle and the Acceleration Principle. These may be summarized as follows:

1. New investment, except for short-run fluctuations in the volume of consumption expenditures, and except for very high values of the Multiplier and Acceleration coefficients, is not affected by the volume of consumption expenditures. Thus (with the exceptions noted), as far as any long-term effect is concerned, the level of consumption in no way affects the level of new investment. A firm grasp of this fundamental conclusion must minimize very much the practical significance of the Acceleration Principle. Replacement investment expenditures are obviously not to be counted at all as a constituent element in the size of the national income, since it is already incorporated in the consumption figures. The value of consumption, of course, consists of the cost of production of such goods, including the cost of replacement of the capital goods required to make the consumption goods in question. The level of consumption determines the volume of replacement investment expenditures. Net investment, however, is a function, in the short run, of *changes* in the level of consumption.

2. There is, therefore, no possibility (except for the case of high leverage values) of raising the income to higher and higher levels by the process of lifting yourself by your boot straps via the interrelation of increased consumption and increased investment in the familiar expansionist process. Instead, as we have shown, the Acceleration Principle, except for temporary fluctuations and the special case of high leverage values, has no effect in lifting the national income at all. The national income can, therefore, in the long run and in the normal case not rise, contrary to commonly accepted but clearly superficial views, by reason of an induced investment springing from an induced rise in consumption.

3. The volume of consumption can be increased, in so far as unemployed resources are available, by net private investment induced by factors, which we shall presently discuss, having no relation whatever to the current level of consumption, or else by governmental expenditures involving the use of new funds and,

therefore, not abstracting from the current level of consumption. How high consumption can be pushed by given increments of private investment expenditures or of governmental expenditures depends upon leakages (which are determined by the propensity to save), as explained under the Multiplier Principle. But the new higher level of consumption rapidly falls to its former level unless the net private investment outlays or the governmental expenditures are continued at a constant level.

4. At a given level of income, consumption equals income, or in other words, the average propensity to consume is equal to one. At this level of income, and at this level alone, a given volume of consumption expenditures is self-perpetuating, and income *tends* to be maintained at a constant level. If income produced temporarily falls below consumption, the gap between the two represents disinvestment. But this situation tends toward a new equilibrium at which income produced and consumption are equal. At this point also there is no *net* investment. The system is self-perpetuating in the sense that 100 per cent of the income received is consumed, and thereby current aggregate demand gives rise to production activities through which a new monetary aggregate demand is created equal to that in the previous period. This is the "circular flow" so vividly described in Schumpeter's *The Theory of Economic Development*.

The national income can, therefore, be divided for analytical purposes into two compartments: the first we shall call the "basic national income," at which the average propensity to consume is equal to one, which income level tends to be self-perpetuating; and the second, the "dynamic income," which, as we have noted, is the margin filled by net investment (private and public) and by the consumption induced by this net investment. It is this dynamic income which is extremely unstable and within the area of which the fluctuations of our economic life occur. This margin need not be wholly filled by net private investment or net income-creating governmental expenditures. But it is these two which are the dynamic factors creating the income above the minimum basic level. According to the size of the leakages (determined by the marginal propensity to save), a part of the margin between the basic income and the full income will be filled by induced consumption expenditures. If the marginal propensity to save that part of the full income which is above the basic minimum income is one half, consumption expenditures will fill one half of this margin. If the marginal propensity to save is one third, consumption expenditures will occupy two thirds of the margin. If the marginal propensity to save is one quarter, consumption expenditures will occupy three quarters of the margin, and so on.

The income level at which consumption equals income may be said to be self-sustaining in the sense that no new, independent, anticipatory investment is necessary to maintain this income level. It is, of course, true that the income may well fall below this basic level owing to dissaving. But this may be regarded as an abnormal, temporary maladjustment, which will sooner or later correct itself. In a progressive society, dissaving can only occur as a temporary phase of the business cycle. If consumption exceeds income (as is true in a serious depression), it follows that replacement capital expenditures are inadequate to sustain the given level of consumption and must sooner or later rise to a point at which no further disinvestment occurs.

Thus, consumption expenditures in a "circular flow" economy in which consumption equals income tend to be self-perpetuating. On the other hand, the net private investment and net income-creating governmental expenditures (together with the secondary consumption expenditures which they induce) are in no sense self-perpetuating. As long as these investment and income-creating expenditures are made, they induce a volume of consumption expenditures above the basic minimum level and thereby have a multiplying effect on the national income.

While from the long-run standpoint the Acceleration Principle (in the usual case) is incapable of raising the level of the national income, it must still be noted that it may have an effect which, under certain conditions, may be very considerable on the cyclical pattern. Without the Acceleration Principle one may argue that private investment or the net income-creating expenditures of the government may lift the national income by a certain Multiplier and hold it there until the investment or net income-creating expenditures cease, whereupon the income rapidly falls to its original level. Under conditions in which, however, the Acceleration Principle is really effective, the stimulated recovery will advance much more rapidly than would otherwise be the case. Still more important, perhaps, is the fact that it may reach a peak and decline with greater or less rapidity, even though the investment and net income-creating expenditures were continued at a constant level. Thus, it is quite possible that a volume of investment or net income-creating expenditures continuously applied may not even be able to sustain the recovery reached. Generally speaking, in the measure that the net income-creating expenditures are extremely effective in creating a burst of recovery, as would be the case when the Multiplier and Acceleration coefficients are high . . ., it may be expected that sooner or later a serious relapse will occur. We may, therefore, conclude (within limits) that the more effectively the investment or net income-creating expenditures operate, the less sustained the recovery is likely to be. This is true, however, only to the extent that the effectiveness in question runs in terms of both the Acceleration and the Multiplier Principles and not in terms of the Multiplier alone. As far as the Multiplier Principle is concerned, the induced recovery can be expected to sustain itself as long as the expenditures continue, but not much longer. If the Acceleration Principle is operative, not even this degree of permanence can be relied upon.

Net income-creating governmental expenditures are undertaken by the government either because the community deliberately wishes to make capital expenditures in order to obtain the utilities directly flowing from the completed projects, or because the community determines to make these capital expenditures in order to raise the national income and thereby escape the wastage incident to unemployed resources. Net private investment is, on the other hand, induced purely in response to the profit motive. Spontaneous net private investment has no relation to the current level of consumption, and any increase in consumption has ordinarily only a temporary and rapidly vanishing effect upon net private investment. Thus, net private investment is fundamentally a function of factors lying quite outside of the current volume of consumption or the current volume of income—factors associated with the dynamics of economic progress. In the absence of new investment outlets adequate to maintain the boom, it is clear that any continued volume of investment, such as would be necessary to maintain income at a full level, would rapidly experience a drastic fall in the prospective rate of profit on new investment (the marginal efficiency of capital). Such a fall progressively weakens the inducement to invest, until net investment equals zero. The classicals were quite right when they argued that without technological progress the price system, including the rate of interest, would progressively drive the economy to the point at which there would be no net investment. They were wrong in assuming that the price system could also ensure a propensity to consume compatible with this investment situation so as to provide full employment.

READING 18

Inflation

THE FOLLOWING READING defines inflation and explains the causes of inflation. The reading also describes some specific terms such as "inflationary gap," "basic inflation," "open inflation," "suppressed inflation," and "galloping inflation." The reader will understand after studying the article that it is a most timely one: we are at present [1960] in a mildly inflationary situation, and we have not experienced the tragic "spiral" or "galloping" aspect of the ailment.

Roy F. Harrod (1900-   ) is Professor of Economics at Oxford University and a distinguished British economist. His most famous contributions to economics have been in the study of prosperity-depression fluctuations. Probably his chief work was his *Trade Cycle* published in 1936. The reading is from "Inflation: A Primer for Today," *The New York Times Magazine,* October 7, 1951. Reprinted by permission.

What Inflation Is

Inflation is the name for that state of affairs in which all or most prices are continually rising. In normal conditions certain prices often rise from time to time, while others fall. During inflation, the general level of prices continues to rise. To put it another way, the purchasing power of the currency deteriorates. This rise in general prices is usually accompanied by wage and salary increases. The increases are sought and given with a view to sustaining living standards in the face of rising prices. But they fail to do this, since it is of the essence of inflation that prices should exceed their normal relation to wages and salaries. The wage and salary increases merely push prices further up; in fact, wages chase prices in vain.

Sometimes this chase becomes hectic and we have what is known as galloping inflation, which may lead to a complete destruction of the currency. At the end of such a process a billion dollars may buy no more than one dollar bought before it began.

A word of warning is needed. The horrors of galloping inflation, with its complete destruction of all existing values, are evident. A moderate inflation, on the other hand, may seem fairly innocuous, and a nation subject to it may complacently believe that the harm ultimately done will also be moderate. Mild inflation develops by insensible stages into galloping inflation and, when the development has got a certain way, it proves impossible to check the process. The German authorities would fain have done so after the first World War, but they had allowed the disease to get too strong a hold and when the tragic consequences showed themselves it was too late to cure it.

The Cause of Inflation

Inflation is sometimes described as the state in which there is "too much money chasing too few goods"; if the available goods were sold at the old prices, people would have money left over which they would want to spend. The process of using the extra money in their pockets drives up prices so that, after all, the inadequate supply of goods absorbs all the money there is.

Why should there ever be more than enough money to match the available goods? It may be simplest to answer this general question with a particular example. The following figures are purely illustrative and do not claim to be assessments of the facts referred to.

Let us suppose that the United States plans to spend for defense purposes $50 billion a year more than she was spending before Korea. This money is paid out as wages, salaries, fees, commissions, profits, etc., to all those who make goods directly or indirectly for the defense effort, as well as to the forces themselves. Prior to the defense effort, all those people (or most of them) were doing something else to serve the economy, and were providing goods or services worth something in the neighborhood of $50 billion. Those goods and services will no longer be available; they have to be cut out, because the people who provided them will now be doing something else.

But those same people will still be earning their living as before—their wages, profits, or what not; they will be earning their living by serving the purposes of the state; having earned the money in a new way, they will want to spend it just as they did before; they must spend some of it to keep alive. And so it happens that there is a shortfall of goods to the value of $50 billion and just as much money as before to spend upon the available goods. There exists what is sometimes called an "inflationary gap" of $50 billion.

Of course, the matter will not be allowed to rest there. Congress gets busy and imposes additional taxes, which take away from consumers some part of the spending power they had before. Let us suppose that Congress imposes $17 billion worth of new taxes. This would seem to reduce the inflationary gap to $33 billion; actually, it does not do quite so much.

The reduction will be fully effective only if all those who pay the new taxes cut their consumption by an exactly equivalent amount. Some of them may pay some part of the additional taxes at the expense of what they would have otherwise have saved; corporations may set aside less to reserve. A country would probably be doing well if $17 billion of new taxes reduced consumption by, say, $14 billion.

Next, an attempt may be made to make people withhold money from consumption by a great campaign for the sale of Government bonds. This is only effective to prevent inflation to the precise extent that purchasers of these bonds actually reduce their own spending on goods. It may help the Government for people to buy bonds out of their bank balances or in lieu of other securities, but it does not help the inflationary problem; to help that they must cut out their personal consumption. We may suppose, for example, that a great bond-selling drive succeeds in reducing consumption by $6 billion; thus taxes and additional savings together would have cut consumer spending by $20 billion. An inflationary gap of $30 billion would still remain.

Those who consider these matters build great hopes upon an increase of production. This is an all-important factor, but it is also important to remember that an increased output of goods does not serve to close the inflationary gap dollar for dollar. There will be increases of income, whether to individuals or corporations, of value equivalent to the new output. Some of this extra money may go to reserve, some be saved, some be taken in taxes. If the United States should increase its output of goods by $20 billion it would be lucky not to have increased spending by more than, say, $10 billion. In that case the increased output would only have tended to close the inflationary gap to the extent of $10 billion. A "gap" of $20 billion (out of the original $50 billion) would still be left. Prices would normally rise in proportion to this gap. Such a rise might or might not be insupportable.

The Inflationary Gap

The inflationary gap is the excess of governmental expenditures and capital expenditures—taken together—over the amounts of money paid in taxes and the amounts of money normally saved, taken together.

Suppose governmental expenditures and capital expenditures together add up to $100 billion; this total sum will be earned by those working on governmental and capital account, and will come into income and constitute part of potential consumer spending. Suppose those who make consumer goods earn $200 billion; then there will be $300 billion in all of potential spending power. Suppose taxes and normal savings take away $80 billion of this; then there will be $220 billion of actual spending power.

But if only $200 billion worth of consumer goods are produced, there will be $220 billion of money running after $200 billion worth of goods. This excess of $20 billion of money applied to spending over goods available for purchase is one and the same thing as the excess of governmental, plus capital, expenditures over taxes plus savings. I call this excess the "basic inflation" in any situation. Basic inflation can always be diagnosed as being a definite limited sum of dollars.

To the extent that this causes prices to rise, wage-earners and salary-earners may demand higher pay with a view to maintaining their standards of living. The employers may feel that they have a good case, and that anyhow it is needful to grant the increases to keep the wheels moving. When this happens, spiral inflation begins.

These increases, taken in bulk, do not help their recipients. No more goods are available. Prices will rise further, to offset the increases. They will rise for two reasons: first, because the increases have sent more money chasing goods and, secondly, because the increases will raise the cost of producing the goods. The further rise of prices may set up increased wage and salary demands, with the same effect again, and so on *ad infinitum*.

It is to be noted that while the amount of *basic* inflation in any situation may be represented by a definite sum of dollars, the amount of *spiral* inflation that may develop is quite unlimited; it all depends on how quickly each new wage increase and each new price increase follow one another. It is spiral inflation that may develop into galloping inflation.

Open Vs. Suppressed Inflation

A given amount of basic inflation does not invariably lead to a fully proportionate rise of prices. A producer, faced with a rising demand for his goods, is not absolutely bound to put up his price so as to clear the market; he may prefer to establish a waiting list. Or the law may intervene with price controls.

These controls do not have the slightest tendency to reduce the basic inflation; they do not alter the factors that make goods in short supply. Instead of the consumers finding that their money will not go so far as before, because prices are higher, they find themselves put on waiting lists and are deprived of what they want that way.

In wartime, controls of this sort may serve to keep down consumption; money may accumulate in the hands of consumers in the form of what has been called "pent-up purchasing power." This may find vent when the war is over. This accumulation will only occur if the controls are very wide-spread and if the consumers, being busy on war work, do not make great efforts to spend the money they have.

In peacetime the consumers are rather likely, if denied certain objects, to spend the money on something else. The burden of "suppressed" inflation may fall on those who have ordered capital goods or on the defense programs. The goods just are not there to satisfy all demands, which is essentially an excess of demand over supply; and if the inflation does not find vent in higher prices but is "suppressed," waiting lists must grow—someone has to bear the brunt of the shortage. If these waiting lists become lengthy inside the industrial process, the efficiency of production is bound to suffer.

Thus "suppressed" inflation has very bad consequences. It gives rise to bottlenecks and delays and tends to slow down the whole productive machine. On the other side, it must be admitted that it has one great virtue compared with open inflation. It is not so likely to lead to a spiral.

The Answer to Inflation

It must already be evident that the correct anti-inflationary policy is to eliminate or reduce *basic* inflation. Without basic inflation, there will be no tendency to a spiral. This can be done by increasing production, by reducing nondefense governmental expenditures, by reducing capital expenditures not essential for the defense effort, by increasing taxes, and by increasing voluntary savings.

Decreases in governmental expenditures and capital expenditures and increases in voluntary savings will provide dollar-for-dollar contributions toward cutting out basic inflation. Increases of production and increases of taxation will tend in the same direction, but are not likely to provide dollar-for-dollar contributions. Every effort should be made along these five roads to eliminate basic inflation, or if this proves impossible to reduce it to quite small dimensions.

If it is proved impossible to eradicate basic inflation completely, then a further decision still has to be made. Shall basic inflation be allowed to eventuate in a proportionate amount of open inflation—namely, an over-all rise of prices—or shall attempts be made to suppress the inflation by means of sundry controls?

The correct answer appears to be this: If the basic inflation has been reduced to really moderate dimensions, it may be wiser to let it eventuate in open inflation. This will allow normal market mechanisms to operate freely, allow those who most need the various goods to have them, prevent the formation of bottlenecks, and keep the production lines running at top efficiency. Even a small degree of open basic inflation may lead to some spiraling; but, if the initiating cause is small, one may hope that the spiraling effects will be moderate. All spiral inflation is an evil, but a small spiral inflation may be a lesser evil than the congestion in the industrial system which results from "suppression."

On the other hand, if a basic inflation of substantial size has been allowed to remain in being, then the wise choice may be to attempt suppression, despite all its evils. A large basic inflation might lead to a large spiral inflation, and there is no greater evil than that. A spiral inflation, too, if it begins to move quickly, can cause chaos in the industrial system. The price mechanism is a delicate one and, in a quickly moving spiral, there is no time for prices to become adjusted to one another. Existing values are destroyed, the basis of free enterprise is sapped, and great confusion results. Lenin is often quoted as having said that inflation is the surest method of destroying the capitalist system.

READING 19

A Social Philosophy

THE SOCIAL PHILOSOPHY delineated in the following pages is that of John Maynard Keynes, considered by some the outstanding economist of this century. Keynes is famous as having welded together theories and thought on the "total economy," or the "macro-economy," into a harmonious whole, thus erecting a framework of "national-income economics." This "national-income economics," or "national-income analysis," is probably the outstanding development of the last few decades in economic thought.

Keynes contemplates in the following reading the condition of society toward which the policies and practices advocated by him in his system of national-income economics would lead. We find in the reading that this system leads to a society in which some degree of "nationalization," or "socialization," of the economy would occur. Keynes states that he makes no case for socialism as such, but that "I can conceive, therefore, that a somewhat comprehensive socialization of investment will prove the only means of securing an approximation to full employment; though this need not exclude all manner of compromises and of devices by which the public authority will co-operate with private initiative."

John Maynard (Lord) Keynes (1883-1946) was, if not the greatest, certainly one of the great economists of this century. Besides being an academic economist he was also active in government affairs. He was Governor of the International Monetary Fund and the International Bank for Reconstruction and Development—the two organizations created at the Bretton Woods Conference held in the United States, in which he participated as representative of the British Government. He was sometime Fellow at Kings College, Cambridge. He was the son of John Neville Keynes, who was also an important English economist. His first widely studied writing was *The Economic Consequences of the Peace,* written as a result of his observations of the peace treaty negotiations at Versailles following World War I. The greatest of his work was *The General Theory of Employment, Interest, and Money,* published in 1935, in which he accomplished the groundwork of the modern "national-income economics." The reading is in Chapter 24, "Concluding Notes on the Social Philosophy Towards which the General Theory Might Lead," pp. 372-384, from *The General Theory of Employment, Interest, and Money* by John Maynard Keynes. Reprinted by permission of Harcourt, Brace and Company, Inc.

I

The outstanding faults of the economic society in which we live are its failure to provide for full employment and its arbitrary and inequitable distribution of wealth and incomes. The bearing of the foregoing theory on the first of these is obvious. But there are also two important respects in which it is relevant to the second.

Since the end of the nineteenth century significant progress towards the removal of very great disparities of wealth and income has been achieved through the instrument of direct taxation—income tax and surtax and death duties—especially in Great Britain. Many people would wish to see this process carried much further, but they are deterred by two considerations; partly by the fear of making skilful evasions too much worth while and also of diminishing unduly the motive towards risk-taking, but mainly, I think, by the belief that the growth of capital depends upon the strength of the motive towards individual saving and that for a large proportion of this growth we are dependent on the savings of the rich out of their superfluity. Our argument does not affect the first of these considerations. But it may considerably modify our attitude towards the second. For we have seen that, up to the point where full employment prevails, the growth of capital depends not at all on a low propensity to consume but is, on the contrary, held back by it; and only in conditions of full employment is a low propensity to consume conducive to the growth of capital. Moreover, experience suggests that in existing conditions saving by institutions and through sinking funds is more than adequate, and that measures for the redistribution of incomes in a way likely to raise the propensity to consume may prove positively favourable to the growth of capital.

The existing confusion of the public mind on the matter is well illustrated by the very common belief that the death duties are responsible for a reduction in the capital wealth of the country. Assuming that the State applies the proceeds of these duties to its ordinary outgoings so that taxes on incomes and consumption are correspondingly reduced or avoided, it is, of course, true that a fiscal policy of heavy death duties has the effect of increasing the community's propensity to consume. But inasmuch as an increase in the habitual propensity to consume will in general (*i.e.* except in conditions of full employment) serve to increase at the same time the inducement to invest, the inference commonly drawn is the exact opposite of the truth.

Thus our argument leads towards the conclusion that in contemporary conditions the growth of wealth, so far from being dependent on the abstinence of the rich, as is commonly supposed, is more likely to be impeded by it. One of the chief social justifications of great inequality of wealth is, therefore, removed. I am not saying that there are no other reasons, unaffected by our theory, capable of justifying some measure of inequality in some circumstances. But it does dispose of the most important of the reasons why hitherto we have thought it prudent to move carefully. This particularly affects our attitude towards death duties; for there are certain justifications for inequality of incomes which do not apply equally to inequality of inheritances.

For my own part, I believe that there is social and psychological justification for significant inequalities of incomes and wealth, but not for such large disparities as exist to-day. There are valuable human activities which require the motive of money-making and the environment of private wealth-ownership for their full fruition. Moreover, dangerous human proclivities can be canalised into comparatively harmless channels by the existence of opportunities for money-making and private wealth, which, if they cannot be satisfied in this way, may find their outlet in cruelty, the reckless pursuit of personal power and authority, and other forms of self-aggrandisement. It is better that a man should tyrannise over his bank balance than over his fellow-citizens; and whilst the former is sometimes denounced as being but a means to the latter, sometimes at least it is an alternative. But it is not necessary for the stimulation of these activities and the satisfaction of these proclivities that the game should be played for such high stakes as at present. Much lower stakes will serve the purpose equally well, as soon as the players are accustomed to them. The task of transmuting human nature must not be confused with the task of managing it. Though in the ideal commonwealth men may have been taught or inspired or bred to take no interest in the stakes, it may still be wise and prudent statesmanship to allow the game to be played, subject to rules and limitations, so long as the average man, or even a significant section of the community, is in fact strongly addicted to the money-making passion.

II

There is, however, a second, much more fundamental inference from our argument which has a bearing on the future of inequalities of wealth; namely, our theory of the rate of interest. The justification for a moderately high rate of interest has been found hitherto in the necessity of providing a sufficient inducement to save. But we have shown that the extent of effective saving is necessarily determined by the scale of investment and that the scale of investment is promoted by a *low* rate of interest, provided that we do not attempt to stimulate it in this way beyond the point which corresponds to full employment. Thus it is to our best advantage to reduce the rate of interest to that point relatively to the schedule of the marginal efficiency of capital at which there is full employment.

There can be no doubt that this criterion will lead to a much lower rate of interest than has ruled hitherto; and, so far as one can guess at the schedules of the marginal efficiency of capital corresponding to increasing amounts of capital, the rate of interest is likely to fall steadily, if it should be practicable to maintain conditions of more or less continuous full employment—unless, indeed, there is an excessive change in the aggregate propensity to consume (including the State).

I feel sure that the demand for capital is strictly limited in the sense that it would not be difficult to increase the stock of capital up to a point where its marginal efficiency had fallen to a very low figure. This would not mean that the use of capital instruments would cost almost nothing, but only that the return from them would have to cover little more than their exhaustion by wastage and obsolescence together with some margin to cover risk and the exercise of skill and judgment. In short, the aggregate return from durable goods in the course of their life would, as in the case of short-lived goods, just cover their labour-costs of production *plus* an allowance for risk and the costs of skill and supervision.

Now, though this state of affairs would be quite compatible with some measure of individualism, yet it would mean the euthanasia of the rentier, and, consequently, the euthanasia of the cumulative oppressive power of the capitalist to exploit the scarcity-value of capital. Interest to-day rewards no genuine sacrifice, any more than does the rent of land. The owner of capital can obtain interest because capital is scarce, just as the owner of land can obtain rent because land is scarce. But whilst there may be intrinsic reasons for the scarcity of land, there are no intrinsic reasons for the scarcity of capital. An intrinsic reason for such scarcity, in the sense of a genuine sacrifice which could only be called forth by the offer of a reward in the shape of interest, would not exist, in the long run, except in the event of the individual propensity to consume proving to be of such a character that net saving in conditions of full employment comes to an end before capital has become sufficiently abundant. But even so, it will still be possible for communal saving through the agency of the State to be maintained at a level which will allow the growth of capital up to the point where it ceases to be scarce.

I see, therefore, the rentier aspect of capitalism as a transitional phase which will disappear when it has done its work. And with the disappearance of its rentier aspect much else in it besides will suffer a sea-change. It will be moreover, a great advantage of the order of events which I am advocating, that the euthanasia of the rentier, of the functionless investor, will be nothing sudden, merely a gradual but prolonged continuance of what we have seen recently in Great Britain, and will need no revolution.

Thus we might aim in practice (there being nothing in this which is unattainable) at an increase in the volume of capital until it ceases to be scarce, so that the functionless investor will no longer receive a bonus; and at a scheme of direct taxation which allows the intelligence and determination and executive skill of the financier, the entrepreneur *et hoc genus omne* (who are certainly so fond of their craft that their labour could be obtained much cheaper than at present), to be harnessed to the service of the community on reasonable terms of reward.

At the same time we must recognize that only experience can show how far the common will, embodied in the policy of the State, ought to be directed to increasing and supplementing the inducement to invest; and how far it is safe to stimulate the average propensity to consume, without forgoing our aim of depriving capital of its scarcity-value within one or two generations. It may turn out that the propensity to consume will be so easily strengthened by the effects of a falling rate of interest, that full employment can be reached with a rate of accumulation little greater than at present. In this event a scheme for the higher taxation of large incomes and inheritances might be open to the objection that it would lead to full employment with a rate of accumulation which was reduced considerably below the current level. I must not be supposed to deny the possibility, or even the probability, of this outcome. For in such matters it is rash to predict how the average man will react to a changed environment. If, however, it should prove easy to secure an approximation to full employment with a rate of accumulation not much greater than at present, an outstanding problem will at least have been solved. And it would remain for separate decision on what scale and by what means it is right and reasonable to call on the living generation to restrict their consumption, so as to establish, in course of time, a state of full investment for their successors.

III

In some other respects the foregoing theory is moderately conservative in its implications. For whilst it indicates the vital importance of establishing certain central controls in matters which are now left in the main to individual initiative, there are wide fields of activity which are unaffected. The State will have to exercise a guiding influence on the propensity to consume partly through its scheme of taxation, partly by fixing the rate of interest, and partly, perhaps, in other ways. Furthermore, it seems unlikely that the influence of banking policy on the rate of interest will be sufficient by itself to determine an optimum rate of investment. I conceive, therefore, that a somewhat comprehensive socialisation of investment will prove the only means of securing an approximation to full employment; though this need not exclude all manner of compromises and of devices by which public authority will co-operate with private initiative. But beyond this no obvious case is made out for a system of State Socialism which would embrace most of the economic life of the community. It is not the ownership of the instruments of production which it is important for the State to assume. If the State is able to determine the aggregate amount of resources devoted to augmenting the instruments and the basic rate of reward to those who own them, it will have accomplished all that is necessary. Moreover, the necessary measures of socialisation can be introduced gradually and without a break in the general traditions of society.

Our criticism of the accepted classical theory of economics has consisted not so much in finding logical flaws in its analysis as in pointing out that its tacit assumptions are seldom or never satisfied, with the result that it cannot solve the economic problems of the actual world. But if our central controls succeed in establishing an aggregate volume of output corresponding to full employment as nearly as is practicable, the classical theory comes into its own again from this point onwards. If we suppose the volume of output to be given, *i.e.* to be determined by forces outside the classical scheme of thought, then there is no objection to be raised against the classical analysis of the manner in which private self-interest will determine what in particular is produced, in what proportions the factors of production will be combined to produce it, and how the value of the final product will be distributed between them. Again, if we have dealt otherwise with the problem of thrift, there is no objection to be raised against the modern classical theory as to the degree of consilience between private and public advantage in conditions of perfect and imperfect competition respectively. Thus, apart from the necessity of central controls to bring about an adjustment between the propensity to consume and the inducement to invest, there is no more reason to socialise economic life than there was before.

To put the point concretely, I see no reason to suppose that the existing system seriously misemploys the factors of production which are in use. There are, of course, errors of foresight; but these would not be avoided by centralising decisions. When 9,000,000 men are employed out of 10,000,000 willing and able to work, there is no evidence that the labour of these 9,000,000 men is misdirected. The complaint against the present system is not that these 9,000,000 men ought to be employed on different tasks, but that tasks should be available for the remaining 1,000,000 men. It is in determining the volume, not the direction, of actual employment that the existing system has broken down.

Thus I agree with Gesell that the result of filling in the gaps in the classical theory is not to dispose of the "Manchester System," but to indicate the nature of the environment which the free play of economic forces requires if it is to realise the full potentialities of production. The central controls necessary to ensure full employment will, of course, involve a large extension of the traditional functions of government. Furthermore, the modern classical theory has itself called attention to various conditions in which the free play of economic forces may need to be curbed or guided. But there will still remain a wide field for the exercise of private initiative and responsibility. Within this field the traditional advantages of individualism will still hold good.

Let us stop for a moment to remind ourselves what these advantages are. They are partly advantages of efficiency—the advantages of decentralisation and of the play of self-interest. The advantage to efficiency of the decentralisation of decisions and of individual responsibility is even greater, perhaps, than the nineteenth century supposed; and the reaction against the appeal to self-interest may have gone too far. But, above all, individualism, if it can be purged of its defects and its abuses, is the best safeguard of personal liberty in the sense that, compared with any other system, it greatly widens the field for the exercise of personal choice. It is also the best safeguard of the variety of life, which emerges precisely from this extended field of personal choice, and the loss of which is the greatest of all the losses of the homogeneous or totalitarian state. For this variety preserves the traditions which embody the most secure and successful choices of former generations; it colours the present with the diversification of its fancy; and, being the handmaid of experiment as well as of tradition and of fancy, it is the most powerful instrument to better the future.

Whilst, therefore, the enlargement of the functions of government, involved in the task of adjusting to one another the propensity to consume and the inducement to invest, would seem to a nineteenth-century publicist or to a contemporary American financier to be a terrific encroachment on individualism, I defend it, on the contrary, both as the only practicable means of avoiding the destruction of existing economic forms in their entirety and as the condition of the successful functioning of individual initiative.

For if effective demand is deficient, not only is the public scandal of wasted resources intolerable, but the individual enterpriser who seeks to bring these resources into action is operating with the odds loaded against him. The game of hazard which he plays is furnished with many zeros, so that the players *as a whole* will lose if they have the energy and hope to deal all the cards. Hitherto the increment of the world's wealth has fallen short of the aggregate of positive individual savings; and the difference has been made up by the losses of those whose courage and initiative have not been supplemented by exceptional skill or unusual good fortune. But if effective demand is adequate, average skill and average good fortune will be enough.

The authoritarian state systems of to-day seem to solve the problem of unemployment at the expense of efficiency and of freedom. It is certain that the world will not much longer tolerate the unemployment which, apart from brief intervals of excitement, is associated—and, in my opinion, inevitably associated—with present-day capitalistic individualism. But it may be possible by a right analysis of the problem to cure the disease whilst preserving efficiency and freedom.

IV

I have mentioned in passing that the new system might be more favourable to peace than the old has been. It is worth while to repeat and emphasise that aspect.

War has several causes. Dictators and others such, to whom war offers, in expectation at least, a pleasurable excitement, find it easy to work on the natural bellicosity of their peoples. But, over and above this, facilitating their task of fanning the popular flame, are the economic causes of war, namely, the pressure of population and the competitive struggle for markets. It is the second factor, which probably played a predominant part in the nineteenth century, and might again, that is germane to this discussion.

I have pointed out in the preceding chapter that, under the system of domestic *laissez-faire* and an international gold standard such as was orthodox in the latter half of the nineteenth century, there was no means open to a government whereby to mitigate economic distress at home except through the competitive struggle for markets. For all measures helpful to a state of chronic or intermittent under-employment were ruled out, except measures to improve the balance of trade on income account.

Thus, whilst economists were accustomed to applaud the prevailing international system as furnishing the fruits of the international division of labour and harmonising at the same time the interests of different nations, there lay concealed a less benign influence; and those statesmen were moved by common sense and a correct apprehension of the true course of events, who believed that if a rich, old country were to neglect the struggle for markets its prosperity would droop and fail. But if nations can learn to provide themselves with full employment by their domestic policy (and, we must add, if they can also attain equilibrium in the trend of their population), there need be no important economic forces calculated to set the interest of one country against that of its neighbours. There would still be room for the international division of labour and for international lending in appropriate conditions. But there would no longer be a pressing motive why one country need force its wares on another or repulse the offerings of its neighbour, not because this was necessary to enable it to pay for what it wished to purchase, but with the express object of upsetting the equilibrium of payments so as to develop a balance of trade in its own favour. International trade would cease to be what it is, namely, a desperate expedient to maintain employment at home by forcing sales on foreign markets and restricting purchases, which, if successful, will merely shift the problem of unemployment to the neighbour which is worsted in the struggle, but a willing and unimpeded exchange of goods and services in conditions of mutual advantage.

V

Is the fulfilment of these ideas a visionary hope? Have they insufficient roots in the motives which govern the evolution of political society? Are the interests which they will thwart stronger and more obvious than those which they will serve?

I do not attempt an answer in this place. It would need a volume of a different character from this one to indicate even in outline the practical measures in which they might be gradually clothed. But if the ideas are correct—an hypothesis on which the author himself must necessarily base what he writes—it would be a mistake, I predict, to dispute their potency over a period of time. At the present moment people are unusually expectant of a more fundamental diagnosis; more particularly ready to receive it; eager to try it out, if it should be even plausible. But apart from this contemporary mood, the ideas of economists and political philosophers, both when they are right and when they are wrong, are more powerful than is commonly understood. Indeed the world is ruled by little else. Practical men, who believe themselves to be quite exempt from any intellectual influences, are usually the slaves of some defunct economist. Madmen in authority, who hear voices in the air, are distilling their frenzy from some academic scribbler of a few years back. I am sure that the power of vested interests is vastly exaggerated compared with the gradual encroachment of ideas. Not, indeed, immediately, but after a certain interval; for in the field of economic and political philosophy there are not many who are influenced by new theories after they are twenty-five or thirty years of age, so that the ideas which civil servants and politicians and even agitators apply to current events are not likely to be the newest. But, soon or late, it is ideas, not vested interests, which are dangerous for good or evil.

READING 20

Taxation

TAXATION MIGHT BE CONSIDERED the most unpopular facet of economics to the layman. Of all aspects of economics, it is the one which is closest to him, possibly because of the painful necessity of periodical payment. While the modern taxpayer may consider his vexations as isolated from other worries and other peoples, we can point out that the subject of taxation has held the close interest of all people from the time at which they chose to live under a government.

Literally hundreds of volumes have been filled with discussions of taxation—systems, policies, and methods. Today economists are devoting great attention to the problems of taxation. Much of all of this work is based, however, upon some of the observations of Adam Smith.

The following reading is the famous statement of Adam Smith on the "canons" of taxation. These four canons, or maxims, have generally stood the test of time. Much of modern taxation theory is built upon these four "canons."

Adam Smith (1723-1790) has often been called the "founder of political economy." His great work, *The Wealth of Nations,* was the first comprehensive statement explaining an economic "system." His work consisted chiefly in a selection from and a tying together of all preceding fragmentary works on economics. From these ideas that had gone before, he erected a system of

economics which we call "classical economics." Three other
economists are usually included among the great "classical" economists: David Ricardo, Thomas Malthus, and John Stuart Mill.

Smith was a Scottish philosopher who was Professor of Moral
Philosophy at the University of Glasgow. Later he was appointed
Commissioner of Customs in Scotland, a post which he held in
Edinburgh until his death. The reading is from *An Inquiry
Into the Nature and Causes of the Wealth of Nations* (New York:
Random House, Inc., Cannan Edition, 1937, 976 pp.), Book V,
"Of the Revenue of the Sovereign or Commonwealth," Chapter I,
"Of the Expences of the Sovereign or Commonwealth," pp. 767-
768, and Chapter II, "Of the Sources of the general or public
Revenue of the Society," pp. 777-779.

The expence of defending the society, and that of supporting
the dignity of the chief magistrate, are both laid out for the
general benefit of the whole society. It is reasonable, therefore,
that they should be defrayed by the general contribution of the
whole society, all the different members contributing, as nearly
as possible, in proportion to their respective abilities.

The expence of the administration of justice too, may, no
doubt, be considered as laid out for the benefit of the whole
society. There is no impropriety, therefore, in its being defrayed
by the general contribution of the whole society. The persons,
however, who give occasion to this expence are those who, by
their injustice in one way or another, make it necessary to seek
redress or protection from the courts of justice. The persons again
most immediately benefited by this expence, are those whom the
courts of justice either restore to their rights, or maintain in
their rights. The expence of the administration of justice, therefore, may very properly be defrayed by the particular contribution of one or other, or both of those two different sets of persons,
according as different occasions may require, that is, by the fees
of court. It cannot be necessary to have recourse to the general
contribution of the whole society, except for the conviction of
those criminals who have not themselves any estate or fund
sufficient for paying those fees.

Those local or provincial expences of which the benefit is
local or provincial (what is laid out, for example, upon the police
of a particular town or district) ought to be defrayed by a local
or provincial revenue, and ought to be no burden upon the

general revenue of the society. It is unjust that the whole society should contribute towards an expence of which the benefit is confined to a part of the society.

The expence of maintaining good roads and communications is, no doubt, beneficial to the whole society, and may, therefore, without any injustice, be defrayed by the general contribution of the whole society. This expence, however, is most immediately and directly beneficial to those who travel or carry goods from one place to another, and to those who consume such goods. The turnpike tolls in England, and the duties called peages in other countries, lay it altogether upon those two different sets of people, and thereby discharge the general revenue of the society from a very considerable burden.

The expence of the institutions for education and religious instruction, is likewise, no doubt, beneficial to the whole society, and may, therefore, without injustice, be defrayed by the general contribution of the whole society. This expence, however, might perhaps with equal propriety, and even with some advantage, be defrayed altogether by those who receive the immediate benefit of such education and instruction, or by the voluntary contribution of those who think they have occasion for either the one or the other.

When the institutions or public works which are beneficial to the whole society, either cannot be maintained altogether, or are not maintained altogether by the contribution of such particular members of the society as are most immediately benefited by them, the deficiency must in most cases be made up by the general contribution of the whole society. The general revenue of the society, over and above defraying the expence of defending the society, and of supporting the dignity of the chief magistrate, must make up for the deficiency of many particular branches of revenue. The sources of this general or public revenue, I shall endeavour to explain in the following chapter.

* * *

The private revenue of individuals, it has been shewn in the first book of this Inquiry, arises ultimately from three different sources; Rent, Profit, and Wages. Every tax must finally be paid from some one or other of those three different sorts of revenue, or from all of them indifferently. I shall endeavour to give the best account I can, first, of those taxes which, it is intended, should fall upon rent; secondly, of those which, it is intended, should fall upon profit; thirdly, of those which, it is intended, should fall upon wages; and, fourthly, of those which, it is intended, should fall indifferently upon all those three different sources of private revenue. The particular consideration of each of these four different sorts of taxes will divide the second part of the present chapter into four articles, three of which will require several other subdivisions. Many of those taxes, it will appear from the following review, are not finally paid from the fund, or source of revenue, upon which it was intended they should fall.

Before I enter upon the examination of particular taxes, it is necessary to premise the four following maxims with regard to taxes in general.

I. The subjects of every state ought to contribute towards the support of the government, as nearly as possible, in proportion to their respective abilities; that is, in proportion to the revenue which they respectively enjoy under the protection of the state. The expence of government to the individuals of a great nation, is like the expence of management to the joint tenants of a great estate, who are all obliged to contribute in proportion to their respective interests in the estate. In the observation or neglect of this maxim consists, what is called the equality or inequality of taxation. Every tax, it must be observed once for all, which falls finally upon one only of the three sorts of revenue above mentioned, is necessarily unequal, in so far as it does not affect the other two. In the following examination of different taxes I shall seldom take much further notice of this sort of inequality, but shall, in most cases, confine my observations to that inequality which is occasioned by a particular tax falling unequally even upon that particular sort of private revenue which is affected by it.

II. The tax· which each individual is bound to pay ought to be certain, and not arbitrary. The time of payment, the manner of payment, the quantity to be paid, ought all to be clear and plain to the contributor, and to every other person. Where it is otherwise, every person subject to the tax is put more or less in the power of the tax-gatherer, who can either aggravate the tax upon any obnoxious contributor, or extort, by the terror of such aggravation, some present or perquisite to himself. The uncertainty of taxation encourages the insolence and favours the corruption of an order of men who are naturally unpopular, even where they are neither insolent nor corrupt. The certainty of what each individual ought to pay is, in taxation, a matter of so great importance, that a very considerable degree of inequality, it appears, I believe, from the experience of all nations, is not near so great an evil as a very small degree of uncertainty.

III. Every tax ought to be levied at the time, or in the manner, in which it is most likely to be convenient for the contributor to pay it. A tax upon the rent of land or of houses, payable at the same term at which such rents are usually paid, is levied at the time when it is most likely to be convenient for the contributor to pay; or, when he is most likely to have wherewithal to pay. Taxes upon such consumable goods as are articles of luxury, are all finally paid by the consumer, and generally in a manner that is very convenient for him. He pays them by little and little, as he has occasion to buy the goods. As he is at liberty too, either to buy, or not to buy, as he pleases, it must be his own fault if he ever suffers any considerable inconveniency from such taxes.

IV. Every tax ought to be so contrived as both to take out and to keep out of the pockets of the people as little as possible, over and above what it brings into the public treasury of the state. A tax may either take out or keep out of the pockets of the people a great deal more than it brings into the public treasury, in the four following ways. First, the levying of it may require a great number of officers, whose salaries may eat up the greater part of the produce of the tax, and whose perquisites may impose another additional tax upon the people. Secondly, it may obstruct the industry of the people, and discourage them from applying to certain branches of business which might give maintenance and employment to great multitudes. While it obliges the people to pay, it may thus diminish, or perhaps destroy, some of the funds which might enable them more easily to do so. Thirdly, by the forfeitures and other penalties which those unfortunate individuals incur who attempt unsuccessfully to evade the tax, it may frequently ruin them, and thereby put an end to the benefit which the community might have received from the employment of their capitals. An injudicious tax offers a great temptation to smuggling. But the penalties of smuggling must rise in proportion to the temptation. The law, contrary to all the ordinary principles of justice, first creates the temptation, and then punishes those who yield to it; and it commonly enhances the punishment too in proportion to the very circumstance which ought certainly to alleviate it, the temptation to commit the crime. Fourthly, by subjecting the people to the frequent visits and the odious examination of the tax-gatherers, it may expose them to much unnecessary trouble, vexation, and oppression; and though vexation is not, strictly speaking, expence, it is certainly equivalent to the expence at which every man would be willing to redeem himself from it. It is in some one or other of these four different ways that taxes are frequently so much more burdensome to the people than they are beneficial to the sovereign.

The evident justice and utility of the foregoing maxims have recommended them more or less to the attention of all nations. All nations have endeavoured, to the best of their judgment, to render their taxes as equal as they could contrive; as certain, as convenient to the contributor, both in the time and in the mode of payment, and in proportion to the revenue which they brought to the prince, as little burdensome to the people. The following short review of some of the principal taxes which have taken place in different ages and countries will show, that the endeavours of all nations have not in this respect been equally successful.

READING 21

Tax Opinion

THE MEANS AND METHODS by which tax laws are enacted present an interesting picture of the activities of "pressure groups." The fact that taxes are imposed by those people who will not pay them upon those who will have to pay them is probably one of the facts of life that we should face. The following reading explains vividly the attitudes toward taxes held by various peoples and groups, the conflicts of interests of various groups, the competition of the various objectives of groups, the influence of the public interest, and the differences in economic analysis resulting from the differing interests involved in the enacting of taxation legislation.

Roy Blough (1901-   ) is a leading American scholar of public finance. He has held various state and Federal appointments; he was a member of the Council of Economic Advisers to President Truman in 1950-52. At present he is Professor of

International Business at Columbia University. The reading is reprinted by permission from *The Federal Taxing Process,* by Roy Blough. © 1952 by Prentice-Hall, Inc., Englewood Cliffs, N. J. pp. 4-11.

THE CLASH OF TAX OPINION

Attitudes Toward Taxes

A few rare souls believe they should be paying more taxes than they do, and actually send voluntary contributions to the Treasury. Occasionally a movie star with a resourceful press agent expresses well-publicized pleasure at having to pay high taxes. Other persons, numbering perhaps in the millions, are reasonably satisfied that their tax bills are justified by the services that are performed by their government, and seek no change. But most people react to taxes in a hostile manner.

They have two major chronic objections to taxes. The first is that taxes in general are too high. This complaint is misdirected, for the level of taxes is a result of the level of governmental spending. The second objection is that the burden of taxes is badly distributed. Attitudes vary in intensity from mild complaints about unfairness and discrimination, through rising degrees of insistence that the tax system is inequitable and should be revised—or is thoroughly bad and requires complete overhauling—to the pathological extreme when blood pressure and choler alike rise at the very mention of taxation. Nearly everyone wants to see the tax system revised; but regardless of what changes are made, criticism continues. Stresses and strains are intensified as taxes take a larger and larger proportion of national income.

Of course, no one really likes to pay the cost of anything. Why are taxes resented more than other costs? The reason is that for the individual the amount of taxes paid is not necessarily related to the amount of governmental benefits received. For excellent reasons there are no price tags on most governmental activities. To be sure, taxes are the price of governmental benefits for the nation as a whole. But for the individual, a change in governmental services may not mean a change in taxes, and a change in taxes paid may not mean a change in governmental services received. From this basic fact about taxation stem the most troublesome problems of federal tax policy. Taxes are resented also because they are compulsory. With respect to most other costs the individual has at least the appearance of freedom of decision; but with respect to taxes, once the law is passed, he has no option but to pay.

Conflicts of Interests

Differences of opinion over tax policy may arise from one or more of three general sources. The first and most important of these is a conflict of private interests. Such conflict arises with respect to both the total cost of government and the distribution of that cost among taxpayers.

One result of the lack of connection between government benefits and tax burdens is that some persons are obliged to pay taxes to support governmental activities from which they derive little or no direct service and in which they see little or no public benefit. To them the cost of government seems too high and they resent the taxes they must pay for its support. Even people who benefit most from government may share this feeling, because almost everyone would like to see some of the activities of government curtailed. Moreover, many services of government are less appreciated than they deserve to be, because their benefits are invisible and intangible. On the other side of the picture, voters are often persuaded to support increased expenditure programs of dubious value in the thought that the cost will be borne by other taxpayers. For these reasons opinions differ among taxpayers over the proper volume and directions of governmental expenditures.

A further result of the separation of tax load and government benefits is a conflict of interest over tax distribution. If a particular taxpayer is able to push part of his tax load onto someone else, his own cost becomes lighter, while he continues to receive the same benefits from the government that he received before. Thus a direct conflict of economic interests arises among taxpayers, which is largely responsible for the intensity of tax controversies. If the economic characteristics of all persons were identical, the tax load distribution among them would not be altered by changes in the form or rate structure of taxes. And obviously if only one tax were available, and only at a uniform rate, there would be no opportunity to alter tax burden distribution. But in our highly specialized economy, persons differ in the amounts and sources of their incomes, the amounts and forms of their wealth, the pattern of their expenditures, and so on. Federal taxes are measured by individual incomes, corporation profits, payrolls, transfers of assets at death and by gift, sales of a large variety of commodities, and in other ways. Some of the taxes have exemptions and graduated rates. By changing the exemptions, or the level of rates, or the degree of rate progression, as well as by imposing new taxes or repealing old ones, the relative amounts of taxes imposed on different persons can be drastically modified.

In pressing for tax reductions, taxpayers rarely admit that they are trying to transfer the tax burden to others, and they may or may not be conscious of trying. However, if the taxes are to paid, lighter loads for some inevitably mean heavier loads for others. Here lies the key to the intensity of tax conflicts. The very possibility of shifting part of the burden encourages the taxpayer to think that he is paying more than his fair share of taxes and that to transfer part of the burden to others would diminish the "unfairness."

Complaints against taxes all too often reflect the feeling of the taxpayer that other taxpayers have pushed part of their taxes onto him, or that he has not succeeded in pushing enough of his tax load onto others. Even if he has been successful in transferring part of the load, his satisfaction soon wears off. The relief is never enough, and as soon as he thinks the time is ripe he will try again. If he has been unsuccessful, he will try again, perhaps next year or when the political climate is more favorable. The most important obstacle to stability in the tax system is this pressure of taxpayer groups for revision every time the political wind shifts in their direction.

Fortunately, many interests of taxpayers are harmonious, and not conflicting. More uniform administration, improved methods of collection, greater simplicity, clarity, and certainty would benefit the great majority of taxpayers. Possibilities for such improvements are a challenge to inventiveness, not to conflict. Even self-interest has its softening aspects. An individual is not merely a consumer, a worker, a real estate owner, a bond-holder, a stockholder, a debtor, a farmer, or an employer. He is usually several of these and sometimes all of them at once. In each capacity, he has a taxpayer interest in a particular direction. When his interests run in several directions, they tend to offset each other, perhaps in large part. Moreover, the prosperity of each taxpayer is in large degree dependent upon the prosperity of others. Taxpayers often fail to realize that they will not gain by pushing taxes onto others to the point where the economic position of the latter is greatly impaired, or that they may stand to gain more from their share of the common good than from a specific tax advantage. Finally, the protection of other groups and classes in society is a kind of personal insurance against the changes and risks of life. Who knows what his position may be tomorrow or in twenty years?

The intensity of tax conflicts is likely to be less when incomes are rising than when they are falling, because people are more aggressive in trying to prevent a decline in their living standards than in trying to raise them. Tax conflicts tend to subside during periods when it is not necessary to change the tax system for a considerable length of time. Emotional and economic adjustments are gradually made to tax measures, which come to seem more nearly right as their age increases. Most persons probably do not think actively about tax policy except when the matter is brought to their attention. The development of more articulate business, labor, and agricultural groups, with ambitious leaders and professional staffs, has a bearing on tax conflict. Eager to benefit their memberships, leaders and staffs have a tendency to keep tax conflicts active that otherwise would die down.

An important influence softening tax conflict stems from the fact that taxpayers are not oblivious to the public interest when they know it is opposed to their private economic interest. No one likes to be put in the position before either public opinion or his own conscience of placing his private interest ahead of the common good. There are many clear cases where the individual deliberately subordinates his own financial interests. Of course, when the direction of self-interest is clear and the pull is strong, the individual is likely to profess and come to believe that the public interest is identical with what he deems to be his own.

Competition of Public Values or Objectives

When harmony of private interests exists, or when the individual subordinates his private interest to the public interest, an important source of tax controversy is removed. However, there may be a difference of views about what will promote the public interest, and this is a second source of clashing opinions over tax policy.

Since the terms are used repeatedly throughout this book, it is desirable to indicate what is meant by the *public interest,* and its synonyms for present purposes, the *general interest,* the *gen-*

eral welfare, and the *national interest.* The author does not look on the public interest as something that can be objectively determined or measured. It is, rather, a highly individual view of what makes the "good society." It is the gleam in a man's eye of the way to promote a better world. It has profound importance for the individual, for without this concept a person could scarcely be expected to rise above narrow self-interest. It is a powerful, and sometimes the dominating, force in the determination of individual actions and decisions. The concept of the public interest likewise is of great importance for society. It supplies a unifying bond that helps to offset the divisive force of self-interest. It channels into social uses enormous amounts of time, energy, and resources.

As will appear later, there are large areas of general agreement about what is in harmony with the public interest. Because of its highly subjective character, however, the concept of the public interest is not identically the same for any two persons, and the differences may be of major importance. Since each person is prone to think that his own idea is the correct one, he seeks to persuade others of its superior validity, as applied to the decisions that must be made. Moreover, when an individual is endeavoring to secure the adoption of a proposal (whether because he believes it would promote his private interest or because he believes it would promote the public interest), he seeks to persuade other persons that his proposal would promote their conception of the public interest. Thus the individual may be trying at the same time to persuade others that his ideas of the public interest are valid and that his proposals will advance their ideas of the public interest. Similarly, he is on the receiving end of both kinds of persuasion brought to bear by many other persons. There is thus a constant interchange and competition of ideas about the public interest, with important consequences for policy.

In the light of these remarks, the reader should note that when the author speaks of something being in the public interest, or opposed to it, he implies the additional words "as I see the public interest," and that he makes no claim to having achieved scientific proof of what is in the public interest.

The public interest, whether it is viewed as a personal ideal or as an instrument of political persuasion, is likely to be expressed in terms of public values or objectives that are shared by virtually everyone. Most taxpayers agree that it is desirable to have a high level of employment, production, and income; a

stable economy free from depression and inflation; a vitally functioning private enterprise system; just and equitable distribution
of the tax burden; neutrality of tax effects on business in general,
to be abandoned only to promote a particular economic or social
objective; awareness by taxpayers of their burdens; simplicity of
taxes and freedom from taxpayer inconvenience; uniform and
nonarbitrary administration; and preservation of state and local,
as well as federal, financial strength and independence.
Agreement on these public values is fortunate, since widespread
disagreement might lead to internal dissension and even
social explosion.

The disagreement over what is in the public interest lies in
the pattern of values—that is, in the relative importance assigned
to the different objectives of taxation. Differences in the pattern
of values are not important if all objectives can be promoted
simultaneously, but often this is impossible. At some point a
choice must be made. Greater justice in tax distribution may at
times be the alternative to a larger volume of production or to
simplicity and convenience in tax compliance. When alternatives
such as these are presented, some persons prefer one choice, some
the other. These choices are made not in the abstract, but in
specific practical situations. There is always a point—for
different people, different points—where the sacrifice in the
direction of one objective is not fully compensated by the gain
toward another.

The proper choice among competing objectives is not something that can be proved or disproved. Each of us may be morally
certain that the kind of society he prefers is by far the best for
the country. But no higher authority exists that is qualified to
pass on questions of value and purpose. One view may dominate
in the final decision, or differences of opinion may be compro-
mised, but no real solution of such differences of opinion is
possible unless there is a willingness on the part of some people
to modify their views.

Differences in Economic Analysis

A possible third source of tax policy controversy is disagreement over the questions of who actually bears a tax and what its
effects are. The problem in this case is not what is desirable or
undesirable, but what will happen if a certain tax measure is
adopted. Two or more persons may agree that tax policy should
be anti-inflationary but may disagree on what kinds and rates of

tax have the most anti-inflationary effects. Again, persons may agree that taxes that are shifted to consumers are undesirable but disagree on whether corporation income taxes are shifted to consumers. Or they may agree that it would be desirable to impose social security taxes on farmers if such taxes could be effectively administered, but may disagree on the evasion that would result.

Determining the effects of a tax change presents a problem not of what ought to be done but of what would happen if the change were made. It is a scientific problem. The question arises: If it is a scientific problem, why are there widely differing beliefs about what would happen if a particular tax change were made? One reason for these differences is that tax changes involve human relations of great complexity. Of the social sciences that deal with human relations the most pertinent to taxation is economics, although effects other than the economic are also significant. Although economics is perhaps the most highly developed of the social sciences, it is far from being an exact science, and perhaps never will be; for this reason, unbiased economists may disagree in their analyses of what will happen if a tax change is made.

Another and more common reason for the wide variation in beliefs about the effects of tax changes is that most people do not understand economics, either in general or as applied specifically to taxation. Even persons who have a fluent vocabulary of economic jargon may have no real economic understanding. There is an old saying that you can teach a parrot to say supply and demand, but you cannot teach him economics.

Finally, there are no completely unbiased social scientists; even the most competent and sincere ones are inevitably influenced by their interests and values. Through known techniques they can partially offset this bias, but it may be doubted that true objectivity is ever achieved.

Relation to the Policy-Making Process

Three sources of tax controversy are, then, (1) conflict of private interests, (2) competition of alternative public purposes, and (3) differences in economic analysis and beliefs. In practice, it is difficult to separate the second and third from the first. Self-interest is so powerful a force in many persons that it dominates their patterns of public values. Economic beliefs are notoriously influenced by a person's interests and values. Conversely, the

ideas that persons hold regarding what promotes their self-interest
and the public interest depend in part on their economic beliefs.
Incorrect economic analysis of personal interests may lead a person to wrong conclusions concerning those things that he believes
to be in his interest. Likewise, the importance that a person
attributes to the promotion of particular industries or even of a
high national product is determined in part by his economic
beliefs about their contribution to the general welfare. Thus, in
practice, private interests, public values, and economic beliefs
are often tightly interwoven.

When the three sources of tax controversy are separated,
their relation to tax policy becomes clear. There are at least three
major elements in the process of making tax policy. The first is
the analytical or scientific function of forecasting the effects that
tax changes would have under the economic and other conditions
that are expected to prevail. This function lies peculiarly within
the field of specialization of the social scientist, primarily
the economist.

The second is the political function of evaluating conflicting
interests of different regional, income, wealth, and occupational
groups, and competing public values—equality, freedom of action
and movement, rate of economic progress, stability of production,
and so on. All of these factors must be weighed, and choices and
compromises must be made in determining what pattern of objectives is to be promoted. The economist can throw a great deal
of light on the problems of making these choices, but they are
not soluble by the application of scientific methods. Any decision
will frustrate some persons' interests and patterns of value. The
making of choices and compromises among the aspirations of
the individuals and groups of the community or nation is the
function of politics in its fundamental sense, because these are
choices that the people should make, either directly or through
their responsible political representatives.

Third is the fact that the political choices must be carried
into effect by specific legislative provisions. This involves a sort
of engineering problem in the solution of which economists (and
other social scientists) join with administrators and lawyers. Since
tax legislation often has unintended effects, the engineering function also requires a variety of supplementary political decisions.
Under our system of government, the political representatives
make the final decisions, whether the determination is at bottom
political or scientific.

Thus, both social scientist and politician are necessary to the process of forming tax policy. Any person who makes choices among interests and values is acting as a politician; any person who analyzes economic effects is acting as an economist. In practice, there is a good deal of overlapping, and the line of demarcation between the two is not clear.

PART III

ECONOMIC PROBLEMS

READING 22

The Leisure Class

WHILE NORTH AMERICAN CIVILIZATION cannot be charged with having a rigid "class" society, it would be far less than the truth to say we have no exhibitions of "class" differences. The caste system of India or the aristocracies of Europe have no counterpart in the United States. At the same time, however, we do possess "class consciousness": witness our feelings toward certain minority groups and our attitude that somehow or other the "wealthy" class is due certain privileges.

The following reading makes no specific case for or against privilege for the "wealthy" class but levels some criticism at the existence of such an institution. Veblen assigns the name of "leisure class" to this special group. This leisure class has what he calls an "instinctive conservatism" and an "aversion to change" which for a number of reasons tend to require a greater effort to be put forth to accomplish any given change in our institutions. This requirement for a greater effort to achieve change in our institutions than would otherwise be the case results in our institutions always being "behind" industrial and technological change. Therefore at any given moment our institutions [our ways of accomplishing things] are never quite adapted to the industrial society we live in since this industrial society is a dynamic one. He points out some additional factors: the unequal distribution of wealth, which is necessitated by a "leisure class," and some of its consequences; and the controlling influence of "pecuniary motives" over "industrial motives," the former of these two motives being those of the "leisure class" and the latter being those of the worker-management interests.

Thorstein Veblen (1857-1929) was a great American economist, professor of economics at several schools—University of Chicago, Stanford University, and others. He is most famous as the originator of the "institutional" school of economics which maintains that man is motivated by a host of different feelings which are noneconomic as well as economic in nature and that therefore economics must concern itself with the whole aspect of man. This school of thought denies the existence of any perfect theoretical framework of economics which would make the study a science. Few men have achieved the distinction of welding together a body of preceding thought into a new statement of a discipline: Adam Smith, the so-called "founder" of the classical school of economics did so in the eighteenth century; Alfred Marshall, leader of the neo-classical school of economics, did so in the nineteenth century; John Maynard Keynes, the leader and fostering influence of the "national income" school did so in the twentieth century; Thorstein Veblen also did so in acting as critic of classical and neo-classical economics in formulating his new approach to economic problems. The reading is in Chapter 8, "Industrial Exemption and Conservatism," pp. 198-211, from *The Theory of the Leisure Class* by Thorstein Veblen. Copyright 1899, 1912 by The Macmillan Company. Reprinted by permission of The Viking Press, Inc., New York.

The leisure class is in great measure sheltered from the stress of those economic exigencies which prevail in any modern, highly organised industrial community. The exigencies of the struggle for the means of life are less exacting for this class than for any other; and as a consequence of this privileged position we should expect to find it one of the least responsive of the classes of society to the demands which the situation makes for a further growth of institutions and a readjustment to an altered industrial situation. The leisure class is the conservative class. The exigencies of the general economic situation of the community do not freely or directly impinge upon the members of this class. They are not required under penalty of forfeiture to change their habits of life and their theoretical views of the external world to suit the demands of an altered industrial technique, since they are not in the full sense an organic part of the industrial community. Therefore these exigencies do not readily produce, in the members of this class, that degree of uneasiness with the existing order which alone can lead any body of men to give up views and methods of life that have become habitual to them. The office of the leisure class in social evolution is to retard the movement and to conserve what is obsolescent. This proposition is by no means novel; it has long been one of the commonplaces of popular opinion.

The prevalent conviction that the wealthy class is by nature conservative has been popularly accepted without much aid from any theoretical view as to the place and relation of that class in the cultural development. When an explanation of this class conservatism is offered, it is commonly the invidious one that the wealthy class opposes innovation because it has a vested interest, of an unworthy sort, in maintaining the present conditions. The explanation here put forward imputes no unworthy motive. The opposition of the class to changes in the cultural scheme is instinctive, and does not rest primarily on an interested calculation of material advantages; it is an instinctive revulsion at any departure from the accepted way of doing and of looking at things—a revulsion common to all men and only to be overcome by stress of circumstances. All change in habits of life and of thought is irksome. The difference in this respect between the wealthy and the common run of mankind lies not so much in the motive which prompts to conservatism as in the degree of exposure to the economic forces that urge a change. The members of the wealthy class do not yield to the demand for innovation as readily as other men because they are not constrined to do so.

This conservatism of the wealthy class is so obvious a feature that it has even come to be recognised as a mark of respectability. Since conservatism is a characteristic of the wealthier and therefore more reputable portion of the community, it has acquired a certain honorific or decorative value. It has become prescriptive to such an extent that an adherence to conservative views is comprised as a matter of course in our notions of respectability; and it is imperatively incumbent on all who would lead a blameless life in point of social repute. Conservatism, being an upperclass characteristic, is decorous; and conversely, innovation, being a lower-class phenomenon, is vulgar. The first and most unreflected element in that instinctive revulsion and reprobation with which we turn from all social innovators is this sense of the essential vulgarity of the thing. So that even in cases where one recognises the substantial merits of the case for which the innovator is spokesman—as may easily happen if the evils which he seeks to remedy are sufficiently remote in point of time or space or personal contact—still one cannot but be sensible of the fact that the innovator is a person with whom it is at least distasteful to be associated, and from whose social contact one must shrink. Innovation is bad form.

The fact that the usages, actions, and views of the well-to-do leisure class acquire the character of a prescriptive canon of conduct for the rest of society, gives added weight and reach to the conservative influence of that class. It makes it incumbent upon all reputable people to follow their lead. So that, by virtue of its high position as the avatar of good form, the wealthier class comes to exert a retarding influence upon social development far in excess of that which the simple numerical strength of the class would assign it. Its prescriptive example acts to greatly stiffen the resistance of all other classes against any innovation, and to fix men's affections upon the good institutions handed down from an earlier generation.

There is a second way in which the influence of the leisure class acts in the same direction, so far as concerns hindrance to the adoption of a conventional scheme of life more in accord with the exigencies of the time. This second method of upper-class guidance is not in strict consistency to be brought under the same category as the instinctive conservatism and aversion to new modes of thought just spoken of; but it may as well be dealt with here, since it has at least this much in common with the conservative habit of mind that it acts to retard innovation and the growth of social structure. The code of proprieties, conventionalities, and usages in vogue at any given time and among any given people has more or less of the character of an organic whole; so that any appreciable change in one point of the scheme involves something of a change or readjustment at other points also, if not a reorganisation all along the line. When a change is made which immediately touches only a minor point in the scheme, the consequent derangement of the structure of conventionalities may be inconspicuous; but even in such a case it is safe to say that some derangement of the general scheme, more or less far-reaching, will follow. On the other hand, when an attempted reform involves the suppression or thorough-going remodelling of an institution of first-rate importance in the conventional scheme, it is immediately felt that a serious derangement of the entire scheme would result; it is felt that a readjustment of the structure to the new form taken on by one of its chief elements would be a painful and tedious, if not a doubtful process.

In order to realise the difficulty which such a radical change in any one feature of the conventional scheme of life would involve, it is only necessary to suggest the suppression of the monogamic family, or of the agnatic system of consanguinity, or of private property, or of the theistic faith, in any country of the Western civilisation; or suppose the suppression of ancestor worship in China, or of the caste system in India, or of slavery in Africa, or the establishment of equality of the sexes in Mohammedan countries. It needs no argument to show that the derangement of the general structure of conventionalities in any of these cases would be very considerable. In order to effect such an innovation a very far-reaching alteration of men's habits of thought would be involved also at other points of the scheme than the one immediately in question. The aversion to any such innovation amounts to a shrinking from an essentially alien scheme of life.

The revulsion felt by good people at any proposed departure from the accepted methods of life is a familiar fact of everyday experience. It is not unusual to hear those persons who dispense salutary advice and admonition to the community express themselves forcibly upon the far-reaching pernicious effects which the community would suffer from such relatively slight changes as the disestablishment of the Anglican Church, an increased facility of divorce, adoption of female suffrage, prohibition of the manufacture and sale of intoxicating beverages, abolition or restriction of inheritance, etc. Any one of these innovations would, we are told, "shake the social structure to its base," "reduce society to chaos," "subvert the foundations of morality," "make life intolerable," "confound the order of nature," etc. These various locutions are, no doubt, of the nature of hyperbole; but, at the same time, like all overstatement, they are evidence of a lively sense of the gravity of the consequences which they are intended to describe. The effect of these and like innovations in deranging the accepted scheme of life is felt to be of much graver consequence than the simple alteration of an isolated item in a series of contrivances for the convenience of men in society. What is true in so obvious a degree of innovations of first-rate importance is true in a less degree of changes of a smaller immediate importance. The aversion to change is in large part an aversion to the bother of making the readjustment which any given change will necessitate; and this solidarity of the system of institutions of any given culture or of any given people strengthens the instinctive resistance offered to any change in men's habits of thought, even in matters which, taken by themselves, are of minor importance.

A consequence of this increased reluctance, due to the solidarity of human institutions, is that any innovation calls for a greater expenditure of nervous energy in making the necessary readjustment than would otherwise be the case. It is not only that a change in established habits of thought is distasteful. The process of readjustment of the accepted theory of life involves a

degree of mental effort—a more or less protracted and laborious
effort to find and to keep one's bearings under the altered circumstances. This process requires a certain expenditure of energy,
and so presumes, for its successful accomplishment, some surplus
of energy beyond that absorbed in the daily struggle for subsistence. Consequently it follows that progress is hindered by
underfeeding and excessive physical hardship, no less effectually
than by such a luxurious life as will shut out discontent by
cutting off the occasion for it. The abjectly poor, and all those
persons whose energies are entirely absorbed by the struggle for
daily sustenance, are conservative because they cannot afford the
effort of taking thought for the day after to-morrow; just as the
highly prosperous are conservative because they have small
occasion to be discontented with the situation as it stands to-day.

From this proposition it follows that the institution of a
leisure class acts to make the lower classes conservative by withdrawing from them as much as it may of the means of sustenance, and so reducing their consumption, and consequently their
available energy, to such a point as to make them incapable of
the effort required for the learning and adoption of new habits
of thought. The accumulation of wealth at the upper end of
the pecuniary scale implies privation at the lower end of the
scale. It is a commonplace that, wherever it occurs, a considerable
degree of privation among the body of the people is a serious
obstacle to any innovation.

This direct inhibitory effect of the unequal distribution of
wealth is seconded by an indirect effect tending to the same
result. As has already been seen, the imperative example set by
the upper class in fixing the canons of reputability fosters the
practice of conspicuous consumption. The prevalence of conspicuous consumption as one of the main elements in the
standard of decency among all classes is of course not traceable
wholly to the example of the wealthy leisure class, but the practice and the insistence on it are no doubt strengthened by the
example of the leisure class. The requirements of decency in this
matter are very considerable and very imperative; so that even
among classes whose pecuniary position is sufficiently strong to
admit a consumption of goods considerably in excess of the
subsistence minimum, the disposable surplus left over after the
more imperative physical needs are satisfied is not infrequently
diverted to the purpose of a conspicuous decency, rather than to
added physical comfort and fulness of life. Moreover, such surplus energy as is available is also likely to be expended in the

acquisition of goods for conspicuous consumption or conspicuous hoarding. The result is that the requirements of pecuniary reputability tend (1) to leave but a scanty subsistence minimum available for other than conspicuous consumption, and (2) to absorb any surplus energy which may be available after the bare physical necessities of life have been provided for. The outcome of the whole is a strengthening of the general conservative attitude of the community. The institution of a leisure class hinders cultural development immediately (1) by the inertia proper to the class itself, (2) through its prescriptive example of conspicuous waste and of conservatism, and (3) indirectly through that system of unequal distribution of wealth and sustenance on which the institution itself rests.

To this is to be added that the leisure class has also a material interest in leaving things as they are. Under the circumstances prevailing at any given time this class is in a privileged position, and any departure from the existing order may be expected to work to the detriment of the class rather than the reverse. The attitude of the class, simply as influenced by its class interest, should therefore be to let well-enough alone. This interested motive comes in to supplement the strong instinctive bias of the class, and so to render it even more consistently conservative than it otherwise would be.

All this, of course, has nothing to say in the way of eulogy or deprecation of the office of the leisure class as an exponent and vehicle of conservatism or reversion in social structure. The inhibition which it exercises may be salutary or the reverse. Whether it is the one or the other in any given case is a question of casuistry rather than of general theory. There may be truth in the view (as a question of policy) so often expressed by the spokesmen of the conservative element, that without some such substantial and consistent resistance to innovation as is offered by the conservative well-to-do classes, social innovation and experiment would hurry the community into untenable and intolerable situations; the only possible result of which would be discontent and disastrous reaction. All this, however, is beside the present argument.

But apart from all deprecation, and aside from all question as to the indispensability of some such check on headlong innovation, the leisure class, in the nature of things, consistently acts to retard that adjustment to the environment which is called social advance or development. The characteristic attitude of the class may be summed up in the maxim: "Whatever is, is right";

whereas the law of natural selection, as applied to human institutions, gives the axiom: "Whatever is, is wrong." Not that the institutions of to-day are wholly wrong for the purposes of the life
of to-day, but they are, always and in the nature of things, wrong
to some extent. They are the result of a more or less inadequate
adjustment of the methods of living to a situation which prevailed
at some point in the past development; and they are therefore
wrong by something more than the interval which separates the
present situation from that of the past. "Right" and "wrong" are
of course here used without conveying any reflection as to what
ought or ought not to be. They are applied simply from the
(morally colourless) evolutionary standpoint, and are intended
to designate compatibility or incompatibility with the effective
evolutionary process. The institution of a leisure class, by force
of class interest and instinct, and by precept and prescriptive
example, makes for the perpetuation of the existing maladjustment of institutions, and even favours a reversion to a somewhat
more archaic scheme of life; a scheme which would be still
farther out of adjustment with the exigencies of life under the
existing situation even than the accredited, obsolescent scheme
that has come down from the immediate past.

But after all has been said on the head of conservation of
the good old ways, it remains true that institutions change and
develop. There is a cumulative growth of customs and habits of
thought; a selective adaptation of conventions and methods of
life. Something is to be said of the office of the leisure class in
guiding this growth as well as in retarding it; but little can be
said here of its relation to institutional growth except as it
touches the institutions that are primarily and immediately of
an economic character. These institutions—the economic structure—may be roughly distinguished into two classes or categories,
according as they serve one or the other of two divergent purposes of economic life.

To adapt the classical terminology, they are institutions of
acquisition or of production; or to revert to terms already
employed in a different connection in earlier chapters, they are
pecuniary or industrial institutions; or in still other terms, they
are institutions serving either the invidious or the non-invidious
economic interest. The former category have to do with "business," the latter with industry, taking the latter word in the
mechanical sense. The latter class are not often recognised as
institutions, in great part because they do not immediately concern the ruling class, and are, therefore, seldom the subject of

legislation or of deliberate convention. When they do receive attention they are commonly approached from the pecuniary or business side; that being the side or phase of economic life that chiefly occupies men's deliberations in our time, especially the deliberations of the upper classes. These classes have little else than a business interest in things economic, and on them at the same time it is chiefly incumbent to deliberate upon the community's affairs.

The relation of the leisure (that is, propertied non-industrial) class to the economic process is a pecuniary relation—a relation of acquisition, not of production; of exploitation, not of serviceability. Indirectly their economic office may, of course, be of the utmost importance to the economic life process; and it is by no means here intended to depreciate the economic function of the propertied class or of the captains of industry. The purpose is simply to point out what is the nature of the relation of these classes to the industrial process and to economic institutions. Their office is of a parasitic character, and their interest is to divert what substance they may to their own use, and to retain whatever is under their hand. The conventions of the business world have grown up under the selective surveillance of this principle of predation or parasitism. They are conventions of ownership; derivatives, more or less remote, of the ancient predatory culture. But these pecuniary institutions do not entirely fit the situation of to-day, for they have grown up under a past situation differing somewhat from the present. Even for effectiveness in the pecuniary way, therefore, they are not as apt as might be. The changed industrial life requires changed methods of acquisition; and the pecuniary classes have some interest in so adapting the pecuniary institutions as to give them the best effect for acquisition of private gain that is compatible with the continuance of the industrial process out of which this gain arises. Hence there is a more or less consistent trend in the leisure-class guidance of institutional growth, answering to the pecuniary ends which shape leisure-class economic life.

The effect of the pecuniary interest and the pecuniary habit of mind upon the growth of institutions is seen in those enactments and conventions that make for security of property, enforcement of contracts, facility of pecuniary transactions, vested interests. Of such bearing are changes affecting bankruptcy and receiverships, limited liability, banking and currency, coalitions of labourers or employers, trusts and pools. The community's institutional furniture of this kind is of immediate consequence only to the propertied classes, and in proportion as they are propertied; that is to say, in proportion as they are to be ranked with the leisure class. But indirectly these conventions of business life are of the gravest consequence for the industrial process and for the life of the community. And in guiding the institutional growth in this respect, the pecuniary classes, therefore, serve a purpose of the most serious importance to the community, not only in the conservation of the accepted social scheme, but also in shaping the industrial process proper.

The immediate end of this pecuniary institutional structure and of its amelioration is the greater facility of peaceable and orderly exploitation; but its remoter effects far outrun this immediate object. Not only does the more facile conduct of business permit industry and extra-industrial life to go on with less perturbation; but the resulting elimination of disturbances and complications calling for an exercise of astute discrimination in everyday affairs acts to make the pecuniary class itself superfluous. As fast as pecuniary transactions are reduced to routine, the captain of industry can be dispensed with. This consummation, it is needless to say, lies yet in the indefinite future. The ameliorations wrought in favour of the pecuniary interest in modern institutions tend, in another field, to substitute the "soulless" joint-stock corporation for the captain, and so they make also for the dispensability of the great leisure-class function of ownership. Indirectly, therefore, the bent given to the growth of economic institutions by the leisure-class influence is of very considerable industrial consequence.

READING 23

Unearned Increment

THE CONCEPT OF THE "UNEARNED INCREMENT" is that some people, chiefly property owners, make gains through no effort of their own: increments in the value of property they possess over decades, or perhaps that have been handed down to them over generations, arise through the sheer growth of society. The situation is stated by John Stuart Mill in the following reading: "The ordinary progress of a society which increases in wealth is at all times tending to augment the incomes of landlords; to give them both a greater amount and a greater proportion of the wealth of the community, independently of any trouble or outlay incurred by themselves. They grow richer, as it were in their sleep, without working, risking, or economizing." This principle is the real foundation of the "land-tax" that existed in Europe, and of the "single-tax" proposal of Henry George, which is explained in the reading immediately following this one.

John Stuart Mill (1806-1873) was, with Adam Smith, Thomas Malthus, and David Ricardo, one of the four great "classical" economists. His father, James Mill, a famous economist himself, tutored John Stuart, so that the son received no school education. John Stuart Mill was an accomplished genius: At eight years of age he was a Greek scholar; at thirteen, an economist of reputation. He was employed by the East India Company for three decades. The latter part of his life was devoted chiefly to economic study and writing. His principal economic work was *Principles of Political Economy* (1848), a reformulation of classical economic doctrine. The reading is from John Stuart Mill's *Principles of Political Economy with Some of Their Applications to Social Philosophy,* edited by W. J. Ashley (London: Longmans, Green and Co., 1909 [text of 7th ed. 1871] 1013 pp.), Book V, "On the Influence of Government," Chapter II, "On the General Principles of Taxation," pp. 817-819. Reprinted by permission of the publisher.

Before leaving the subject of Equality of Taxation, I must remark that there are cases in which exceptions may be made to it, consistently with that equal justice which is the groundwork of the rule. Suppose that there is a kind of income which constantly tends to increase, without any exertion or sacrifice on the part of the owners: those owners constituting a class in the community, whom the natural course of things progressively enriches, consistently with complete passiveness on their own part. In such a case it would be no violation of the principles on which private property is grounded, if the state should appropriate this increase of wealth, or part of it, as it arises. This would not properly be taking anything from anybody; it would merely be applying an accession of wealth, created by circumstances, to the benefit of society, instead of allowing it to become an unearned appendage to the riches of a particular class.

Now this is actually the case with rent. The ordinary progress of a society which increases in wealth is at all times tending to augment the incomes of landlords; to give them both a greater amount and a greater proportion of the wealth of the community, independently of any trouble or outlay incurred by themselves. They grow richer, as it were in their sleep, without working, risking, or economizing. What claim have they, on the general principle of social justice, to this accession of riches? In what would they have been wronged if society had, from the beginning, reserved the right of taxing the spontaneous increase of rent, to the highest amount required by financial exigencies? I admit that it would be unjust to come upon each individual estate, and lay hold of the increase which might be found to have taken place in its rental; because there would be no means of distinguishing in individual cases between an increase owing solely to the general circumstances of society, and one which was the effect of skill and expenditure on the part of the proprietor. The only admissible mode of proceeding would be by a general measure. The first step should be a valuation of all the land in the country. The present value of all land should be exempt from the tax; but after an interval had elapsed, during which society had increased in population and capital, a rough estimate might be made of the spontaneous increase which had accrued to rent since the valuation was made. Of this the average price of produce would be some criterion: if that had risen, it would be certain that rent had increased, and (as already shown) even in a greater ratio than the rise of price. On this and other data, an approximate estimate might be made, how much value had been added to the land of the country by natural causes; and in laying on a general land-tax, which for fear of miscalculation should be considerably within the amount thus indicated, there would be an assurance of not touching any increase of income which might be the result of capital expended or industry exerted by the proprietor.

But though there could be no question as to the justice of taxing the increase of rent, if society had avowedly reserved the right, has not society waived that right by not exercising it? In England, for example, have not all who bought land for the last century or more, given value not only for the existing income, but for the prospects of increase, under an implied assurance of being only taxed in the same proportion with other incomes? This objection, in so far as valid, has a different degree of validity in different countries; depending on the degree of desuetude into which society has allowed a right to fall, which, as no one can doubt, it once fully possessed. In most countries of Europe, the right to take by taxation, as exigency might require, an indefinite portion of the rent of land, has never been allowed to slumber. In several parts of the Continent, the land-tax forms a large proportion of the public revenues, and has always been confessedly liable to be raised or lowered without reference to other taxes. In these countries no one can pretend to have become the owner of land on the faith of never being called upon to pay an increased land-tax. In England the land-tax has not varied since the early part of the last century. The last act of the legislature in relation to its amount, was to diminish it; and though the subsequent increase in the rental of the country has been immense not only from agriculture, but from the growth of towns and the increase of buildings, the ascendency of landholders in the legislature has prevented any tax from being imposed, as it so justly might, upon the very large portion of this increase which was unearned, and, as it were, accidental. For the expectations thus raised, it appears to me that an amply sufficient allowance is made, if the whole increase of income which has accrued during this long period from a mere natural law, without exertion or sacrifice, is held sacred from any peculiar taxation. From the present date, or any subsequent time at which the legislature may think fit to assert the principle, I see no objection to declaring that the future increment of rent should be liable to special taxation; in doing which all injustice to the landlords would be obviated if the present market-price of their land were secured to them; since that includes the present value of all future expectations. With reference to such a tax, perhaps a safer criterion than either a rise of rents or a rise of the price of corn, would be a general rise in the price of land. It would be easy to keep the tax within the amount which would reduce the market value of land below the original valuation: and up to that point, whatever the amount of the tax might be, no injustice would be done to the proprietors.

READING 24

The Single Tax

THE "SINGLE TAX" PROPOSAL of Henry George rests ultimately upon the idea that, since landlords receive an "unearned increment" in the value of their land not due to their own efforts, it is just to tax this unearned increment and use it to support the government. George proposed that this "unearned increment" on land, which is "rent," should be taxed away completely. The tax would be sufficient to support the government without any other source of income whatever and what could be more just, he asked, than that the government of the people should be supported by gains which result from the natural growth of population and the society which the government is serving? George did not advocate the seizure of property by the government and is not therefore to be confused with the socialist or communist. His proposal has received great attention, probably greater elsewhere in the world than in the United States. His proposal can be criticized in that it is not consistent with our contemporary institutional and social framework in America.

Henry George (1839-1897) was an American publisher and economist. He was a keen observer of the world of his time, witnessing the industrialization of the country. His intense sympathy with the industrial worker was the motivating force resulting in the fruition of his plan to abolish poverty and to support government without injury to any individuals in the society. His book *Progress and Poverty* is one of the all-time best sellers, having been translated into scores of languages and sold in millions of copies. The reading is from *Progress and Poverty* (New York: Robert Schalkenbach Foundation, 1940, Fiftieth Anniversary Edition, 571 pp.), Book VIII, "Application of the Remedy," Chapter 2, "How Equal Rights to the Land May Be Asserted and Secured," pp. 403-407. Reprinted by permission.

We have traced the want and suffering that everywhere prevail among the working classes, the recurring paroxysms of industrial depression, the scarcity of employment, the stagnation of capital, the tendency of wages to the starvation point, that exhibit themselves more and more strongly as material progress goes on, to the fact that the land on which and from which all must live is made the exclusive property of some.

We have seen that there is no possible remedy for these evils but the abolition of their cause; we have seen that private property in land has no warrant in justice, but stands condemned as the denial of natural right—a subversion of the law of nature that as social development goes on must condemn the masses of men to a slavery the hardest and most degrading.

We have weighed every objection, and seen that neither on the ground of equity or expediency is there anything to deter us from making land common property by confiscating rent.

But a question of method remains. How shall we do it?

We should satisfy the law of justice, we should meet all economic requirements, by at one stroke abolishing all private titles, declaring all land public property, and letting it out to the highest bidders in lots to suit, under such conditions as would sacredly guard the private right to improvements.

Thus we should secure, in a more complex state of society, the same equality of rights that in a ruder state were secured by equal partitions of the soil, and by giving the use of the land to whoever could procure the most from it, we should secure the greatest production.

Such a plan, instead of being a wild, impracticable vagary, has (with the exception that he suggests compensation to the present holders of land—undoubtedly a careless concession which he upon reflection would reconsider) been indorsed by no less eminent a thinker than Herbert Spencer, who ("Social Statics," Chap. IX, Sec. 8) says of it:

> "Such a doctrine is consistent with the highest state of civilization; may be carried out without involving a community of goods, and need cause no very serious revolution in existing arrangements. The change required would simply be a change of landlords. Separate ownership would merge into the joint-stock ownership of the public. Instead of being in the possession of individuals, the country would be held by the great corporate body—society. Instead of leasing his acres from an isolated proprietor, the farmer would lease them from the nation. Instead of paying his rent to the agent of Sir John or his Grace, he would pay it to an agent or deputy agent of the

community. Stewards would be public officials instead of private ones, and tenancy the only land tenure. A state of things so ordered would be in perfect harmony with the moral law. Under it all men would be equally landlords, all men would be alike free to become tenants. * * * Clearly, therefore, on such a system, the earth might be enclosed, occupied and cultivated, in entire subordination to the law of equal freedom."

But such a plan, though perfectly feasible, does not seem to me the best. Or rather I propose to accomplish the same thing in a simpler, easier, and quieter way, than that of formally confiscating all the land and formally letting it out to the highest bidders.

To do that would involve a needless shock to present customs and habits of thought—which is to be avoided.

To do that would involve a needless extension of governmental machinery—which is to be avoided.

It is an axiom of statesmanship, which the successful founders of tyranny have understood and acted upon—that great changes can best be brought about under old forms. We, who would free men, should heed the same truth. It is the natural method. When nature would make a higher type, she takes a lower one and develops it. This, also, is the law of social growth. Let us work by it. With the current we may glide fast and far. Against it, it is hard pulling and slow progress.

I do not propose either to purchase or to confiscate private property in land. The first would be unjust; the second, needless. Let the individuals who now hold it still retain, if they want to, possession of what they are pleased to call *their* land. Let them continue to call it *their* land. Let them buy and sell, and bequeath and devise it. We may safely leave them the shell, if we take the kernel. *It is not necessary to confiscate land; it is only necessary to confiscate rent.*

Nor to take rent for public uses is it necessary that the State should bother with the letting of lands, and assume the chances of the favoritism, collusion, and corruption this might involve. It is not necessary that any new machinery should be created. The machinery already exists. Instead of extending it, all we have to do is to simplify and reduce it. By leaving to land owners a percentage of rent which would probably be much less than the cost and loss involved in attempting to rent lands through State agency, and by making use of this existing machinery, we may, without jar or shock, assert the common right to land by taking rent for public uses.

We already take some rent in taxation. We have only to make some changes in our modes of taxation to take it all.

What I, therefore, propose, as the simple yet sovereign remedy, which will raise wages, increase the earnings of capital, extirpate pauperism, abolish poverty, give remunerative employment to whoever wishes it, afford free scope to human powers, lessen crime, elevate morals, and taste, and intelligence, purify government and carry civilization to yet nobler heights, is— *to appropriate rent by taxation.*

In this way the State may become the universal landlord without calling herself so, and without assuming a single new function. In form, the ownership of land would remain just as now. No owner of land need be dispossessed, and no restriction need be placed upon the amount of land any one could hold. For, rent being taken by the State in taxes, land, no matter in whose name it stood, or in what parcels it was held, would be really common property, and every member of the community would participate in the advantages of its ownership.

Now, insomuch as the taxation of rent, or land values must necessarily be increased just as we abolish other taxes, we may put the proposition into practical form by proposing—

To abolish all taxation save that upon land values.

As we have seen, the value of land is at the beginning of society nothing, but as society develops by the increase of population and the advance of the arts, it becomes greater and greater. In every civilized country, even the newest, the value of the land taken as a whole is sufficient to bear the entire expenses of government. In the better developed countries it is much more than sufficient. Hence it will not be enough merely to place all taxes upon the value of land. It will be necessary, where rent exceeds the present governmental revenues, commensurately to increase the amount demanded in taxation, and to continue this increase as society progresses and rent advances. But this is so natural and easy a matter, that it may be considered as involved, or at least understood, in the proposition to put all taxes on the value of land. That is the first step, upon which the practical struggle must be made. When the hare is once caught and killed, cooking him will follow as a matter of course. When the common right to land is so far appreciated that all taxes are abolished save those which fall upon rent, there is no danger of much more than is necessary to induce them to collect the public revenues being left to individual land holders.

Experience has taught me (for I have been for some years

endeavoring to popularize this proposition) that wherever the idea of concentrating all taxation upon land values finds lodgment sufficient to induce consideration, it invariably makes way, but there are few of the classes most to be benefited by it, who at first, or even for a long time afterward, see its full significance and power. It is difficult for workingmen to get over the idea that there is a real antagonism between capital and labor. It is difficult for small farmers and homestead owners to get over the idea that to put all taxes on the value of land would be unduly to tax them. It is difficult for both classes to get over the idea that to exempt capital from taxation would be to make the rich richer, and the poor poorer. These ideas spring from confused thought. But behind ignorance and prejudice there is a powerful interest, which has hitherto dominated literature, education, and opinion. A great wrong always dies hard, and the great wrong which in every civilized country condemns the masses of men to poverty and want, will not die without a bitter struggle.

READING 25

The Laboristic Economy

THE RISE IN IMPORTANCE OF LABOR in the United States is well expressed in the accompanying reading. When we reflect that before the Civil War approximately 90 per cent of the working population consisted of self-employed farmers and only about 10 per cent of the working population worked for "hire" in factories, while at the present time the situation is reversed, with 90 per cent of our gainfully employed workers being wage-paid employees and only 10 per cent, self-employed, we may recognize the force of Slichter's statements. In a society in which nearly all of the people are dependent upon a single source of money income for subsistence and are dependent upon institutions such as corporations for their very lives, we may expect vastly different problems from those of a society in which the people are independent and self-sustaining.

Slichter points out in this reading that "although an increasing proportion of the workers in the United States are employees, the economy is not developing a proletariat in the sense of an oppressed and propertyless class." Karl Marx' observation that the development of such a class is inevitable in an industrial society and will eventually be engaged in a revolution is an observation not applying to the United States. Slichter points out three important factors: Technological gains have come to the employees and only secondarily to capitalists; second, technological progress demands increased knowledge, skill, and responsibility from the workers and therefore their contribution increases; third, a larger and larger proportion of American workers own property by way of homes, common stock evidencing ownership in corporations, and other kinds of property—and thus there would seem to be little danger of a "propertyless class" arising.

Sumner H. Slichter (1892-1959) was an outstanding American economist, late Lamont University Professor at Harvard University. Slichter was a prolific writer of stimulating articles and books, writing as well for the layman as for the professional economist. The reading is in Chapter I, "The American Economy," pp. 7-13, reprinted from *The American Economy Its Problems and Prospects* by Sumner H. Slichter, by permission of Alfred A. Knopf, Inc. Copyright 1948 by Alfred A. Knopf, Inc.

The American economy is a laboristic economy, or at least is rapidly becoming one. By this I mean that employees are the most influential group in the community and that the economy is run in their interest more than in the interest of any other economic group. A community composed almost entirely of employees must be expected to have its own distinctive culture—its own scales of value, its own industrial institutions, its own public policies, and its own jurisprudence. The fact that employees are supplanting businessmen as the most influential group in the community means that basic and far-reaching changes are impending in the civilization of the United States.

Employees have great and growing influence, because over three out of four persons who work for a living in the United States are employees, and less than one out of four are self-employed. In addition, about fourteen million of the thirty-five million nonsupervisory and nontechnical employees in private industry are organized into trade unions. The trade-union movement in the United States is the largest and most powerful the world has ever seen.

Communities composed in the main of free employees are new in the history of the world. In ancient times or in the Middle Ages the bulk of the work was done by slaves or serfs. In early modern times there grew up economies composed predominantly of self-employed. The United States was such an economy until about 1840. Only within the last hundred years have there appeared economies composed almost entirely of free employees. Even today such economies are limited to a few countries. In Russia, eastern Europe, and many other parts of the world, the workers are vassals of the state rather than citizens—they lack civil rights and are not expected to think for themselves. They are not bound to the land as were the serfs of the Middle Ages, or even to a particular industry or occupation, but they work under conditions determined by a government in which they have no voice. In a rough way they may be compared to the "king's peasants" of Ptolemaic Egypt.

Evidence of the influence of employees is found in factory legislation prescribing standards to protect the safety and health of workers, in workmen's compensation legislation (applying to industrial accidents a different principle of liability from that generally prevailing), in restrictions on the terms of labor contracts in the interest of employees (maximum hours of work and minimum wages), in arrangements for compensating persons who lose their incomes because of unemployment or retirement, and, most of all, in laws encouraging employees to combine for the purpose of raising the price of their labor. Only employees and farmers who form co-operatives are permitted to combine in order to control selling prices. Any other kinds of sellers who do this commit a crime and are liable to fine or imprisonment.

Many people will deny that the United States is becoming a laboristic community. They are used to thinking of this country as the stronghold of capitalism. It is true that many other groups have great influence—especially the self-employed, who include the farmers, many small retailers, and most professional workers. It is true also that on many matters of public policy, employees have not yet had time to develop a common and distinctive point of view. Although their influence has been growing for several generations, not until the political revolution resulting from the great depression of the thirties did employees become the strongest single influence in the community. Hence it is not surprising that on many matters employees continue to accept the ideas that prevailed when employers and the self-employed dominated the country.

Some tendency to underestimate the influence of employees results from the habit of assuming that trade unions invariably are the authentic spokesmen for all workers. As a general rule this assumption is correct, but it is not always so. Especially with respect to the problem of protecting the community against strikes or lockouts in certain key industries, or with respect to safeguarding the right of employees to join unions or remain members of unions, there have been divergencies between the official position of trade unions and the preference of employees. Hence the failure of unions to control public policy on certain matters does not mean that the employee point of view is not influential.

Although an increasing proportion of the workers in the United States are employees, the economy is not developing a proletariat in the sense of an oppressed and propertyless class. The view of Marx and other nineteenth-century socialists that industrial evolution would produce greater and greater poverty among workers, and greater and greater concentration of wealth and income in the hands of employers, has turned out to be contrary to fact. Indeed, if Marx were able to visit the United States today, he would undoubtedly be amazed at the trouble enterprises have in providing adequate parking space for the "proletariat." Several observations on the failure of industrial evolution to take the course predicted by Marx are worth making.

In the first place, the gains of technological progress have not gone in the main to capitalists, as Marx thought they would, or even to consumers, but to employees. Between 1840 and 1940 the hourly earnings of nonagricultural workers increased about eightfold. The level of wholesale prices in 1940 was about 10 per cent higher than in 1840. The index of prices has an upward bias. Hence, the real price level in 1940 was moderately lower than in 1840. It is plain, however, that the principal effect of technological progress has been to raise the wages paid to employees rather than to reduce the prices paid by consumers. In spite of the steady increase in the use of capital in industry (three times as much per worker in 1940 as in 1880), the share of the national income going to property in the form of profits, interest, and rent has been declining. In 1880 profits, interest, and rent were about one fourth of the national income; in 1940, about one fifth; and in 1947, about one sixth.*

In the second place, technological and business changes are making increased demands upon the knowledge, skill, and responsibility of the workers. This fact is in conflict with a widely held popular superstition that technological progress has been robbing workers of skill and responsibility and reducing men to automatons or robots. As a matter of fact, common labor is the one principal class of employees that is not increasing. In 1940 the number of common laborers was scarcely any greater than in 1910. Between 1910 and 1940, common laborers dropped from 36 per cent of the labor force to 25.9 per cent. On the other hand, managerial, technical, professional, and clerical jobs are increasing faster than the [total of] gainfully employed. Between 1910 and 1940 professional persons increased from 4.4 per cent of the labor force to 6.5 per cent, and clerical workers from 10.2 per cent to 17.2 per cent. Skilled workers remained a constant proportion of the labor force, and the semiskilled increased faster than the labor force. Between 1870 and 1940, technical engineers, physicists, and chemists increased from 10 to 14 times as fast as the gainfully employed; bookkeepers, cashiers, and accountants, 8 times; artists, sculptors, and art teachers, 5 times; editors and reporters, 3.75 times; musicians and teachers of music, 3 times; dentists, 3.7 times; clergymen and social and welfare workers, 1.6 times.

In the third place, a large and growing proportion of the people in the United States own property. For example, about thirty-six million people have life insurance policies, thirty million have savings accounts, twenty million own their own homes, and about nine million are stockholders in business corporations. No one knows what proportion of these property owners are employees, but since over three fifths of income payments consist of wages and salaries, a high proportion of property must have been acquired out of wages or salaries, and hence must belong to employees.

---

* [Some economists would disagree with this observation, pointing out that over the last several years to 1953, wages have constituted approximately 70 per cent of the national income, profits 20 per cent, and interest and rent about 5 per cent each. This means that profits, interest, and rent together would be about one third of national income at present. Much depends on how the figures are made up.]

READING 26

Social Security

IT HAS ONLY BEEN SINCE the 1930s that the economics of social security has received much attention in the United States. The establishment of a social security system in the United States was in considerable part the result of the great depression of the 1930s. Among other industrialized nations, which had already established such systems, the depression offered further impetus for change and improvement.

The great, and probably increasing, importance of a system of social or "economic" security for people in a highly industrialized economy makes the study of the subject necessary. The following article defines the terms used in social security, compares our attitudes and our system with that of Great Britain, and delineates some of the dangers we must guard against in the development of our social security system.

Edwin E. Witte (1887-1960) was Professor and Chairman of the Department of Economics at the University of Wisconsin. Dr. Witte was a member of many important government commissions dealing with problems of labor and economic security. His chief contributions in economics were in these two fields. Among the books he authored is *The Government and Labor Disputes* (1932); he published numerous articles in economic and social journals. The reading is from "What to Expect of Social Security" (*American Economic Review*, Volume 34, March, 1944, Papers and Proceedings), pp. 212-220. Reprinted by permission.

Social security is today an immensely popular term. Everybody in public life is for social security and nearly all discussion of the subject concerns improvement and extension. It remains, however, a term of uncertain meaning, which conveys very different ideas to different people. To many Americans it means nothing more than old age pensions; to others, it is a socialized form of insurance protection against hazards whose normal consequences are poverty and dependency; to still others, a governmentally guaranteed minimum income in all contingencies of life; to others, again, an economic system which operates to afford plenty for everybody. These are only some of the concepts of social security widely prevalent in this country. This lack of precise meaning to some extent accounts for the popularity of social security. Social security is in fact more of an ideal than an institution or group of institutions. Yet if we are to intelligently discuss the place which social security should have in postwar America or how social security can be improved, we need to give an institutional content to the term.

What is called "social security" differs from country to country. Social security is a part of the total institutional pattern of the nations in which it exists and is most soundly conceived in conformity with such total patterns. It is something different in totalitarian countries like Germany and Japan from what it is in democratic countries like the United States and the nations of the British Commonwealth, and something else still in Soviet Russia. The existing governmental structure, the economic system which prevails, the stage of economic development attained, the history and traditions of the nation will all have their influence upon the social security institutions of the country and even upon what is considered to be social security. So will such social and economic factors as the state of family life, the economic position of women, the nobility of labor, the extent of union organization, and, above all, the nation's economic productivity. This holds true also for psychological factors such as the public attitude toward government, the degree to which security is valued as contrasted with the opportunities presented by risks, and the prevailing concepts of progress.

In this paper I shall use the term social security as it was defined in the report on *Approaches to Social Security,* published in 1942 by the International Labour Office. This includes within the term both social assistance and social insurance and also social security systems. Social security systems represent an integration of social insurance and social assistance. Social assistance stems from the old institution of poor relief and "expresses the obligation of the community toward its needy members." It includes noncontributory pensions to the aged and to invalids (the American old age assistance and aid to the blind), mothers' pensions (officially called "aid to dependent children" in this country), unemployment assistance, medical assistance, rehabilitation of the disabled, and general public assistance (or relief). It is financed from general tax sources and is free to the beneficiaries. Social insurance, in contrast, "is situated between social assistance and commercial insurance." It is established by law and serves social purposes, but utilizes insurance principles. Today it includes workmen's compensation (which is known as industrial accident insurance in continental Europe), sickness (or health) insurance, old age, invalidity and survivors' insurance, and unemployment insurance (or compensation).

As thus defined, social security is broader than social insurance, although the latter term is sometimes applied to the entire scope of social security. It is narrower than the English social services and the Scandinavian social policy, which include, besides the social security institutions which have been enumerated, such other governmental services as public education, public health and medical services, public housing developments, minimum wage legislation, and still other publicly financed and directed programs for the benefit of people in low income groups. It is also narrower than economic security, which includes in addition to social security many other institutions whose objective is economic stability and an assurance of a satisfying minimum income for everybody.

As I conceive social security, it is oriented toward family and individual welfare rather than the functioning of the economic system. It is social in the sense that it is provided for by law and is compulsory in at least some of its aspects. It is usually administered by public officials and is always strictly controlled by the government. Its approach, however, is from the point of view of the welfare of the family and the individual rather than that of the nation as an entity or of society in the abstract. Its concern is with the immediate hazards confronting the family and the individual, or, rather, with their economic consequences, not with ultimate causes, as they appear to an economist.

Such a concept of social security is consistent with the totality of our existing institutions and calls for no revolutionary changes. Far from being inconsistent with our free enterprise system and our democratic government, it is a bulwark to these basic institutions, vitally necessary, under present conditions, for their preservation and continued successful functioning. Such a concept of social security is also in accord with the past history of the development of social security in the United States and, more specifically, with the statements regarding social security which were made by the President, the Congressional committees in charge of the legislation, and the Committee on Economic Security, which drafted the measure, at the time of the enactment of the Social Security Act.

In its present connotation, the term social security does not seem to go back further than 1933, when the late Dr. Abraham Epstein expanded his Association for Old Age Security into the Association for Social Security. It did not come into general use until the House Ways and Means Committee, in order to emphasize that the measure it recommended was not the Administration's Economic Security bill, changed its title to the Social Security Act. As a group of institutions, however, social security goes back to the earliest Colonial days. Social security in this country, as in England, had its beginnings in the Elizabethan Poor Law, which was brought here by the earliest settlers. Its subsequent development, however, was quite different.

England was far ahead of us in becoming industrialized. Economic conditions there were such as to bring home to public consciousness much earlier than here, that unemployment and poverty are not always the fault of the unemployed and the poor. England's racial unity and its unitary government facilitated earlier action and a more orderly development of social security than in the United States. This has often been noted, but it is less familiar that the differing history, concepts, and conditions also account for most of the differences in the present content of social security legislation in the two countries. We have never had a Poor Law Commission or a Beveridge Report in the United States, but on the other hand, England to this day does not have a workmen's compensation act developed on social insurance principles. The major social security legislation of England had its origin in dissatisfaction with the poor law but had the same objective of relieving distress. Social insurance developed as a substitute for poor relief, and retains many aspects to this day which plainly point to this origin. Completely absent in the development of social security in England has been the police power approach, which regards social insurance as a form of labor legislation, justified as a regulation of employment relations in the interests of the public welfare.

In contrast, social security in the United States has stemmed from labor legislation quite as much as from poor relief. Workmen's compensation developed as labor legislation, without even a realization at the time that it is social insurance. Unemployment compensation and health insurance were both first advocated as logical complements of workmen's compensation. For twenty years before the American Association for Social Security was organized, the American Association for Labor Legislation championed social insurance measures and cited the police power as their legal justification. It was not until the great depression had set in that the point of view that unemployment insurance should serve primarily as a relief institution had any popularity in this country. No unemployment insurance law was enacted until that time, but the legislation we got was something between the British unemployment insurance and American workmen's compensation. Similarly, health insurance proposals in this country have departed far from European models.

The great depression furnished the impetus for the swift advances in social security which we made in the thirties. But it was less dissatisfaction with the disgraceful administration of poor relief than sheer need for financial assistance to the local and state governments which brought the national government into the social security picture. By this time, the national government again does not concern itself with relief in any manner, and our relief laws and their administration have reverted pretty much to their predepression status. In many other respects also the depression now seems to have produced far less change in relation to social security than appeared to be the case a few years ago. Social security is approved of by everybody and there is very general agreement that it should be expanded and "liberalized." But there is very little interest in social security and a great lack of understanding as to what it is all about. Particularly, there is almost no appreciation on the part of the prospective beneficiaries that social security involves costs as well as benefits, while to businessmen social security is nothing more than a matter of taxes. The word insurance in the terms social insurance, old age and survivors' insurance, and unemployment insurance is one of the reasons for the popularity of these institutions in this country where everybody has an insurance policy. However, confusion and doubt are now being created by the view that social insurance is not "insurance" at all. Americans generally still regard private enterprise, initiative, and thrift as the best assurance of security. Unlike the British and despite all the gibes about the WPA, they believe that work is the best cure for unemployment and that government should provide employment when private industry cannot do so. They distrust their government, and, particularly, the "Washington bureaucrats." Yet it is a certainty that if serious trouble develops they, almost as one man, will turn to their government to help them and it will be the national government to which they will turn.

These are the broad outlines of the present American concepts and attitudes in relation to social security. This is the foundation now available on which we can and must build. This is not a very secure foundation—and not so much because our social security legislation is defective in content or poor in administration as a consequence of confused thinking about social security. This confusion is largely attributable to the absence of any precise concept of what the term means and of all popular understanding as to the values and limitations of the institutions which are described by this term.

* * *

This requires giving social security a narrower meaning than "freedom from want." Freedom from want cannot be guaranteed through social security measures. The possibilities of providing even a minimum satisfying income to all people and in all contingencies of life depend first of all upon total production. At this time when we are producing so prodigiously for war purposes, it may appear that production does not constitute any limitation to the attainment of freedom from want. But it remains undetermined whether we can produce for purposes of peace as much as we are now producing for purposes of war. Personally, it is my view that full employment, as we now know it, is too costly to be a practical objective for peacetime, although I believe that we can and must organize our economy so that we will have a much greater production than we had prior to the war, and an ever increasing production. This is an essential for the attainment of freedom from want. Most economic goods and services are so ephemeral that production must be continuous; moreover, what is a minimum satisfying income and even freedom from want is variable and in a progressive society will ever rise. Social security cannot assure the high and rising level of production which is essential to the attainment of such an objective. It may even be organized in such a way as to hold back production. It is my belief that it can be made a factor promoting production. It cannot become a substitute for industry, initiative, and invention, or for the proper organization and controls of our economic system.

This does not mean that social security does not matter, nor that social security proposals should be judged primarily on the basis of their probable effects upon the functioning of the economic system. It is my view that the economic planners who look upon social security as one means for reshaping the economic system towards ends they deem desirable are a greater menace to the improvement of our social security institutions than are the Townsendites—and, as I shall develop later, I do not underrate the still present dangers from that source. It is a perversion of the concept of social security to look upon it as being primarily designed for the control of the business cycle, to insure full employment, or to redistribute income and purchasing power. Its effects in these respects should be considered and discussed, but should not overshadow its major objective—the protection of the individual and the family against the immediate economic hazards confronting them. Economists, interested as they are in the functioning of the economic system as a whole, are prone to look upon this objective as secondary; and perhaps it is, but it surely is not unimportant. Without maintenance of individuals and families in all contingencies of life, the hope of fundamental remedies for economic ills is but illusory.

It is very certain also that the economic system will never function so as to render unnecessary any social security measures. There is want and suffering even at this time of abnormally great production. Full employment and maximum production do not keep people from growing old and do not guarantee that many old people will not be in want and from reasons which are not their fault. There is some unemployment even in wartime and everyone knows that, under the most favorable circumstances, there will be a much greater volume of unemployment in the transition period. Sickness and invalidity have little relation to employment conditions and industrial accidents actually increase with increases in employment. Regardless of the functioning of the economic system, many breadwinners will die young and when this happens their surviving small children usually will be in poverty; and we cannot afford to overlook the fact that the great majority of all our children, upon whom depends the future of our country, are in the homes of the poor.

* * *

Equally unsound is the view that social security is principally a tax problem. This appears to be the predominant view in Congress and may well produce even greater havoc in the future than it has already created. In part, at least, this view has developed because in the United States we had to label the employer and employee contributions to the social insurance funds as "pay roll taxes"—which has not been done in any other country. The attitude toward taxes in this country has always been antagonistic, with an almost complete failure to appreciate that in its entirety it is a two-way, not a one-way, process. Social security is not, at least mainly, an additional cost to society, but an orderly redistribution of costs which the American people have to bear in any event. Even from the point of view of the government's expenditures alone, the costs of a well-conceived social security system will be offset to a very considerable extent by reduced relief and salvage costs.

It is equally, if not more, dangerous that the largest groups of prospective beneficiaries think of social security in terms of benefits only and that this has also been the attitude of most of its champions in the ranks of the academicians and social workers. This is again a typically American point of view. Our economic growth has been so great that we have not had to think very much about where the money is coming from. America is the land of plenty and there is widespread belief that we can do anything. This is so infectious that it is not unnatural that even people who thoroughly understand what costs are involved, generally are willing to take the chance of a possible financial breakdown in the future to get improvements now about whose costs they do not dare to talk. England, while it has something like "pay as you go" financing for old age insurance, provides for increasing government, employer, and employee contributions as disbursements increase with the lapse of the years. In contrast, when the Social Security Amendments were passed in 1939 no estimates of costs whatsoever were given Congress and language was written into the act which can be interpreted as implying that we should not look ahead more than five years. This has been followed, in three successive years, by the "freezing of social security taxes" (which is really a reduction in taxes already levied), although no one claims that the accruing costs do not far exceed the amounts collected from present taxes. Many of the people who understand what is happening still see nothing very alarming in these developments because they are confident that a future Congress will come to the rescue with large government contributions from general tax sources. Time may justify their hopes, but it is a fact that Congress to date has refused to make any such commitments, even in committee reports, and in 1939 struck from the original law the actual government contributions provided therein, in the form of a high interest rate on the reserve funds.

*   *   *

I view with similar concern the playing down of the "insurance" in social insurance, which has developed since the passage of the Social Security Act. It is understandable that insurance company executives and actuaries should look upon private insurance as the only kind of insurance meriting the esteem and confidence which Americans attach to that term. It is even clearer why certain politicians see political advantages in creating distrust of the government's handling of the social security funds. It would be extremely unfortunate, however, if they persuaded the workers that their funds were not safe with the government. Equally dangerous is any weakening of the contributory principle. The several forms of social insurance differ from private insurance, but not more so than do the several kinds of private insurance from each other. It is anomalous, to say the least, that the very people who justified reducing the pay roll tax rates by denouncing reserves as having no place in social insurance also were responsible for the provisions in the Social Security Act Amendments of 1939 limiting benefits to currently insured and fully insured persons. These are clearly concepts taken from private insurance, and they are likely to work out in such a way that many millions of war workers will get nothing at all for their social security deductions from pay rolls.

I also do not accept the view that social security is nothing more than a relief institution. I include social assistance within the concept of social security. But I object to making of social insurance but another form of relief. In the English environment and with the background of the history of social security in England, the concept that social insurance is a substitute for poor relief may be adequate. In the United States, where social security developed from labor legislation as well as from relief, there is still value in retaining something of the police power approach, although it alone also is not adequate. It is a defeatist attitude to say that, because the hazards against whose consequences social insurance is designed to provide protection cannot be wholly prevented, no attempt should be made to utilize it for preventive purposes. Such a position is illogical and is bound to provoke much unnecessary opposition to proposals for the improvement of social security. It is also to be noted that the world over, social security is increasingly coming to mean not merely cash payments but also social services with a preventive objective.

READING 27

Conservation

NATURAL RESOURCES may be classified into those resources which are *renewable* and those which are *exhaustible*. The latter are chiefly mineral resources like coal, petroleum, and metals, which once removed and used by man cannot be "replaced," or "renewed," since they have been formed over great spans of geologic time. The former, *renewable,* resources are the soil, the forests, and wild life. All of these mentioned resources are important, of course; but of them possibly the resource of greatest importance is that furnishing the sustenance of man: soil. It is from the soil that man secures his food, and food is one of the three basic necessities of life: food, clothing, shelter.

With an increasing population—and therefore an increasing need for food—the condition of soil in any given country becomes of greater and greater importance. While there may be evidence of "increasing returns" in agriculture, meaning that on a given acreage of land more and more food may be produced because of an improving technology employing superior machines and methods, nevertheless some point of diminishing returns must eventually be reached. It is certainly patent that a given acreage of land cannot support an infinite population. In the United States, soil conservation has received more and more study and emphasis since 1908 when Theodore Roosevelt founded the National Conservation Commission. In the 1930s the Soil Conservation Service was created in the United States Department of Agriculture. This Service has contributed considerably to the increase in productivity in agriculture. The following reading explains the history and present condition of the soil resources of the United States.

Hugh Hammond Bennett (1881-   ) is probably America's foremost living soil conservation leader. He has been employed chiefly by the United States Government in many capacities in conservation: He has participated in and directed explorations and soil surveys in Alaska and Central America, as well as in the United States. He was soil scientist in the United States Department of Agriculture 1903-1909. From 1935 until retirement in 1952, he was Chief of the Soil Conservation Service. He has published many articles and books dealing with the problem of conservation. The reading is reprinted by permission from *Soil Conservation*, by Hugh Hammond Bennett. Copyright 1939. McGraw-Hill Book Company, Inc., pp. 1-15.

The Virgin Land

The earliest settlers arriving on the North American continent found a land richly endowed by nature and virtually unexploited by man. Except in an inconsequential way, the aborigines had done little to cultivate this land or change its virgin character. Before the gaze of the transplanted Europeans lay a vast wilderness teeming with apparently inexhaustible stores of game, fish, fur, timber, grass, and soil. Across the broad expanses of the country, from semitropical to boreal climates, from humid to arid regions, spread an infinite variety of soil types, topographic and climatic conditions, and vegetative types and patterns. Almost everywhere the fertile land supported some kind of vegetation—trees or grasses, shrubs or chaparral. In all but a few scattered barren areas, dense stands of perennial plants sheltered the ground from the elements and enriched it with their decaying material. Soil nourished vegetation, and vegetation protected soil, in a compact of mutual advantage and growth.

Rains fell on the land, and snows melted with the changing seasons; but water tended to move slowly over the ground surface, checked and kept clear by the tangled canopy of vegetative growth. The deep, humus-charged, granular topsoil, perforated even into the subsoil by decaying plant roots and burrowing earthworms, insects, and animals, soaked up the raindrops, which filtered down to nourish the growth of vegetation or to replenish underground reservoirs and springs. Rivers ran clear, except in flood, when abrasive rushing waters tore soil from the banks, sometimes muddying even the Missouri and the Mississippi. Generally speaking, however, the natural circulation of waters was a uniform and orderly process. Flood heights and silt-laden streams were the spasmodic exceptions in a land of prevailing harmony and balance. Topsoil was removed from the land surface no faster than it was built up from beneath by the slow, complex processes of nature.

The March of Occupation

Into this virgin land the eager colonists entered with energy and enthusiasm. They began a transformation of the earth's surface that is probably without parallel in the history of the world. The occupation of the continent was accomplished not through steady infiltration of population into undeveloped regions but rather through a remarkably rapid advance over a wide front by farmers, stockmen, prospectors, miners, trappers, loggers, explorers, and adventurers. Along the line of advance, there was little thought of conservation or of depleting resources. With a country of immense potential wealth beckoning for development, it is small wonder that the emphasis lay, unconsciously, on speedy exploitation.

For a time, the advance was checked by an extensive belt of forest land bordering the Atlantic and eastern Gulf. Cutting, girdling, and burning acres of timber required hard work and patience. For more than a hundred years, settlement was largely confined to a relatively narrow strip lying along the Eastern seaboard. Eventually, however, with the pressure of new population from Europe, the westward trek began. Moving slowly at first, the pioneers set to work on the virgin forests with axe and fire. Little by little, the land was cleared for farmsteads; vast quantities of timber were burned at the "logrollings" of the settlers; trails and roadways were opened into the heart of the continent.

By about 1830, most of the better land east of the Mississippi was occupied. Then, across the grasslands lying west of the river, the migration moved at a much swifter pace. Over vast areas the prairie sod of the tall-grass country was broken with amazing speed. Before long the short-grass country of the Great Plains was also invaded, first by buffalo hunters, then by ranchmen, and finally by farmers. By 1890, most of the better lands lying within the borders of the United States had been settled. After little more than 200 years from the beginning of the westward movement, the last frontier was dissolved in the Pacific Ocean.

History records the daring of the early pioneers, who blazed the path for a new nation, and the heroic suffering of the settlers who followed. In many respects it is a thrilling story of adventure, hardihood, and courage. The march across the continent was accomplished in the face of great odds and sometimes at tragic costs in human misery. It was followed by a rapid and energetic development in agriculture, industry, commerce, transportation, and communications, which finally produced one of the greatest nations on the face of the earth.

Depletion of Natural Resources

Both the march of land occupation and the ensuing national development were accompanied, however, by a prodigious wastage of the resources with which nature originally stocked the land. The white inhabitants of this country, in their "conquest of the wilderness" and their "subjugation of the West," piled up a record of heedless destruction that nearly staggers the imagination. Slopes once clothed with mighty forests now lie bare and stark. Formerly rich lands are riddled with gullies. Level plains country that once supported lush stands of native "short" grasses is overgrown with weeds or covered with shifting sands left in the wake of dust storms.

What caused this tragic transformation? What happened to the bountiful land that inspired early explorers to enthusiastic comment and rhapsodic description? The answer lies largely in a false philosophy of plenty, a myth of inexhaustibility, which prevailed generally for many years and persists, in some quarters, even at the present time.

Yet in the time of our forefathers this was a normal, perhaps an inevitable, reaction to environmental conditions. Nearly everywhere the early settlers faced rich farm and grazing lands which stretched away as far as the eye could see. There was every reason to conclude that the agricultural domain was limitless and inexhaustible. Free land extended to the far horizons. Occupation was encouraged by the Federal Government, by the territories and states, by railroads and land companies. Go West, and take your choice of free land or cheap land, was the advice to young and old. It was a dramatic era—an era of empire building. For a hundred years the settlers came by ox cart, covered wagon, and railway. For a hundred years this hurried settlement of the West absorbed the rapidly increasing population of the nation. It was only natural that those who took over the West, like those who occupied the East, should look upon the grasses of the virgin prairies, plains, and tablelands and upon the trees of the valleys as nothing more than obstacles in the way of human progress.

The fact remains, however, that much of the land was abused, mined, and ravaged. In the turmoil of national growth, abundant resources were reduced to a state of impoverishment or near-extinction. Buffaloes were slaughtered by the thousands, merely for their hides. Trappers took their harvest of pelts without restriction or restraint. Protective forests were cut from sloping hillsides and entire watersheds; immense areas of grassland were broken or bared by the onrushing settlers with their plows and their livestock. Minerals were extracted, and their wealth dissipated in a surge of exploitation.

The story of the passenger pigeon is characteristic. The last of these birds died in a Cincinnati zoo in September, 1914. Ornithologists say that once this species was one of the most abundant game birds ever known in any country. Their flights frequently darkened the skies; the branches of trees are said to have been broken off by the very weight of their numbers settling to roost. Yet within a few generations, the legions of this species have been effaced from the earth. Should man dwell upon this planet for millions of years, he would never behold another passenger pigeon.

In like manner, other valuable resources have been exhausted and continue to be exhausted. What the final result will be in terms of the national economy no one can predict with accuracy. One fact, however, is eminently clear. The potential wealth and living standard of this nation, or of any nation, depend ultimately on its store of natural resources. If, through carelessness and neglect, these resources are wasted beyond a certain point, the whole structure of national achievement must be impaired.

Soil Erosion

Out of the long list of nature's gifts to man, none is perhaps so utterly essential to human life as soil. And topsoil is the most vital part of soil (made up of topsoil plus the layers beneath). Lying at an average depth of about 7 or 8 inches over the face of the land, this upper layer of the soil is the principal feeding zone of the plants, which provide food for human or livestock consumption, fiber for clothing, and timber for shelter. Soil constitutes the physical basis of our agricultural enterprise; it is a *sine qua non* in the production of practically all food (except fish), of all fiber (without exception), and of all wood (without exception). Under many conditions, however, it is the most unstable of all major natural resources.

Water or wind, in moving across the ground surface, exerts an abrasive force which picks up soil particles and carries them away in suspension. In a natural, undisturbed environment, the dense cover of vegetation retards this surface transposition of soil to a pace so slow, generally, that new soil is formed from the parent materials beneath as rapidly as the finished product (topsoil) is carried away from above. Under such conditions, the removal of topsoil is known as *normal erosion,* sometimes referred to as *geological erosion* or the *geologic norm of erosion.* It is a normal process, proceeding with the tediousness of centuries. It abrades at one place and builds (aggrades) at another. In slowly sculpturing the highlands of the world, it contributes material for the development of alluvial plains, valley fills, and aeolian deposits.

Where the land surface is bared of protective vegetation—as it must be under cultivation—the soil is exposed directly to the abrasive action of the elements. Transposition processes of an extremely rapid order are set in motion. Stripped of the protective cover that normally anchors soil to the landscape, this indispensable material frequently is moved a thousand times faster than under natural conditions. This accelerated phenomenon of soil removal is known as *soil erosion.* Unless steps are taken to check its progress, it becomes the most potent single factor in the deterioration of productive land.

Wastage of Soil in the United States

National habits of waste in this country have nowhere been exhibited more flagrantly than in the use of agricultural land. From erosion surveys, soil surveys, and other measurements of soil losses, it is estimated that erosion in the United States already has ruined, or seriously impoverished, approximately 282 million acres. From an additional 775 million acres, erosion has stripped away varying proportions of the fertile topsoil. Considering only cropland, it is estimated that erosion has ruined about 50 million acres for further practical cultivation. Another area of cropland approximating 50 million acres is bordering on the same condition. Nearly 100 million acres more, still largely in cultivation, has been severely damaged by the loss of from one-half to all the topsoil. On at least another 100 million acres of cropland, erosion is getting actively under way.

Examining the details, it must be admitted that there was in this country a large aggregate area of inferior land to begin with, much of which was so obviously poor that it has never, to this day, been touched by the plow. Vast areas in the West were too rough, too steep, too stony, or too arid for any use other than limited grazing or forestry. In the East there were large tracts too steep, too stony, too wet, or too sandy for plowing.

Nevertheless, many fundamental principles of sound land use were grossly violated—tens of thousands of acres of excessively steep land were plowed. Within 10 years, 20 years, 50 years, more or less, the soil has been washed away, and a condition of permanent, or near-permanent, ruin is the result. Even where the land itself was not too steep for a limited and conservative agriculture, farmers waded in with plow and axe, stripped nature's protective cover from the ground, and indiscriminately, without regard for the future, laid bare the rich soil to the erosive forces of wind and water. This was not done maliciously but simply without thought of the consequences.

Soil an Irreplaceable Resource

Lack of foresight and restraint, starting in the early Colonial period and continuing through the present day, has created in this country a land problem of tremendous implications. What makes the situation so grave is the irreplaceable nature of soil. Once this valuable asset leaves a field, it is as irretrievably lost as if consumed by fire, as far as that particular field is concerned. It cannot be hauled back economically even though temporarily stranded only a short distance down the slope. A thousand tons would be required to cover one acre to a depth of 7 inches.

Soil is reproduced from its parent material so slowly that we may as well accept as a fact that, once the surface layer is washed off, land so affected is, from the practical standpoint, generally in a condition of permanent impoverishment. As nearly as can be ascertained, it takes nature, under the most favorable conditions, including a good cover of trees, grass, or other protective vegetation, anywhere from 300 to 1,000 years or more to build a single inch of topsoil. When 7 inches of topsoil is allowed to wash away, therefore, at least 2,000 to 7,000 years of nature's work goes to waste. The time involved may be much longer; the building of the second inch may require many more years than the building of the first inch at the surface, and so on downward. Studies of old eroded areas abandoned to trees or other types of vegetation indicate that the building of soil by the natural process generally proceeds from the surface downward.

Widespread Damage of Erosion

Probably the most reliable picture of the extent of erosion in this country can be obtained from the results of a nation-wide reconnaissance survey, made by the Soil Erosion Service of the United States Department of the Interior during the summer of 1934. The figures gathered at that time, together with more detailed studies in numerous problem areas, make it possible to estimate with reasonable accuracy the amount of land affected in varying degrees. The survey revealed that erosion is much more widespread in the United States than had previously been imagined. Some evidence of its damaging effects was found over more than a billion acres of crop and grazing land.

In addition to the 50 million acres of cropland now virtually useless for further production, because it has been stripped of topsoil or riddled with gullies, another 150 million acres of arable land has declined far enough to make farming difficult or unprofitable. Over an additional area of nearly 680 million acres of all kinds of land, traces of water erosion are now discernible; and on much of this land the damage is constantly increasing in severity. Finally, a large area, located in the Great Plains from Texas to North Dakota and in other parts of the West, is characteristically subject to wind erosion, wherever exposed through the activities of man. The survey indicates that this form of erosion is active in some degree over more than 200 million acres of farm and grazing land.

Annual Losses of Soil

Available measurements indicate that at least 3,000,000,000 tons of solid material is washed out of the fields and pastures of America every year. It is estimated that about 730,000,000 tons of solid matter is discharged annually into the Gulf of Mexico by the Mississippi River alone. These materials come largely from the farms of the Mississippi Basin; as alluvial deposits, they form land richer than the flood plains of the Nile. But the sediment entering the oceans represents merely a fraction of the soil washed out of fields and pastures. The greater part is piled up or temporarily lodged along lower slopes, often damaging the soil beneath; or it is deposited over rich, alluvial stream bottoms or in channelways, harbors, reservoirs, irrigation ditches, and drainage canals.

Losses of Plant Food

The vast quantity of our soil wasted every year contains 92,172,300 tons of the five principal elements of plant food (phosphorus, potassium, nitrogen, calcium, and magnesium), as computed from the average of analyses of 389 samples of surface soils collected throughout the country (1.55 per cent potash, 0.15 per cent phosphoric acid, 0.10 per cent nitrogen, 1.56 per cent lime, 0.84 per cent magnesia). Of this total, 43,361,000 tons consists of phosphorus, potassium, and nitrogen, the principal ingredients of commercial fertilizer. According to estimates, approximately 668,000 tons of phosphorus, potassium, and nitrogen was used in the United States during the fiscal year ending June 30, 1934. The same authority estimates the value of commercial fertilizers sold in the United States during the calendar year 1934 at $158,500,000.

In other words, erosion removes from the country's fields and pastures every year available and potential plant food amounting to about sixty times the available plant food returned to the soil in various forms of commercial fertilizers, assuming 1934 to be a fairly representative year with respect to fertilizer usage. Furthermore, erosion removes not only the plant food itself but actually the entire body of the soil—plant nutrients, humus, beneficial microscopic organisms, and all other constituents. Plant food can be restored to soil worn lean by cropping or leaching; but when the soil itself is washed into the streams and oceans, nature can rebuild its counterpart only after centuries of activity.

Subsoil Farming

Where farmers operate on land stripped of its vitally important surface layer of topsoil, they frequently have but the slimmest opportunity to make a satisfactory living, whether prices are up or down. They have, in short, been reduced to the status of subsoil farmers; and subsoil farming too often is the equivalent of bankrupt farming on bankrupt land. According to measurements on a variety of types of important agricultural lands, the productivity of these eroded slopes, as compared with the original soil, has been reduced by 35 to 97 per cent.

In the last analysis, soil is the raw material of agriculture—the primary source of its output. Without it a farmer has no more chance of producing a satisfactory crop than an automobile manufacturer has of turning out motor cars without steel or rubber. Nevertheless, many of these subsistence or submarginal farmers, operating on erosion-impoverished land, continue to produce something and, in the aggregate, enough to compete, in a price-depressing way, with those farmers who are tilling good land.

Indirect Damage of Erosion

Aside from the destruction and impoverishment of farm land, erosion has indirect consequences which threaten the permanence of investments amounting to billions of dollars in navigation, power, municipal water supply, and irrigation developments. Products of surface wash and gully excavation are carried away by storm waters and often deposited in stream channels or reservoirs. Yawning gullies concentrate rainfall and discharge it at maximum speed to gorge the channelways of tributaries and trunk streams with destructive floods. As erosion strips away the absorptive top layers of soil, rainwater finds more difficulty in penetrating the frequently less permeable layers lying beneath. In many sections of the country, the effects of drought on plant life have been aggravated by progressive soil removal.

Cost of Erosion

Conservative estimates indicate that the annual monetary cost of erosion in the United States amounts to at least $400,000,000 in terms of lost productivity alone. This loss already totals probably not less than $10,000,000,000; and unless erosion is effectively curbed, the probable future costs will be equally gigantic. The annual $400,000,000 direct loss would, within fifty years, accumulate to not less than $20,000,000,000; and since unrestrained erosion progresses at an increasing rate (the subsoil usually being more erodible than the topsoil), the cost may extend to $30,000,000,000 or beyond. To this would have to be added huge losses due to (1) clogging of great reservoirs and shoaling of stream channels with the sedimentary products of erosion; (2) the abandonment of irrigated areas dependent on reservoirs; (3) the virtual abandonment of large agricultural sections; (4) the economic devastation of large western areas dependent on grazing; and (5) the disintegration of rural communities and transfer of large farm populations to relief rolls or to new means of livelihood. Furthermore, soil wasted by erosion is irreplaceable; accordingly, from the long-time view, from the

standpoint of a nation that would be permanent, the real value
of land is indeterminate.

History of Erosion

Accelerated erosion of the soil is not merely a recent threat
to human security; it is as old as agriculture. In all probability,
it began when the first rain struck the first furrow turned by a
crude implement in the hands of prehistoric man. It has been
going on ever since, wherever man's efforts to gain a livelihood
from the soil have led him to remove the natural cover of protective vegetation.

History is largely a record of man's efforts to wrest the land
from nature, because man relies for sustenance on the products
of the soil. Yet too frequently man's conquest of the land has
been disastrous; over extensive areas, his culture of the earth has
resulted in extreme impoverishment or complete destruction of
the very soil resources upon which he is dependent. When this
has occurred on a wide scale, the consequence has been the disappearance of civilization from the affected region. Recent
archeological evidence indicates that erosion doubtless played a
large part in undermining and obliterating many ancient civilizations in Africa, in the Near East, and in Central Asia.

Susceptibility of the United States

In 1934, the United States had, according to available statistics, approximately 414 million acres of cropland, including
idle fields and plowable pastures. Of this total area, about 100
million acres was in corn, 28 million in cotton, and 20 million
in potatoes, tobacco, sorghums, and other clean-tilled crops that
leave the soil exposed to wind and rain during the growing season. In Europe, excluding Russia, there is approximately the
same number of acres of cropland as in the United States, but
only 65 million acres is devoted to row crops, as compared with
150 million acres in this country. In other words, the United
States, with about the same area of cultivated land as western
Europe, exposes two and a half times as many acres to the more
serious forms of erosion. Moreover, the rains over much of Europe
do not come in such sudden, dashing downpours as over most of
that part of the United States where clean tillage is practiced.
This combination of dashing rains and vast acreages in row
crops in the United States is largely responsible for the present
terrific erosion damage.

Disappearance of the Frontier

In short, little has been left undone to accentuate the gravity of the erosion problem over a large portion of continental United States. The plain truth is that Americans, as a people, have never learned to love the land and to regard it as an enduring resource. They have seen it only as a field for exploitation and a source of immediate financial return. In the days of expanding frontier it was customary, when land was washed, cropped, or grazed to a condition of impoverishment, to pull up stakes and move on to fresher fields and greener pastures. Today such easy migration is no longer possible. The country has expanded to the full limits of its boundaries, and erosion is causing a progressive shrinkage of the tillable area. The early frontier psychology of land treatment must be abandoned once and for all. In its place a new frontier has appeared. A restricted area of land—an indispensable area, subject to still further restriction by the inroads of uncontrolled erosion—has taken the place of a former abundance of land. Now, man must move rapidly over this diminishing area in order to clear away not trees or prairie grasses but old methods of wasteful land use and substitute therefor new methods of conservation that will provide security for the soil and for those living by the soil.

Necessity for Erosion Control

As matters now stand, control of erosion is the first and most essential step in the direction of correct land utilization on about 75 per cent of the present and potential cultivated area of the nation. Looking to the future, it appears, on the basis of past experience, that within the next hundred years at least 100,000,000 acres of the remaining valuable agricultural land will become severely impoverished through erosion unless adequate protection is provided. This progressive impoverishment, if permitted to continue unchecked, eventually will reduce the fertile area of farm land from the present total of about 450,000,000 to not more than about 150,000,000 acres. Such an area might easily prove insufficient for the maintenance of a satisfactory national standard of living. And beyond a hundred years, which is not a long time in the life of a nation (or should not be), rain and wind will still be moving soil from vulnerable areas.

In other words, accelerated soil erosion presents the nation, not merely the individual farmer, with a physical land problem of enormous importance to the continuing welfare of agriculture in particular and the entire social structure in general. Moreover, beyond this whole land problem exists the intimate physical relationship of eroding land to mounting flood heights and to damaging silt deposits. No permanent solution of these latter two problems appears possible without better control of runoff all the way from the crests of ridges down across the watersheds, where floods originate and silt loads are picked up, on to the very channelways of streams and rivers. Control of runoff means control of erosion; the one necessarily involves the other.

Techniques of Erosion Control and Water Conservation

Over a period of many generations, farmers in America and in foreign lands have developed, largely by a process of trial and error, a number of devices and practices for the control of erosion and the retardation of runoff. In recent years, agricultural technicians have studied these measures, tested their effectiveness under varying conditions, and made some valuable improvements. Today there is a practical solution, or a partial solution at least, for virtually every erosion problem with which the farmer or stockman may be confronted.

Responsibility for Soil Defense

Conservation of the soil, in a national sense, requires the adoption of sound land-use principles and practices by agriculture as a whole. The attainment of this objective involves the widespread use of physical measures of land defense and the adjustment of certain economic and social forces tending to encourage exploitation of the soil.

The responsibility for such a national program falls upon both the nation and the individual. National responsibility involves the protection of society's interest in a natural resource of vital importance to the whole people. Government functions properly in discharging this responsibility. Equally strong, however, is the interest of the individual in the land that he owns. National action may be led and aided by government, but the soil must be conserved ultimately by those who till the land and live by its products. Without a widespread recognition of this latter responsibility, any governmental program of soil conservation must be doomed to eventual futility and failure.

READING 28

Too Many Farmers

MANY ECONOMISTS MIGHT AGREE that the basic problems of agriculture in the United States are essentially twofold: a relatively high degree of competition and low productivity. Actually, if properly measured, the supposedly low productivity of farming in the country may be a mistaken notion; there seems considerable evidence that agriculture in the United States is an industry of "increasing returns" rather than "diminishing returns." At any rate, farms in America, with a very slowly growing total acreage and a rapidly increasing application of capital to these acres, are producing vast quantities of food products—quantities undreamed of even a few short decades ago. This increasing output of food year by year is accomplished with a continuing decrease in the total number of farmers producing it. It is maintained by many economists, and by Theodore Schultz in the following article, that one reason for our unbalanced agriculture in America is that farmers, while they are year by year leaving the farm for the city, are not leaving the farm rapidly enough. The case for this situation is carefully and clearly stated.

Theodore W. Schultz (1902-   ) is Professor of Economics at the University of Chicago. He is one of the leading contemporary agricultural economists. The reading is reprinted by permission from *Agriculture in an Unstable Economy,* by Theodore W. Schultz. Copyright 1945. McGraw-Hill Book Company, Inc., pp. 85-88.

The low earnings of people engaged in farming are a surface manifestation of a more fundamental dislocation. Apart from war years and the effects of cyclical fluctuations, the rates of growth of the supply and demand for farm products have been so unequal as to cause most parts of agriculture to be chronically depressed. As the output outdistances the demand, agriculture finds itself with an excess supply of resources consisting primarily of labor. Low earnings for farm people result from this excess.

The burden of equilibrating the excess supply of resources in agriculture falls mainly upon the labor force. First, labor is quantitatively the major part—upward of seven-tenths—of the resources employed in farming in the United States. Second, the improvements in farm technology have been largely laborsaving in their effects. Advances in farm technology have made capital resources, such as power-driven farm machinery and equipment, highly productive. Thus, in spite of the excess supply of labor in agriculture, these new types of capital have been increased. Third, labor is more readily transferable than other resources. The rate of disinvestment in land is usually very slow. Rents under these conditions may drop and the capitalized value of land may decline relatively; yet most of the land stays in production because the new technology has increased its productivity. Many of the advances in farm technology have been of such a kind that they not only have held land in use but have actually drawn additional land, low in productivity, into cultivation.

Consequently, we should expect a redistribution of the labor force with relatively fewer workers engaged in agriculture. The statistics on this point are conclusive. The proportion of the labor force engaged in agriculture has been dropping, not only in the United States and the older industrial countries in Europe, but also in the more largely agricultural countries and in parts of the Orient. The universality of this decline is striking. It has been going on for decades. It suggests that there are powerful and persistent forces at work with no signs that these forces have run their course. On the contrary, there are reasons for believing that a decade or two hence the proportion of the labor force that will be needed to produce farm products will be considerably below present figures.

*   *   *

Since it is desirable from the point of view of the economy as a whole to encourage rather than to discourage advances in labor-saving technology for agriculture, and since farm people for many years to come are likely to have a very considerable natural increase in their numbers, and inasmuch as the growth of demand is likely to be less for farm products than it is for goods and services of other producers—*the primary adjustment that is necessary to approach an equilibrium involves the migration of many people out of agriculture into other fields of endeavor. We have here a transfer problem, a redistribution of the working population, to relieve agriculture of the excess supply of labor engaged in, and dependent upon, farming for its income.*

That the farm problem is exceedingly complex is evident from the many types of difficulties that arose during the interwar years. The question is therefore often put: Where does one start in formulating a national policy with regard to agriculture? Between the two wars, the main focus fell upon low farm prices attributed to loss of markets and to excessive output. Crop control was initiated to hold production of basic crops in check. Efforts to ameliorate the farm problem also involved better use of land, storage, soil conservation, subsidies, foreign trade, new uses for farm products, better nutrition, credit, marketing arrangements, and farm management. When properly viewed, each of these contributes to understanding farm problems. With so many approaches at hand, however, it is all the more essential to discover the more fundamental elements in the farm problem to make sure that attacks on these many fronts are consistent and necessary.

We have set forth in the preceding chapter, in considerable detail, the forces at work aggravating the maldistribution of the nation's labor forces—that is, continually diminishing the number of workers needed on the farms. The crucial question in policy formulation is: Should these forces be checked or counterbalanced? It is not desirable, in the main, to check these forces associated with a developing economy, since they are essentially positive in their contribution. If they are not to be checked, how can they be counterbalanced? It is necessary to improve the capacity of the economy to equalize earnings by helping people move out of farming. *A national agricultural policy, therefore, should have as its primary goal the attainment of a better equilibrium in the distribution of the labor force.*

*   *   *

The overlarge supply of labor in agriculture increased considerably during the interwar years, especially after 1930. This escaped the notice of the general public chiefly because it is not so visible as is industrial unemployment. Excess labor in agriculture expresses itself primarily in much underproductive employment; this is harder to detect and measure than industrial unemployment. Some headway has been made—through the Census—in counting and classifying the unemployed, and some headway has been made in social legislation to aid workers unable to find work. But no technique has as yet been developed for counting the excess labor in agriculture, nor has legislation been framed to aid such workers. It is not an easy thing to do.

One would have supposed that while programs were being developed to help subsistence and low-income farmers, it should have been evident that agriculture was burdened with excess labor. But even those who contributed to these schemes of assistance—though aware of differential birth rates between the agricultural and industrial sectors of our society, the migratory pattern that had prevailed for several decades, and the differences in economic opportunities among regions and occupations—did not have anything like a full realization of the man power forced into uneconomic uses in farming. It has taken the mobilization for war to show us how great an excess of man power was attempting to derive a living from farming.

The excess labor in agriculture is concealed in part by what would be comparable to a spread-work policy in industry. Labor is not left unemployed, but farm workers generally, both self-employed and hired, are at a greater disadvantage, with consequent lowered earnings. The nature of farm work is such that the surplus labor does not show up in a shorter day, or in fewer work days per year. The overlarge supply of labor does, however, lower both the physical and value productivity per worker. In the main, it reduces the value both of hired and of family labor, decreasing the earnings of both. Family workers, including farm operators, constitute about three-fourths of all workers in agriculture, and there is much effective substitution between nonhired and hired labor.

Why does agriculture absorb this excess labor force and in so doing reduce its per capital earnings? Why doesn't the labor in agriculture become unemployed, as it does in industry? As we have seen, farm production and employment continue at a steady, even gait, regardless of boom or depression. This certainly is not because farmers have less self-interest in the returns they receive for their effort than do other entrepreneurs. The explanation may be found first in the competitive structure of agriculture, and second in its high proportion of fixed costs.

The competitive structure of agriculture forces resources to stay employed, which is not the case in much of industry. Farms being small and numerous, a farmer acting alone cannot affect the price either of the products he sells or the factors he buys. He gains nothing through curtailing production by letting part of his farm lie idle. A like situation prevails in any industry in which the firms are small and numerous, the labor is self-employed, and that which is hired is unorganized. Production is maintained simply because prices, wages, and profits do not become obstacles to production.

Production costs on most farms are in large part fixed costs that go on regardless of the amount the farm produces. Fixed labor costs are of course the most important expense. Farmers, with few exceptions, cannot dismiss their labor during a depression; to do so would usually mean dismissing themselves and members of their families. (When farm prices fall, theoretically they could leave agriculture and find industrial jobs, but as we have seen, unemployment in industry forces them to stay on the farm.) Nor is labor the farmer's only fixed cost: mortgage payments, taxes, and installments on farm equipment must be met, no matter whether the farmer receives low or high prices for his product.

Thus he has no alternative but to keep his farm in full production. When the demand for farm products contracts, it is not within the power of the farmer to make output the variable and treat his selling price and "wage" as constants. With farm-product supply remaining roughly constant, a contraction in the demand causes farm prices to fall unless the government intervenes.

There can be no doubt that society as a whole gains from the steady production effort of agriculture, though agriculture becomes the recipient of earnings both low and highly unstable. Society also gains from the fact that agriculture continues to absorb labor when industry is stagnant, thereby keeping more people in employment, each doing something of some value. It reduces the numbers on relief; it also makes food cheap. But it seriously lowers the per capital earnings of farm people.

It is apparent, therefore, that the test for ascertaining the amount of excess labor in agriculture lies in per capita earnings. What we want to know is how the earnings of workers in farming compare with earnings in other industries, for work which farm people are prepared to do. Stated thus, the test depends on the value productivity of workers, assuming that the worker receives the amount he contributes to total production. In this way the weighing of labor requirements in agriculture is linked to the larger task of attaining a general equilibrium in the distribution of resources between agriculture and other industries. For the twenty-year span, 1920-1939, earnings per worker in agriculture were declining relative to earnings in industry. This decline is, in itself, sufficient proof that the excess of labor in agriculture was increasing.

READING 29

Population

THE MALTHUSIAN THEORY of population is studied sometime by every student of economics. It is one of the most important single statements in the field of economics. Malthus, observing the pressure of population upon the means of subsistence in the Scandinavian and other Western European countries, was able to formulate a concise theory explaining the facts. His theory states that population tends to increase faster than the means of subsistence but is held in check by certain powerful restraints such as war, pestilence, disease, and moral restraint. This theory has been criticized voluminously and has also been upheld by many. The condition of most of the peoples in the world—in India, for example, or in China, where vast numbers of people perish in years when the harvest is lean and where population multiplies in periods when a series of good years brings good harvests—illustrates that there is a basic validity to the theory.

The vast quantities of food stuffs raised on American farms, indicating a suspected condition of "increasing return" in American agriculture, would seemingly invalidate Malthus' theory; but we must keep in mind that Malthus was speaking of the "long run"—a period of time involving decades or centuries in time; he was speaking of the growth and decline of nations— and our observation of America may be over too short a span of time to observe the possible working out of the Malthusian theory.

Thomas Robert Malthus (1766-1834) was a famous English economist, one of the four great classicists, along with Adam Smith, David Ricardo, and John Stuart Mill. He was interested in social and economic problems and reforms. His great contribution to economics was his theory of population. The reading is in *An Essay on the Principle of Population*, Book I, "Of the

In an inquiry concerning the improvement of society, the mode of conducting the subject which naturally presents itself, is

1. An investigation of the causes that have hitherto impeded the progress of mankind towards happiness; and,

2. An examination into the probability of the total or partial removal of these causes in future.

To enter fully into this question, and to enumerate all the causes that have hitherto influenced human improvement, would be much beyond the power of an individual. The principal object of the present essay is to examine the effects of one great cause intimately united with the very nature of man, which, though it has been constantly and powerfully operating since the commencement of society, has been little noticed by the writers who have treated this subject. The facts which establish the existence of this cause have, indeed, been repeatedly stated and acknowledged; but its natural and necessary effects have been almost totally overlooked; though probably among these effects may be reckoned a very considerable portion of that vice and misery, and of that unequal distribution of the bounties of nature, which it has been the unceasing object of the enlightened philanthropist in all ages to correct.

The cause to which I allude, is the constant tendency in all animated life to increase beyond the nourishment prepared for it.

It is observed by Dr. Franklin, that there is no bound to the prolific nature of plants or animals, but what is made by their crowding and interfering with each other's means of subsistence. Were the face of the earth, he says, vacant of other plants, it might be gradually sowed and overspread with one kind only; as, for instance, with fennel: and were it empty of other inhabitants, it might in a few ages be replenished from one nation only; as, for instance, with Englishmen.[1]

---

[1] Franklin's Miscell. p. 9.

This is incontrovertibly true. Throughout the animal and vegetable kingdoms Nature has scattered the seeds of life abroad with the most profuse and liberal hand; but has been comparatively sparing in the room and the nourishment necessary to rear them. The germs of existence contained in this spot of earth, with ample food, and ample room to expand in, would fill millions of worlds in the course of a few thousand years. Necessity, that imperious, all-pervading law of nature, restrains them within the prescribed bounds. The race of plants and the race of animals shrink under this great restrictive law; and man cannot by any efforts of reason escape from it.

In plants and animals, the view of the subject is simple. They are all impelled by a powerful instinct to the increase of their species; and this instinct is interrupted by no doubts about providing for their offspring. Wherever, therefore, there is liberty, the power of increase is exerted; and the superabundant effects are repressed afterwards by want of room and nourishment, which is common to plants and animals; and among animals, by their becoming the prey of each other.

The effects of this check on man are more complicated. Impelled to the increase of his species by an equally powerful instinct, reason interrupts his career, and asks him whether he may not bring beings into the world, for whom he cannot provide the means of support. If he attend to this natural suggestion, the restriction too frequently produces vice. If he hear it not, the human race will be constantly endeavouring to increase beyond the means of subsistence. But as by that law of our nature which makes food necessary to the life of man, population can never actually increase beyond the lowest nourishment capable of supporting it; a strong check on population, from the difficulty of acquiring food, must be constantly in operation. This difficulty must fall somewhere; and must necessarily be severely felt in some or other of the various forms of misery, or the fear of misery, by a large portion of mankind.

That population has this constant tendency to increase beyond the means of subsistence, and that it is kept to its necessary level by these causes, will sufficiently appear from a review of the different states of society in which man has existed. But before we proceed to this review, the subject will perhaps be seen in a clearer light, if we endeavour to ascertain what would be the natural increase of population if left to exert itself with perfect freedom; and what might be expected to be the rate of increase in the productions of the earth, under the most favourable circumstances of human industry. A comparison of these two rates of increase will enable us to judge of the force of that tendency in population to increase beyond the means of subsistence, which has been stated to exist.

It will be allowed, that no country has hitherto been known, where the manners were so pure and simple, and the means of subsistence so abundant, that no check whatever has existed to early marriages from the difficulty of providing for a family; and no waste of the human species has been occasioned afterwards by vicious customs, by towns, by unhealthy occupations, or too severe labour. Consequently in no state that we have yet known, has the power of population been left to exert itself with perfect freedom.

Whether the law of marriage be instituted or not, the dictate of nature and virtue seems to be an early attachment to one woman; and where there were no impediments of any kind in the way of a union to which such an attachment would lead, and no causes of depopulation afterwards, the increase of the human species would be evidently much greater than any increase which has been hitherto known.

In the northern states of America, where the means of subsistence have been more ample, the manners of the people more pure, and the checks to early marriages fewer, than in any of the modern states of Europe, the population was found to double itself, for some successive periods every twenty-five years. Yet, even during these periods, in some of the towns, the deaths exceeded the births; and they consequently required a continued supply from the country to support their population.

In the back setlements, where the sole employment is agriculture, and vicious customs and unwholesome occupations are little known, the population was found to double itself in fifteen years. Even this extraordinary rate of increase is probably short of the utmost power of population. Very severe labour is requisite to clear a fresh country; such situations are not in general considered as particularly healthy; and the inhabitants probably were occasionally subject to the incursions of the Indians, which might destroy some lives, or at any rate diminish the fruits of industry.

According to a table of Euler, calculated on a mortality of 1 in 36, if the births be to the deaths in the proportion of 3 to 1, the period of doubling will be only 12⅘ years. And these proportions are not only possible suppositions, but have actually occurred for short periods in more countries than one.

Sir William Petty supposes a doubling possible in so short a time as ten years.[2]

But to be perfectly sure that we are far within the truth, we will take the slowest of these rates of increase, a rate in which all concurring testimonies agree, and which has been repeatedly ascertained to be from procreation only.

It may safely be pronounced therefore, that population, when unchecked, goes on doubling itself every twenty-five years, or increases in a geometrical ratio.

The rate according to which the productions of the earth may be supposed to increase, it will not be so easy to determine. Of this, however, we may be perfectly certain, that the ratio of their increase must be totally of a different nature from the ratio of the increase of population. A thousand millions are just as easily doubled every twenty-five years by the power of population as a thousand. But the food to support the increase from the greater number will by no means be obtained with the same facility. Man is necessarily confined in room. When acre has been added to acre till all the fertile land is occupied, the yearly increase of food must depend upon the melioration of the land already in possession. This is a stream, which, from the nature of all soils, instead of increasing, must be gradually diminishing. But population, could it be supplied with food, would go on with unexhausted vigour; and the increase of one period would furnish the power of a greater increase the next, and this, without any limit.

From the accounts we have of China and Japan, it may be fairly doubted, whether the best directed efforts of human industry could double the produce of these countries even once in any number of years. There are many parts of the globe, indeed, hitherto uncultivated and almost unoccupied; but the right of exterminating, or driving into a corner where they must starve, even the inhabitants of these thinly-peopled regions, will be questioned in a moral view. The process of improving their minds and directing their industry, would necessarily be slow; and during this time, as population would regularly keep pace with the increasing produce, it would rarely happen that a great degree of knowledge and industry would have to operate at once upon rich unappropriated soil. Even where this might take place, as it does sometimes in new colonies, a geometrical ratio increases with such extraordinary rapidity, that the advantage could not

---

2 Polit. Arith. p. 14.

last long. If America continue increasing, which she certainly will do, though not with the same rapidity as formerly, the Indians will be driven further and further back into the country, till the whole race is ultimately exterminated.

These observations are, in a degree, applicable to all the parts of the earth where the soil is imperfectly cultivated. To exterminate the inhabitants of the greatest part of Asia and Africa, is a thought that could not be admitted for a moment. To civilize and direct the industry of the various tribes of Tartars, and Negroes, would certainly be a work of considerable time, and of variable and uncertain success.

Europe is by no means so fully peopled as it might be. In Europe there is the fairest chance that human industry may receive its best direction. The science of agriculture has been much studied in England and Scotland; and there is still a great portion of uncultivated land in these countries. Let us consider at what rate the produce of this island might be supposed to increase under circumstances the most favourable to improvement.

If it be allowed that by the best possible policy, and great encouragements to agriculture, the average produce of the island could be doubled in the first twenty-five years, it will be allowing probably, a greater increase than could with reason be expected.

In the next twenty-five years, it is impossible to suppose that the produce could be quadrupled. It would be contrary to all our knowledge of the properties of land. The improvement of the barren parts would be a work of time and labour; and it must be evident to those who have the slightest acquaintance with agricultural subjects, that in proportion as cultivation extended, the additions that could yearly be made to the former average produce, must be gradually and regularly diminishing. That we may be the better able to compare the increase of population and food, let us make a supposition, which, without pretending to accuracy, is clearly more favourable to the power of production in the earth, than any experience we have had of its qualities will warrant.

Let us suppose that the yearly additions which might be made to the former average produce, instead of decreasing, which they certainly would do, were to remain the same; and that the produce of this island might be increased every twenty-five years, by a quantity equal to what it at present produces: the most enthusiastic speculator cannot suppose a greater increase than this. In a few centuries it would make every acre of land in the island like a garden.

If this supposition be applied to the whole earth, and if it be allowed that the subsistence for man which the earth affords might be increased every twenty-five years by a quantity equal to what it at present produces, this will be supposing a rate of increase much greater than we can imagine that any possible exertions of mankind could make it.

It may be fairly pronounced therefore, that, considering the present average state of the earth, the means of subsistence, under circumstances the most favourable to human industry, could not possibly be made to increase faster than in an arithmetical ratio.

The necessary effects of these two different rates of increase, when brought together, will be very striking. Let us call the population of this island eleven millions; and suppose the present produce equal to the easy support of such a number. In the first twenty-five years the population would be twenty-two millions, and the food being also doubled, the means of subsistence would be equal to this increase. In the next twenty-five years, the population would be forty-four millions, and the means of subsistence only equal to the support of thirty-three millions. In the next period the population would be eighty-eight millions, and the means of subsistence just equal to the support of half that number. And, at the conclusion of the first century, the population would be a hundred and seventy-six millions, and the means of subsistence only equal to the support of fifty-five millions, leaving a population of a hundred and twenty-one millions totally unprovided for.

Taking the whole earth, instead of this island, emigration would of course be excluded; and, supposing the present population equal to a thousand millions, the human species would increase as the numbers, 1, 2, 4, 8, 16, 32, 64, 128, 256, and subsistence as 1, 2, 3, 4, 5, 6, 7, 8, 9. In two centuries the population would be to the means of subsistence as 256 to 9; in three centuries as 4096 to 13, and in two thousand years the difference would be almost incalculable.

In this supposition no limits whatever are placed to the produce of the earth. It may increase for ever, and be greater than any assignable quantity; yet still the power of population being in every period so much superior, the increase of the human species can only be kept down to the level of the means of subsistence by the constant operation of the strong law of necessity, acting as a check upon the greater power.

*   *   *

The checks to population, which are constantly operating with more or less force in every society, and keep down the number to the level of the means of subsistence, may be classed under two general heads; the preventive and the positive checks.

The preventive check, is peculiar to man, and arises from that distinctive superiority in his reasoning faculties, which enables him to calculate distant consequences. Plants and animals have apparently no doubts about the future support of their offspring. The checks to their indefinite increase, therefore, are all positive. But man cannot look around him, and see the distress which frequently presses upon those who have large families; he cannot contemplate his present possessions or earnings, which he now nearly consumes himself, and calculate the amount of each share, when with very little addition they must be divided, perhaps, among seven or eight, without feeling a doubt, whether if he follow the bent of his inclinations, he may be able to support the offspring which he will probably bring into the world. In a state of equality, if such can exist, this would be the simple question. In the present state of society, other considerations occur. Will he not lower his rank in life, and be obliged to give up in great measure his former society? Does any mode of employment present itself by which he may reasonably hope to maintain a family? Will he not at any rate subject himself to greater difficulties, and more severe labour than in his single state? Will he not be unable to transmit to his children the same advantages of education and improvement that he had himself possessed? Does he even feel secure that, should he have a large family, his utmost exertions can save them from rags, and squalid poverty, and their consequent degradation in the community? And may he not be reduced to the grating necessity of forfeiting his independence, and of being obliged to the sparing hand of charity for support?

These considerations are calculated to prevent, and certainly do prevent, a great number of persons in all civilized nations from pursuing the dictate of nature in an early attachment to one woman.

If this restraint do not produce vice, as in many instances is the case, and very generally so among the middle and higher classes of men, it is undoubtedly the least evil that can arise from the principle of population. Considered as a restraint on an inclination, otherwise innocent, and always natural, it must be allowed to produce a certain degree of temporary unhappiness;

but evidently slight, compared with the evils which result from any of the other checks to population.

When this restraint produces vice, as it does most frequently among men, and among a numerous class of females, the evils which follow are but too conspicuous. A promiscuous intercourse to such a degree as to prevent the birth of children, seems to lower in the most marked manner the dignity of human nature. It cannot be without its effect on men, and nothing can be more obvious than its tendency to degrade the female character, and to destroy all its most amiable and distinguishing characteristics. Add to which, that among those unfortunate females with which all great towns abound, more real distress and aggravated misery are, perhaps to be found, than in any other department of human life.

When a general corruption of morals, with regard to the sex, pervades all the classes of society, its effects must necessarily be, to poison the springs of domestic happiness, to weaken conjugal and parental affection, and to lessen the united exertions and ardour of parents in the care and education of their children; effects, which cannot take place without a decided diminution of the general happiness and virtue of society; particularly, as the necessity of art in the accomplishment and conduct of intrigues, and in the concealment of their consequences, necessarily leads to many other vices.

The positive checks to population are extremely various, and include every cause, whether arising from vice or misery, which in any degree contribute to shorten the natural duration of human life. Under this head therefore may be enumerated, all unwholesome occupations, severe labour and exposure to the seasons, extreme poverty, bad nursing of children, great towns, excesses of all kinds, the whole train of common diseases and epidemics, wars, pestilence, plague, and famine.

On examining these obstacles to the increase of population which are classed under the heads of preventive and positive checks, it will appear that they are all resolvable into moral restraint, vice, and misery.

Of the preventive checks, that which is not followed by irregular gratifications, may properly be termed moral restraint.

Promiscuous intercourse, unnatural passions, violations of the marriage bed, and improper arts to conceal the consequences of irregular connections, are preventive checks that clearly come under the head of vice.

Of the positive checks, those which appear to arise unavoidably from the laws of nature, may be called exclusively misery; and those which we obviously bring upon ourselves, such as wars, excesses, and many others which it would be in our power to avoid, are of a mixed nature. They are brought upon us by vice, and their consequences are misery.

In every country, some of these checks are, with more or less force, in constant operation; yet, notwithstanding their general prevalence, there are few states in which there is not a constant effort in the population to increase beyond the means of subsistence. This constant effort as constantly tends to subject the lower classes of society to distress, and to prevent any great permanent melioration of their condition.

These effects, in the present state of society, seem to be produced in the following manner. We will suppose the means of subsistence in any country just equal to the easy support of its inhabitants. The constant effort towards population, which is found to act even in the most vicious societies, increases the number of people before the means of subsistence are increased. The food therefore which before supported eleven millions, must now be divided among eleven millions and a half. The poor consequently must live much worse, and many of them be reduced to severe distress. The number of labourers also being above the proportion of work in the market, the price of labour must tend to fall; while the price of provisions would at the same time tend to rise. The labourer therefore must do more work to earn the same as he did before. During this season of distress, the discouragements to marriage, and the difficulty of rearing a family are so great, that population is nearly at a stand. In the meantime, the cheapness of labour, the plenty of labourers, and the necessity of an increased industry among them, encourage cultivators to employ more labour upon their land; to turn up fresh soil, and to manure and improve more completely what is already in tillage; till ultimately the means of subsistence may become in the same proportion to the population as at the period from which we set out. The situation of the labourer being then again tolerably comfortable, the restraints to population are in some degree loosened; and, after a short period, the same retrograde and progressive movements, with respect to happiness, are repeated.

This sort of oscillation will not probably be obvious to common view; and it may be difficult even for the most attentive observer to calculate its periods. Yet that, in the generality of old states, some such vibration does exist, though in a much less marked, and in a much more irregular manner, than I have described it, no reflecting man who considers the subject deeply can well doubt.

One principal reason why this oscillation has been less remarked, and less decidedly confirmed by experience than might naturally be expected, is, that the histories of mankind which we possess, are, in general, histories only of the higher classes. We have not many accounts, that can be depended upon, of the manners and customs of that part of mankind where these retrograde and progressive movements chiefly take place. A satisfactory history of this kind, of one people and of one period, would require the constant and minute attention of many observing minds in local and general remarks on the state of the lower classes of society, and the causes that influenced it; and, to draw accurate inferences upon this subject, a succession of such historians for some centuries would be necessary. This branch of statistical knowledge has, of late years, been attended to in some countries, and we may promise ourselves a clearer insight into the internal structure of human society from the progress of these inquiries. But the science may be said yet to be in its infancy, and many of the objects, on which it would be desirable to have information, have been either omitted or not stated with sufficient accuracy. Among these perhaps may be reckoned the proportion of the number of adults to the number of marriages; the extent to which vicious customs have prevailed in consequence of the restraints upon matrimony; the comparative mortality among the children of the most distressed part of the community, and of those who live rather more at their ease; the variations in the real price of labour; the observable differences in the state of the lower classes of society with respect to ease and happiness, at different times during a certain period; and very accurate registers of births, deaths, and marriages, which are of the utmost importance in this subject.

A faithful history, including such particulars, would tend greatly to elucidate the manner in which the constant check upon population acts; and would probably prove the existence of the retrograde and progressive movements that have been mentioned; though the times of their vibration must necessarily be rendered irregular from the operation of many interrupting causes; such as, the introduction or failure of certain manufactures; a greater or less prevalent spirit of agricultural enterprise; years of plenty, or years of scarcity; wars, sickly seasons, poor laws, emigration, and other causes of a similar nature.

A circumstance which has perhaps more than any other, contributed to conceal this oscillation from common view, is, the difference between the nominal and real price of labour. It very rarely happens that the nominal price of labour universally falls; but we well know that it frequently remains the same, while the nominal price of provisions has been gradually rising. This is, in effect, a real fall in the price of labour; and, during this period, the condition of the lower classes of the community must be gradually growing worse. But the farmers and capitalists are growing rich from the real cheapness of labour. Their increasing capitals enable them to employ a greater number of men; and, as the population had probably suffered some check from the greater difficulty of supporting a family, the demand for labour, after a certain period, would be great in proportion to the supply, and its price would of course rise, if left to find its natural level; and thus the wages of labour, and consequently the condition of the lower classes of society, might have progressive and retrograde movements, though the price of labour might never nominally fall.

In savage life, where there is no regular price of labour, it is little to be doubted that similar oscillations take place. When population has increased nearly to the utmost limits of the food, all the preventive and the positive checks will naturally operate with increased force. Vicious habits with respect to the sex will be more general, the exposing of children more frequent, and both the probability and fatality, of wars and epidemicks will be considerably greater; and these causes will probably continue their operation till the population is sunk below the level of the food; and then the return to comparative plenty will again produce an increase, and, after a certain period, its further progress will again be checked by the same causes.

But without attempting to establish in all cases these progressive and retrograde movements in different countries, which would evidently require more minute histories than we possess, the following propositions are proposed to be proved:

1. Population is necessarily limited by the means of subsistence.

2. Population invariably increases, where the means of subsistence increase, unless prevented by some very powerful and obvious checks.

3. These checks, and the checks which repress the superior power of population, and keep its effects on a level with the

means of subsistence, are all resolvable into moral restraint, vice, and misery.

READING 30

Progress and Population

IN INQUIRING INTO POPULATION THEORY, it may be wise not only to study the Malthusian theory itself but also to read what a modern economist might have to say concerning the population conditions in the world today and the possible influence of the Malthusian theory. In the following reading Kenneth E. Boulding points out that in the underdeveloped countries of the world the Malthusian theory evidently has considerable validity, for certainly in those countries population presses on the means of subsistence. On the other hand, he points out that in those greatly industrialized nations like the United States, England, and the countries of Western Europe seemingly the birth rate has declined while the standard of life has risen rapidly.

Kenneth E. Boulding (1910-   ) is Professor of Economics at the University of Michigan. He was educated chiefly at Oxford in England but has done most of his teaching in the United States. He is an outstanding contemporary economic theorist. His chief works are: *Economic Analysis* (1941) and *The Economics of Peace* (1945). The reading is reprinted by permission from *The Economics of Peace,* by Kenneth E. Boulding. © 1945 by Prentice-Hall, Inc., Englewood Cliffs, N. J. pp. 97-101.

It is clear that the standard of life of a people depends not only on its techniques and its natural resources, but also on the size of its population. After a certain point, any increase in the population which has to be supported with given resources and techniques must lead to a reduction in the standard of life. The more children there are around the table, the more difficult it is to feed, clothe, and house them. This is the basis of the "Dismal

Science" of Malthus and Ricardo—dismal not so much because it was dull reading, but because its conclusions were so completely depressing. If nothing can stop the growth of population but starvation, then nothing can prevent the growth of the population till it starves. There in a nutshell is the Malthusian specter. No amount of technical progress can do us any good in the long run, for though it enables us to live better for a while, the fact that we live better means that the population grows, and hence the standard of life will decline until it is down at the starvation level again, where the sickle of death keeps pace with the harvest of the womb.

The argument is logically flawless. It fortunately has a minor premise that is not necessarily correct. This is the assumption that only starvation can check the growth of population. Even Ricardo and Malthus recognized that this assumption might not be true, if people limited their families voluntarily. Now, in the technically advanced parts of the world, the voluntary limitation of families has reached the point where we have reason to fear not over-, but underpopulation. In hardly any Westernized country is the population reproducing itself; each generation as it dies leaves a smaller generation in its stead, and unless present trends are reversed, the technically advanced countries will suffer a fairly rapid decline in population before the end of this century.

This does not mean, however, that the Malthusian specter is finally laid. In the East, and to a smaller extent even in eastern Europe and southern United States, and in some parts of the tropics, there is real pressure of population on the means of subsistence. The disappointing results of British rule in India have been in large part due to the fact that the gain from improved techniques has been swallowed up in an avalanche of new mouths. The very density of population of China is the main physical obstacle to the reformation of Chinese agriculture. If only one could lift about 250 million Chinese up bodily, hang them in the air for a few years while tractors rooted out the old boundaries and while her pocket-handkerchief farms were consolidated into something on which a tractor could be used, and while factories and schools to receive the suspended Chinese could be built, then the problem of China would be easy! But if China is really to be reconstructed, millions must be driven off the farms *first* before the farms can be consolidated. How to accomplish this revolution painlessly is a problem that no country has yet been able to solve: England had her enclosures and "sturdy beggars," Russia her dispossessed Kulaks and starving peasantry. Perhaps it is not beyond the wit of man to devise a painless solution, or perhaps pain is the price of a new world.

Fertility falls as the standard of life rises

There seems to be a clear relationship between the fertility of a people and its standard of life: the higher the standard of life, at least up to a certain point, the lower the fertility. The causes of this phenomenon are imperfectly understood; everything from soap and hot baths to contraceptives has been suggested as a reason. Probably the most important reason is the growth of economic consciousness and the clearer realization of the *cost* of children that comes about when the standard of life rises. Whatever the reasons for the phenomenon, it is as clearly established as any empirical fact can be. It is a fact of momentous significance, for it means that if a society can improve its techniques, and therefore its standard of life *fast enough,* the rise in the standard of life will be permanent, for the rising standard of life will inhibit the growth of population. If, however, a society improves its techniques too slowly, the old habits will persist and the rise in population will keep pace with the improvement in techniques, thus preventing any improvement in the standards of life. The only result of improved techniques in such a case would be that *more* people would be able to live in abject misery than before!—a dismal conclusion indeed. Yet, without outside help, the masses of the East may actually be in that position.

Improvements in techniques lead to rise in population

When a country first begins a rapid improvement of techniques, there is always a sharp rise in the population. This happened in the Western World between 1760 and the present day; it is just beginning in Russia, Mexico, and Turkey where the technical revolution has just started; it may still lie ahead for the rest of the world. The reason is plain: improvements, especially in the food supply and in medical care, lead to a marked fall in mortality, and particularly to a fall in the infant mortality. The fall in the birth rate however does not take place for some time—perhaps not for a hundred years. In that interval death rates are low, birth rates are high, and the population grows accordingly. In Britain, for instance, the death rate fell dramatically between 1740 and 1760; the birth rate stayed up until about 1880. A similar course of events took place, or is still taking place, in all countries affected by the technical revolution.

Thus, we may expect a large growth in population in Russia, in Mexico, in Turkey, and in all rapidly developing countries during the next fifty years. The population of all these countries may be expected to double or treble in that time. If the technical revolution comes to India or China in an effective form, one trembles to think of the result. The very density of population of these countries, however, effectively prevents the technical revolution from spreading. It is significant that the most rapidly developing countries today are those with room to expand. The problem of China and India, of Poland and Java is therefore significantly different from the problem facing Russia. Russia, with her vast resources, can easily take care of an expanding population; she will continue to expand into Siberia, just as the United States expanded westward. Even now Sverdlovsk rivals Kansas City, and in another generation two great industrial-agricultural "heartlands" will face each other across the North Pole. But China cannot expand her population, or she will starve. Even if she utilized her land to the full, and doubled her yields (as technically she might do) even then she could only give a reasonably adequate diet to her 400 or 450 million people. She could not possibly support a billion people, any more than the United States could, no matter how chromium-plated her equipment. In her case, technical progress must go hand-in-hand with a vigorous program to check population growth and to shift people from the land. There is no other way for her. The same is true of the other densely populated countries.

Even migration in their case is of little use, unless it is carried out on a scale vaster than any we have hitherto conceived. The settlement of, say, 200,000,000 Asiatics in the Amazon Valley in 25 years might provide an answer. But anything much less than this would be useless. For every emigrant leaves food to support another child. Where infant mortality due to malnutrition is the main check on population growth, emigration then does nothing to solve the population problem. For every emigrant that leaves, one child—or perhaps even two children—grow up to take his place.

READING 31

Technology

THE WORD "TECHNOLOGY" refers to techniques of production. The aspect of technology receiving most attention is that of substituting machines for men. Thus a "high" degree of technology implies a large amount of capital equipment by way of machinery and power equipment applied to the production of goods. The great importance of an advancing technology is that it results in increasing productivity, i.e., output of goods per worker employed. The greater the productivity, of course, the more goods and services are produced with a given expenditure of cost and effort; therefore the greater the consumption that is made possible, resulting in a continually higher standard of living.

The following reading describes the immense advances that have been made in the technology of farming which has a two-fold aspect: the substitution of machinery for labor effort and the direct scientific advance in husbandry. The reading next describes our advancing technology in the field of mining. Finally, the significance of capital in our economy is explained, for it is chiefly in the application of huge amounts of capital that our improving technology is most evident.

Harold G. Moulton (1883-   ) is a prominent American economist. He taught at the University of Chicago until 1922, when he became president of The Brookings Institution. He has written widely on a variety of economic topics, directing his interest chiefly toward historical and institutional aspects of the economy. The reading is from *Controlling Factors in Economic Development* (Washington, D. C.: The Brookings Institution, 1949, 397 pp.), Part I, "Looking Backward," Chapter II, "Factors Overlooked," pp. 14-22, 27-29. Reprinted by permission.

Science and Technology

The most fundamental of the several developments which combined to transform the economic world during the last century has been the phenomenal advance in science. Without scientific discoveries and their application through engineering to the processes of production, the limiting factors discussed by the early economists might well have operated to prevent any great improvement in living standards.

The economists of a century ago had witnessed only the beginnings of the technological revolution. There had been numerous important inventions in the field of textile production, and a considerable range of small-scale manufacturing had developed. Of much greater potential significance was the beginning made in the use of steam power in manufacturing and in transportation. But most of the great scientific discoveries and inventions were yet to come. Engineering was still in the infancy stage, and the epoch-making developments in the fields of metallurgy, electricity, oil, and chemistry belonged to the future. While as events proved economic society was on the threshold of a technological revolution, observers of the time could scarcely be expected to perceive the economic significance of coming developments.

In every field of production—agriculture, mining, manufacturing, transportation, public utilities—the developments which have occurred have increased manyfold the productive power of the individual worker. Instead of diminishing returns from natural resources—agriculture and mining—we have witnessed constantly increasing returns. This outcome, as we shall see, is not so much a result of the discovery of *new* agricultural and mineral resources as of a more efficient use of *known* resources.

The Revolution in Agriculture

Until well into the nineteenth century there had been very little improvement in methods of agricultural production for many centuries. Indeed, in 1800 farmers were in the main employing the production techniques of 3,000 years earlier. The crude wooden plows were so antiquated that in many areas hand tools for preparing the soil were preferred. Small grains were broadcast by hand; hoes were used in planting cotton and corn; haying and harvesting were done with the scythe and the cradle, and threshing with the flail.

The great era of technological progress in agriculture may be said to have begun in the second quarter of the nineteenth century. In the succeeding 100 years, two distinct types of development combined to revolutionize agricultural production methods. One was the introduction of labor-saving machinery—made possible by preceding developments in the field of manufacture. The other was the direct use of scientific knowledge in agricultural production—a development, in the main, since 1900.

The use of labor-saving machinery in agriculture has involved two stages: the first was the replacement of hand tools by machines—the mowing machine for the scythe, the reaper for the cradle, the cultivator for the hoe. The second stage came with the introduction of power-driven machinery during the last thirty years.

The significance of farm machinery is found in reduced labor requirements and net costs.

The increase in man-hour output resulting from the introduction of labor-saving machines was truly extraordinary, even before the advent of power machinery. For example, the Department of Agriculture estimates that around 1830 about 50 to 60 man-hours of labor were required to produce one acre (20 bushels) of wheat—with walking plow, brush for harrow, hand broadcast of seed, sickle, and flail; while in the nineties to produce 20 bushels of wheat on an acre with gang-plow, seeder, harrow, binder, thresher, wagon and horse, only 8 to 10 man-hours of labor were required. This represents a saving in labor amounting to as much as 85 per cent. The labor saving in corn production between 1850 and the nineties was roughly 50 per cent. In a broad group of farm products—including grains, cotton, hay, and potatoes, the saving in labor time during the course of the nineteenth century averaged nearly 80 per cent.

These savings in labor requirements were not offset by the added cost of the machines. In the group of farm products referred to above, the *dollar* costs of production decreased more than 50 per cent in fifty years—and this despite a four-fold increase in farm wage rates.

Since 1900 the increasing variety of farm machines and the extensive use of mechanical power have brought large additional labor economies in agriculture. In wheat, for example, only 3 to 4 man-hours of labor were required in 1939 to produce one acre of wheat with three-bottom gang plow, tractor, ten-foot tandem disk harrow, twelve-foot combine, and trucks. In American agriculture as a whole the increase in output per worker between 1900 and 1939 was as much as 90 per cent.

The primary significance of the development of farm machinery in the nineteenth century is found in its effect upon costs rather than upon yields per acre. With some crops the yield may have been increased somewhat as a result of the better tillage which machines make possible, but in other cases the output may have been adversely affected. In any case, the statistics of crop production reveal no important changes in the decades here under review—in contrast with the results achieved in the period of scientific agriculture which followed.

The significance of the direct use of science
in agriculture lies in increased yields.

The scientific age in agriculture is the result of the scientific research fostered by the Department of Agriculture, agricultural colleges and experiment stations, and also by industries dependent upon agricultural markets. These scientific developments have been directed along the following principal lines:

(1) Better systems of crop rotation.

(2) Soil fertility improvement—by studies of the chemical requirements of plants; the development of fertilizer formulas for different soils and crops; the better placement of fertilizers in relation to plants; the various types of soil conservation.

(3) Plant disease control—by means of spraying and dusting, quarantines, and baits; the discovery and importation of "natural enemies"; and the wholesale destruction of infested plants.

(4) Plant breeding or genetics—for the double purpose of obtaining more productive plants and stronger disease-resistant organisms.

(5) Animal breeding—through the process of careful selection of the best specimens and the rapid elimination of poor producers—with special attention in recent years to the development of disease-resistant qualities.

(6) Control of animal diseases—such as hog cholera, the cattle tick, bovine tuberculosis, and the hoof and mouth disease.

(7) Animal nutrition, involving the use of scientific knowledge of food values and the requirements for balanced rations.

These developments have served directly to increase output per acre. They have also conserved and increased the food value of plants, and they have increased the productivity of livestock. It is only within the last 25 years, however, that the effects upon yields have become important. Future potentialities along these lines . . . are very great.

As a result of the technological improvements thus briefly sketched, the percentage of the working population engaged in agricultural production steadily declined over the century under review, while at the same time per-capital consumption of food-stuffs steadily expanded. Whereas in 1830 as much as 70 per cent of the labor force was engaged in agriculture, by 1940 the figure had been reduced to less than 18 per cent.

The Revolution in Mineral Production

During the century under review, mineral exploration and prospecting uncovered vast resources unknown to our forefathers. But important as these discoveries have been they are of less significance than the expansion of mineral resources that has resulted from improvements in the arts of mining and mineral processing.

Mineral technology has both increased resources and reduced costs of production.

The application of scientific knowledge in this field has brought improvements of many types. The more important of these may be briefly summarized as follows:

Prospecting has been greatly facilitated by geology, aided by equipment devised in the laboratories of physicists and seismologists.

Deeper mining has been made possible by improved ventilation and air conditioning, which combat both high temperatures and high humidity.

The rotary drill and the development of superior steel alloys, and special cements adapted to high temperatures have made it possible to drill oil wells to great depths, thereby making available enormous additional reservoirs of oil, and uncovering huge new fuel resources in the form of natural gas.

Blasting, by means of low freezing and low density explosives, has greatly decreased the cost of mining operations.

The development of the pneumatic rock drill has led, even

within the last 25 years, to a three-fold increase in drilling speed.

Block caving methods have made it possible to mine economically much lower grade ores.

Power shovels for loading by compressed air, and electric locomotives have greatly reduced the cost of moving ores.

During this period there were developed: the cyanide process in gold and silver mining; the open-hearth method in steel production, froth flotation in copper mining; the electrolytic process in aluminum, copper, zinc, and lead refining; and the debismuthizing of lead by the addition of calcium and antimony. It has been said that: "At least once every generation technical advances in methods of treatment make new mines out of old dumps or revive abandoned mining districts."

These improvements in metallurgical methods have brought a great reduction in the amount of labor required to turn out a given quantity of product. In the mineral industry as a whole, one man in 1939 could turn out in an hour 3.67 times as much as in 1902; in the oil and gas division the increase in man-hour efficiency was nearly five-fold. Since these progressive decreases in labor requirements were not matched by corresponding increases in capital requirements, there was a continuous decline in over-all costs of production.

Modern methods have improved the quality of minerals and also furnished additional metals.

There have been many improvements in the quality of minerals to meet specific consumption requirements. Washeries and cleaning plants installed at mines have reduced ash and sulphur content. Uniform sizing has increased efficiency in blast furnaces. The efficiency of fuel has been improved by better heating devices such as residential stokers. The development of large public utility power plants has reduced the amount of coal required to produce a kilowatt hour of electric power from over 7 pounds in 1899 to an average of 1.4 pounds in 1936. Special analyses have been made to determine the relative yield of gas, coke, and by-products for particular purposes.

Improved methods of production have also given us important additional by-product metals. For example, silenium is obtained from copper residues, palladium from electrolytic nickel production, and cadmium from lead refining.

Because of the vast importance of oil, an additional statement is desirable with respect to this mineral. The first American oil well was opened in 1859. In the next 60 years oil—because of its combined uses in lighting and heating and as lubricant and source of power—came to be regarded as indispensable to modern civilization. But exploitation of this rich mineral resource had been so rapid that by the end of World War I grave fears were expressed over its prospective early exhaustion. Twenty-eight billion barrels of oil had been produced in the United States between 1860 and 1920; and remaining reserves were estimated at only 7 billion barrels. By the end of 1943, however, 27 billion barrels of additional oil had been produced, and the proved reserves were then estimated at 20 billion barrels. As a leading oil geologist points out:

The recoverable oil reserve is not a fixed quantity. . . . As time proceeds, more oil is discovered by existing techniques, new methods of discovery are devised, the areas of search are extended both regionally and vertically. The efficiency of recovery is raised, the effectiveness of processing and utilization is improved, and entirely new resources are created by chemical science through its ability to rearrange molecular structures. . . .[1]

Modern methods of oil processing have, moreover, greatly increased efficiency in the use of oil, thereby lessening the amount required for a given purpose. This is of course equivalent to an increased quantity of oil reserves.

In summary, the revolution in mining processes has furnished us abundant supplies of mineral products. Instead of expected shortages, we have had in many lines chronic surpluses. Thus the mineral foundations for an expanding economy proved altogether adequate.

* * *

The Fundamental Significance of Capital

* * *

The ever-increasing efficiency of machines and tools has multiplied man-hour productivity.

The increasing productivity of capital instruments as measured by man-hour output has come from the invention of new types of materials and machines, from improvements in the quality of tools, from greater durability of materials, and from

---

[1] Joseph E. Pogue, *Oil and the Americas* (1944).

the increased size of plant, fixed installations, and movable equipment. Modern machine tools are incomparably superior in performance to those of only two decades ago. The Diesel engine has multiplied traction power. The efficiency of the present steam electric turbine is many times that of its prototype.

In consequence of developments such as these, a new machine may have an efficiency double or triple that of the one it replaces, although the dollar cost may be the same. Or, a larger machine, costing twice as much as its predecessor, may have a producing capacity five times as great. Adding better units of capital is a wholly different matter from adding like units, which was the assumption of earlier economists.

The increasing productivity of capital instruments, aided by improvements in the organization and layout of industrial establishments, has greatly increased man-hour output during the course of the last century. Between the Civil War and the end of the century, machine methods were introduced in a wide range of manufacturing industries. Perhaps the most striking advance in productivity accompanying the shift from hand to machine methods was that which occurred in the manufacture of shoes and textiles. At the end of the period as compared with the beginning, there could be produced in a given time about 8 times as many pairs of shoes, 74 times as many pounds of cotton thread, and 80 times as many yards of gingham. The accompanying reduction in the cost of labor per unit of output during these three and a half decades was equally dramatic. For shoes the reduction was from $4.60 a pair to 60 cents, for cotton thread from 87 cents a pound to 2 cents, and for gingham from 20 cents a yard to 1 cent.

After 1900 improvements in machine technique were rapidly extended throughout the greater part of the economy. While precise data are not available for all the various lines of industry, it appears that for the economy as a whole output per man-hour during the first four decades of the twentieth century "doubled or more than doubled." In manufacturing as a whole the increase was at least threefold.

In the fifteen-year period of rapid technological advance from 1923 to 1937, man-hour output in the major divisions of American industry increased as follows: in manufacturing, 50 per cent; in railroads, 43 per cent; in mining, 89 per cent; and in public utilities, 111 per cent. This increase in efficiency was more or less continuous, occurring both in periods of prosperity and depression.

Improvements in the *quality* of capital instruments have been the cutting edge of economic progress.

READING 32

Economic Causes of War

THE ECONOMIC CAUSES of war have received attention in the past from historians rather than from economists. The vast convulsion called modern war, however, has brought more and more attention to its problems by modern economists. A. C. Pigou in the accompanying reading delineates some of the fundamental economic causes of war at the same time that he cautions that such economic causes can in no sense be regarded as the *sole* causes of war. The two basic causes of war, he maintains, are the urge to domination and the desire to loot. The latter of these two is economic; and it manifests itself in a search for markets by nations, in a search for concessions (in spheres of influence) by great financiers, and finally in a search for markets by armaments manufacturers. The author, however, is careful to point out that some of these economic influences, for example the desire for expanded trade, may conversely be influences toward peace.

Arthur Cecil Pigou (1877-1959) was Professor of Economics at the University of Cambridge. He was a student of, and "successor" to, Alfred Marshall, the great leader of the "neo-classical" school. His contribution to economics was chiefly in "welfare economics," although he did important work in business cycles. The reading is from *The Political Economy of War* by Arthur Cecil Pigou (New York: The Macmillan Company, 1941, 169 pp.), Chapter II, "Economic Causes of War," pp. 19-28. Reprinted by permission of St. Martin's Press, Inc., New York, and Macmillan & Co., Ltd., London.

The immediate occasions of war are manifold and, maybe, trivial—an "insult to the flag", the murder of an official personage, the rash act of some panic-stricken commander of troops or warships, the falsification of a telegram by some astute diplomatist. But these occasions are not the causes of war. They are the match to the powder magazine. The real fundamental causes are those that lie behind the assembling of the powder. In the last analysis these are two in number, the desire for domination and the desire for gain.

The desire for domination for its own sake, apart from any economic advantages it may confer, is a real and effective motive for action. The English schoolboy who asserts himself by bullying smaller boys, the self-styled Aryan who bullies Jews, the white man in tropical countries who exacts special marks of respect and subordination from his 'inferiors', all at bottom are displaying a desire for domination. There is no doubt at all that the average Englishman or Frenchman does have this sort of desire; and, moreover feels that it is somehow gratified by the fact that he is a citizen of a 'Great Power', not of Holland or Switzerland or Spain. In 1914 and again in 1939 many Germans have really desired their country to hold Europe in a thrall of fear, and to hear their country's sabre rattling behind its diplomacy. It does not happen, indeed, that modern nations go to war for the avowed purpose of discovering which is "the better man". But this element is certainly present in their rivalry. Furthermore, the desire for domination makes nations extraordinarily unwilling to relax their hold on any territory they have come once to 'possess'. They are humiliated, outraged, dishonoured if a subject population passes out from their yoke. For continuing to hold these peoples against their will, ruling Powers have offered many reasons—their duty to civilisation, the white man's burden, the need for a strategic frontier and so forth. These reasons are often put forward sincerely; sometimes they are sound; but, in addition to and behind everything else, there is the will of dominant Powers to continue dominant. Against that clashes the will of the dominated to be free. There is the seed of wars of liberty, of irredentist wars, of wars of nationality! This explosive force has little to do with economics. It is outside the scope of this discussion, but it is none the less real. To ignore it and to seek an exclusively economic interpretation of war would be to neglect evident truths. The desire for gain, whose subtle workings are the subject of study here, is not the only ferment that makes for international war. It is important, in concentrating attention upon it, not to forget that the part it plays is limited.

Civilised nations do not go to war with one another with the

avowed and direct purpose of loot. It is not, indeed, as was sometimes urged before 1914, in the nature of things impossible for a
victorious nation to make an economic profit by exacting a war
indemnity. An indemnity is equivalent to the wiping out of a
foreign debt or to the receipt of a foreign loan on which no
interest need be paid. It may, of course, happen, if the indemnity
is received all at once in a form unwisely chosen, that industry
will be disturbed and incidental damage suffered in the process
of adjustment. But to assert in a general way that a nation which
receives an indemnity *must* suffer a net economic injury from it
is to uphold a paradox. It will generally gain, just as an individual will gain if somebody gives him a present. So soon,
however, as this is admitted, it follows that the amount of the
gain *may* be greater than the cost of the war through which it
was won. This must be fully acknowledged. Nevertheless, in view
of the enormous expense of modern military and naval operations, and of the chance that a war begun on a small scale may
draw in other Powers, it is extremely *improbable* that there will
be to any country in the end any balance of economic gain. For
a government to enter on war in the hope of such a gain would
be a colossal stupidity as well as a colossal crime. This is so far
recognised that wars motivated by the hope of loot in the form of
huge indemnities are not practically to be feared. It is not in this
crude way that economic influences foster modern war.

The traders of industrialised countries naturally desire
profitable markets for their goods. Owing to the general vogue
of protective and preferential tariffs they often find themselves
exposed, in territories controlled by governments other than
their own, to fiscal handicaps as against the citizens of the controlling governments. Consequently, as a safeguard against these
handicaps, they prefer to see as large a part of the world as
possible controlled by their own government. Having secured this
much, they reflect that the situation would be still further improved if their government could be induced to place a fiscal
handicap in the way of their competitors. There is thus in many
countries a tendency on the part of traders and manufacturers
interested in exportation to favour self-assertion by the
government of their country in regions where expansion or the
earmarking of spheres of interest is feasible without too great risk.
Manufacturers of goods, the raw materials of which come from
tropical lands, may also expect a greater complaisance in satisfying
their wants in regions controlled by their own, rather than by
rival, governments. They, therefore, tend to back up the traders

interested in exportation. When the amount of trade actually done by civilised countries with the regions of Africa and Asia controlled by them is compared with the amount done with regions politically outside the range of their influence, it is, indeed, apparent that the economic prize that merchants and manufacturers have looked for is not a great one. This is the more obvious when it is recalled, first, that the figures of exports and imports measure, as it were, the *turnover,* and, therefore, very greatly exceed the *profit* of the trade; secondly, that the absence of national control, though it might involve a reduction, certainly would not involve the disappearance, of national trade (and the resultant profit) from controlled regions; and, thirdly, that the manufacturing and trading activity directed to any particular market is never a net addition to the aggregate manufacturing and trading activity of a country, but is, in great part, a mere diversion of it from other markets or other products. These considerations suggest that the eagerness of manufacturers and traders to support policies of expansion in the search for markets is based on an imperfect realisation of the economic consequences of these policies. But, however this may be, the fact remains that many manufacturers and traders do believe that political imperialism is, or may be made, a great factor in benefiting trade and industry. This belief they succeeded over many decades in imposing upon the governments of the United Kingdom, France, Italy, Germany, Russia and Japan. Since the same territory cannot be controlled by two governments at the same time, the necessary result has been competition and diplomatic contests among these governments.

It is not, however, chiefly as agencies for promoting the trade of their nationals in relatively undeveloped parts of the world that European governments have come into conflict with one another. They have also been pushed forward towards imperialism by the influence of financiers in search of profitable concessions. Here the gain to be looked for is larger. There are openings for highly profitable investments in loans to weak governments whose officials can be bribed or cajoled, in building railways for such governments on favourable terms, in developing the 'natural resources' of oil fields, or in establishing rubber plantations on land taken from Africans and worked by the forced or 'stimulated' labour of Africans at a very low wage. When the government of some civilised country has annexed, or is protecting, or has established a sphere of influence over, any undeveloped region, these valuable concessions are apt to flow, even when they are not formally reserved, to financiers among its own nationals. These financiers are often rich and powerful. They have means of making their voices heard through newspapers, of influencing opinion and of putting pressure on governments. In Mr. Woolf's book on *Empire and Commerce in Africa* there is a lurid account of the methods they sometimes employ. It is not my business to go through that sordid tale. All that is important here is that the desire for gain through concessions, as well as, and more powerfully than, the desire for gain through trade has impelled civilised governments into a competition for influence and control in relatively undeveloped regions of the world.

This competition means diplomatic backing by governments of their traders and concession-seekers in weak States, coupled at once with attempts to acquire spheres of influence, protectorates or annexations for themselves and with resistance to similar attempts on the part of others. Thus, the rivalry of the traders and financiers of different nations leads to a contest among their governments for "places in the sun". In this contest allies and associates are helpful, and so the area of contest is extended. In the background of it all stands military power. No government wants to fight for a sphere of influence or a concession for its nationals, but every government knows that, unless there is some point at which people believe that it will fight, its diplomacy will be relatively ineffective; and it knows too that, once it enters upon a game of bluff, the bluff may unexpectedly be called. In this way the economic interest of private persons, reacting upon the policy of governments, piles up further explosive material alongside of that already prepared by desires for and resistance to political domination.

Moreover, there is one private economic interest which operates in a peculiar manner. This is the private interest of makers of armaments. These persons wish to sell their goods. It need not be suggested that any among them are so callous to human suffering as to desire actual war for that end. But they certainly desire preparations for war. If they can persuade one government that another government is arming against it, they may obtain a lucrative order for ships or guns. The leading armament firms of different countries do not limit themselves to supplying the needs of their own governments, nor are they wholly independent of, or dissociated from, one another. It is to the interest of all of them to promote war scares and international competition in armaments. If they can induce one government to buy from them some new instrument of war, this of itself affords them a powerful lever with which to induce other governments to do the same. They are not without influence in the press, and, through the press, on public opinion. It is not necessary to assume that the persuasion they exercise is corrupt, or that they deliberately disseminate false alarms. It is enough to know that they find a profit in stimulating the purchase of armaments; that, so far as they succeed, mutual suspicions and mutual fears among governments are fostered; and that thus the explosive material, out of which the flame of war may burst, is piled higher.

This explosive material, we may next remark, has a peculiar quality. Once piled up under the several influences I have described, it tends, like a living thing, to grow. The fear of war itself forces governments to adopt policies that make war more likely. If there were no fear of war there would be no purpose in achieving strategic frontiers. One of the objects sought in conquering African colonies, namely, the recruitment of black troops, would exist no longer. Two of the grounds for refusing independence to subject populations desirous of independence, namely, the desire to draw soldiers from them, and the desire to prevent rival nations from drawing soldiers from them and using their territory as the base for an attack, would also disappear. But the search for strategic frontiers, the absorption of uncivilised regions rich in potential conscripts, and the refusal to set subject peoples free are important factors in building up the war-like mind. Nursed by the fear of war, they themselves make war more likely and are the cause of further fears.

So far attention has been confined to sorts of economic activity that promote conditions of war between governments. Naturally there are also important economic factors making for peace. The great nations afford very important markets for one another's goods, and people do not wish, if it can be avoided, to fight with their customers. Moreover, trade and travel and the development of means of communication promote an improved understanding of one another in the peoples of different countries. It was the hope of Cobden and his friends that increasing freedom of trade among nations might go hand in hand with increasing friendliness and ever-diminishing danger of war. That hope has not been fulfilled, but it was, none the less, a reasonable hope. Moreover, besides the co-operation of individual citizens of different nationalities in trade, there is also scope for co-operation among governments in connection with economic interests extending beyond the range of single States. Of this kind of co-operation the international postal convention affords the classical example. Under the aegis of the League of Nations more and more occasions for joint economic effort have been found and utilised. This might well have been expected to lessen international rivalries and jealousies, to make possible diminished armaments, and so to lessen that fear of war, which is, both directly and through its indirect influence on policy, one of its principal causes. That these forces making for peace have been overpowered is not a proof that they are feeble, still less that they are unreal.

READING 33

The Planned Economy: Pro

THE GREAT CONTEMPORARY CONTROVERSY between socialism, or communism, and capital, between totalitarianism and democracy, or between the planned economy and the free-enterprise economy, has brought forth extended treatments of the arguments for and against these ideals. The following reading presents the argument in favor of a planned economy. The stand taken in this statement is that a planned economy does not impair freedoms of individuals; but that larger freedoms are maintained or increased by sacrificing some of the lesser economic freedoms. The case against the planned economy, which is explained in the reading immediately following this one, maintains that the fundamental objection to the planned economy is the loss of freedom individuals must suffer.

Barbara F. Wootton (1897-) was Professor of Social Studies at the University of London and is one of the principal proponents of the planned economy. She is the author of several works in this field. The reading is from *Freedom Under Planning* (Chapel Hill, North Carolina: The University of North Carolina Press, 1945, 180 pp.), Chapter I, "Introduction," pp. 3-13, 15-19. Reprinted by permission.

The freedoms that matter in ordinary life are definite and concrete; and they change with the changing ways of different ages and different civilizations. Freedom today might mean, for instance, freedom to ask for your cards and sweep out of an objectionable job; freedom to say what you think of the government in language of your own choosing; freedom to join, or to refuse to join, the Transport and General Workers' Union; freedom to start a rival Union on your own; freedom to be a Freemason, a Catholic or a Plymouth Brother; freedom from concentration camps, official spying and detention without trial; freedom to stand for Parliament or the Parish Council on any program that you like; freedom to strike or not to strike; freedom to wear a nightdress or pyjamas as you prefer. No one would suggest that all these freedoms are of equal importance; nor do these examples necessarily cover all the freedoms that we actually have, can have, or ought to have. The relative value of different freedoms, and the conditions under which they can in fact be realized are difficult and debatable matters, and are, in fact, debated in the pages that follow. But a random list of typical contemporary freedoms is useful as a reminder that free*dom* has to be perpetually reinterpreted into free*doms*. You can philosophize endlessly about freedom; but in daily life it is freedoms that you want. This book would in fact have been called *Freedoms Under Planning*, had not the title been so impossibly ugly.

At the same time all freedoms have a common quality—the quality, in fact, of freedom. If the discussion is to be practical and realistic, it is necessary to have a working notion of what this particular quality is. For the purpose of this book, which is severely practical, freedom may be simply defined as ability to do what you want. Behind every word in that definition there lurks, admittedly, a mass of philosophic doubts and subtleties. In practice one must turn a blind eye to these, and build on the assumption that in ordinary life most people recognize the difference between ability to do what they want, and inability to do this. Lack of freedom, at all events, is unmistakable enough. Most of us know only too well the peculiar emotion of frustration by which denial or deprivation of freedom is accompanied.

Taking this earthy, commonsense view of the nature of freedom, we admittedly bypass the complex issues raised by the child who, on returning to a progressive school after the holidays, is said to have asked: "Mummy, shall I still have to do what I want to do?" Equally we suspend judgment on the implications of the (no doubt apocryphal) Treasury Minute[1] which declared

---

[1] Quoted by Mallalieu: *Pass to you, Please*, p. 105.

that: "It is one thing to compel an officer to retire voluntarily, another to permit him to retire compulsorily. Please keep the two distinct, lest worse confusion befall." What is more important, we deny the validity, for all practical purposes, of any distinction between what people want to do, and what they "really" want to do. Any such distinction is extremely dangerous, and may be the cloak for some of the most wicked, because the most insidious, attacks upon freedom. For sooner or later what I "really" want to do turns out to be a polite paraphrase for what you think I ought to want to do. But freedom means freedom to do what I want, and not what anybody else wants me to want— or else it has no meaning at all. How my wants come to be what they are is, no doubt, the result of a complex social and personal process which had best be left to the psychologist to explore. So far as freedom is concerned, what people want to do must be taken as something to be discovered, not changed.

There is another reason for emphasizing this. Freedom for everybody to do what he wants is not necessarily the sole purpose of organized society. There may be other admirable social ends which conflict with, or demand, limitations upon freedom. The possibility of one such conflict and the methods by which it may be resolved is indeed the theme of this book. It is, however, possible to use the word freedom in such a comprehensive way that it covers practically every conceivable social end. For instance, a full belly and an educated mind are commonly thought of today as good things in themselves; and the view is widely held that it is the business of the state to see that people are in fact in a position to enjoy these blessings. But the use of the terms "freedom from want" and "freedom from ignorance" to describe these desirable conditions is liable to confuse any serious discussion of freedom, and to obscure real problems. For in this way the term freedom is easily stretched so wide as to be emptied of distinctive meaning; and the very possibility of conflict, real enough in experience, between freedom and other praiseworthy social ends is disposed of by a verbal trick. The fact is, of course, that people's freedom—their ability to do what they want—is affected in many and complex ways by nearly every kind of organized social activity. Thus, one of the reasons for desiring a full stomach is that, if your stomach is empty, you will not be free to do anything else until you have filled it. But it is absurd to infer from this either that freedom consists in, and is identical with, a state of repletion, or that the limitation which the pangs of hunger impose on your freedom is the only reason for wishing to be rid of those pangs. A condition of well-fed, well-housed, well-clad, even well-entertained, slavery is not an imaginary impossibility. It is only too possible. But it is not freedom. Freedom should not be defined in terms which, even by implication, deny the possibility that a high degree of material well-being may be accompanied by deprivation of freedom. Prisoners would not become free men even if they were looked after as well as race horses.

Where all the terms are so highly charged with political bias it is necessary to be unusually careful about definitions. What then is meant by planning? Planning, in the sense that is relevant here, may be defined as the conscious and deliberate choice of economic priorities by some public authority. Economic activity consists essentially of choice. Shall I spend this shilling on a pint of mild or send a greetings telegram to my mother on her birthday? Shall I buy a house or rent one? Shall this field be plowed, left as pasture or built over? The first two of these choices may be said to be concerned with priorities of consumption, the third with priorities of production. There must of course always be some connection between the two kinds of choice, since it is not possible to consume that which is not produced. In the long run the pattern of consumption, apart from saving and waste (both of which, by a stretch of language not greater than is customary in the peculiar vocabulary of economics, may be included as special forms of consumption) is identical with the pattern of production. It does not, however, follow that whoever determines the general pattern of production also necessarily decides just exactly what each individual will consume.

It is this planning of production which is the heart of the matter. Since it is not possible to produce indefinite quantities of everything in a given place, as for instance in this island, there must be choice, and there must be priority. You cannot feed a cow off a suburban villa; to that extent there is on every acre a conflict between agriculture and building, in which one must eventually give way to the other. In every case, therefore, priorities of production must somehow be eventually determined. In the world as we know it there are, in principle, two ways, in one or other or both of which these questions can be settled. They can be settled consciously and deliberately as part of a plan, or they can be left to settle themselves through the higgling of the market (more politely known as the market mechanism). In the latter case, the final picture emerges as the unpremeditated result of the decisions of perhaps thousands of people, each

of whom is concerned only with his own particular part (and
that often a very tiny one) of the whole. Planning, on the other
hand, implies that there is a known target to be aimed at. In
the Soviet Union, the planned output of coal, for instance, in the
third year of the second five-year plan, was 110 million tons. The
output actually realized was 108.9 million tons. The plan figure
thus stands as a measure by which to judge the results that were
in fact recorded. In this country, at about the same time, the
annual output of coal was 226.5 million tons. Nobody planned
that. It happened.

It will be noticed that I have confined the term planning to
the determination of priorities by a public authority. In this
context "public authority" means a state or government (with
police and military power to give effect to its decisions if necessary); or some other body which the state has itself created, or to
which it has expressly devolved certain rights and duties—such
as the London County Council, created by Act of Parliament in
1888, or the London Passenger Transport Board, also created by
Act of Parliament in 1933. This limitation on the meaning of
planning is a matter of convenience. In ordinary speech the
decision to put a shilling on a horse may well be spoken of as
part of an *individual's* economic plan; and in some instances
large-scale economic planning may be undertaken by other than
public bodies. The total output of certain chemicals in this
country, for instance, must be fairly closely planned by Imperial
Chemical Industries. The policy of that firm will make a most
significant difference to the total. As has been said, however, the
uncoordinated small-scale plans of individuals generally add up
to a result which is completely unplanned; and the large-scale
planning of private monopolies raises issues which, though alarming and important enough, are different from those characteristic
of what is coming to be called a "planned economic system."

The use of the phrase "economic system" must not be held
to imply that the world is neatly divided into planned economies
on the one hand, and unplanned economies on the other.
Planning is a matter of degree. It is nowhere completely absent
nor does it anywhere cover 100 per cent of all economic activity.
Yet the span that divides the Soviet Union from New Deal
America may be wide enough to justify the use, as a convenient
shorthand, of the respective labels "planned" and "unplanned"
"*system.*" Even in the Soviet Union, the collective farmer can
grow and sell what he likes as he likes on his own modest
allotment, not bothering about anybody's plans but his own. In

real life a pure economy is as improbable as a pure race. Economic hybrids are scarcely less varied than biological.

If, for practical purposes, economic planning is to mean *state* economic planning, it follows that, in the present stage of political development, plans must be confined within national boundaries. M. Stalin's government can make and execute most comprehensive plans of production throughout the vast areas over which they rule. If they wish to extend the geographical scope of their plans, they must first find some way of incorporating the territory of their neighbors into the Soviet Union. International economic planning is indeed possible in the sense that independent governments may agree to co-operate in certain economic activities, or create joint organs to regulate the output of particular commodities. The production of rubber and other raw materials was internationally planned in this way before the war. The status of plans of this kind is, however, necessarily quite different from that of those imposed by a government within the limits of its own authority. If the members of the Blankshire County Council fail to carry out their statutory duty to provide education for the children of the county in accordance with plans laid down by Parliament, they will personally be compelled by force of law to conform, or to get out: and it will be no use pleading that the people of Blankshire, holding as they do that ignorance is bliss, do not therefore wish to be bothered with education. But if the Dutch government took a dislike to the rubber control scheme and decided to disregard its provisions, they would have been amenable to no effective authority. The Dutch electors might refuse at their next opportunity to re-elect a government that had proved so careless of its bond. But that would still be a matter only between Dutch and Dutch. The remaining parties to the agreement, outside Holland, must confine themselves to protests, or in the last resort to economic or military sanctions directed, not against the offending members of the Netherlands government, but against the Dutch people as a whole. If the Blankshire County Council ignores the law, there is no question of blockading or bombing the County.

This difference between the activities of governments inside and outside their own boundaries is as plain as a pikestaff as well as quite fundamental. But it is sometimes forgotten in practice. The members of an international planning authority (the phrase, in a world of still sovereign states, is actually a contradiction in terms) are either severally responsible to the several governments by whom they have been appointed (each one of which may at any time change its mind about the whole business); or else they are responsible to no one—self-appointed dictators in fact. Incidentally, this dilemma necessarily tempers, though it does not invalidate, the hope that international political unity will eventually emerge from, rather than precede, international economic integration. For present purposes its chief significance is that it unavoidably limits the scope of the discussion. A plan which has the force of law is at most, as things are, a national plan. A planned economy can only mean an economy which is predominantly planned by the government of one state (or its appointees) for the people of that state. This of itself creates certain special problems affecting freedom, different from those which would be raised by the world-wide plans of a government of world-wide authority.

It is perhaps worth adding that state planning of priorities in production, even if it covered much the greater part of our economic life, is not necessarily identical with socialism. Socialism is generally held to mean (among other things) public ownership and operation of industry. Now, in theory at least, it is quite possible for the state to make all major decisions about how much of what is to be produced, without itself undertaking anything approaching the whole of that production. That is indeed, near enough, what happens in war. Production and priorities are officially planned and are carried out to government order; but by no means all these orders are executed in firms in which the workers are directly government employees. In principle, therefore, the distinction between socialism and economic planning is parallel with the distinction between doing something yourself and telling, or paying, somebody else to do it. How far such planning without socialism would be practicable except in the special circumstances of war is a question to which experience gives as yet no clear answer. The convinced socialist (if he can be persuaded to proceed beyond dogmatic assertion that the two are inherently incompatible) will argue that government plans which are not also government-executed will either founder on the rocks of vested interest, or be wrecked by exploitation. In a world where business men are accustomed to make their own plans with an eye on their own or their firm's profit, very strong pressure may be put on the government to frame its own programs to suit the wishes at least of those private concerns which are large enough to make themselves heard. If this fails, the business world, it is said, will bring up a large armory of weapons with which to defeat the substance, while accepting the letter, of a government program; and finally the apparatus of controls (price regulation, profit limitation, quotas, perhaps concentration of industry, to name only a few complexities) which government will need to establish to prevent such tricks—will prove so formidable that in the end the conclusion that it would be more sensible to do the job yourself will become irresistible. That is, anyhow, how it looks to the socialist. What people will put up with in the war, he will say, is no guide to what can be done with them in peace; and, even in war, it cannot be said that the enforcement of the controls necessary for comprehensive planning is either frictionless or easy. The amount of effort which is devoted to circumventing government regulations seems to be considerable: the amount of effort devoted to circumventing such efforts to circumvent the law is even greater. And even so there are still black markets and prosecutions. If this is what happens in war, the socialist will write off the possibilities of public planning without public production in peacetime, when the danger and the glory are past, as hopeless. Necessarily, however, this remains a question of opinion. Nor is it certain that the answer is the same for all communities at all times. Business men vary both in their predatory qualities, and in their sense of public responsibility. Until the weight of experience is conclusive one way or the other, the problems of freedom under planning must be treated as distinct from those of freedom under socialism. But the prudent will remember the possibility that the one may lead to the other.

* * *

The task is, then, to inquire how significant contemporary freedoms are likely to be affected by authoritative public choice of economic priorities. On this, extreme opinions are held. On the one hand we read (near the *beginning* of a book in a *discussion* series): "Public planning means that enterprise, labour, distribution must be strictly regulated. It means, therefore, that one's chance to choose one's occupation must be reduced, since the plan cannot possibly be worked unless enough labour is directed into the occupation where it is needed, regardless of whether enough people want to do that kind of work or not. . . . In the same way, hours, pay, conditions will have to be standardised. Strikes, as also lock-outs, must become illegal. . . . Ambitious people will not be at liberty to take chances with their careers unless the proper officials allow it (and officials are not commonly venturesome) . . . public authorities must obviously take a larger and larger part in cultural activities if these are not to be allowed to languish . . . teachers and teaching must be more or less standardised. . . ."[2]

These dogmatic statements do not seem to leave much room for discussion. In this case, however, one dogmatism is answered by another. Contrast the following:—

"A planned society can be a far more free society than the competitive *laissez-faire* order which it has come to replace. Its greater freedom lies in its ability to offer those who work in it the sense, on the one hand, of continuous opportunity for the expression of capacity, and the power, on the other, to share fully in making the rules under which they work. The failure of the pre-war order was the degree to which, in the daily economic life of the worker, it made freedom and security dependent on privilege. Men feel that a social order is just only when their hopes are not frustrated and their future not in constant danger: justice is the parent of freedom."[3] "The alternatives before us are stark. . . . There is no remedy now for our ills save, with all its complexities, the planned production of our economic resources for community consumption. . . . And it cannot be too strongly emphasised that those who seek the new social order are in this hour the soldiers of freedom. . . . A society like ours . . . is incapable of the security which, as this book has argued, is the basic condition of freedom. Not only so. The greater the effort to restore its security upon its present foundations, the greater the attack upon freedom that is involved."[4]

It was, I think, Bertrand Russell who remarked that, should the temperature of a room unhappily become the subject of political controversy, two political parties would hold two views—one would stand for boiling-point, the other for freezing.

It does not, however, follow that where strong opinions conflict the right answer is found by splitting the difference. That might be true of a dispute about temperature: it is not likely to be true in the freedom-under-planning controversy, except in a qualitative sense. The sensible answer is not that freedom is best promoted by a judiciously moderate dose of planning—something between that prescribed by Miss Jaeger and Professor Laski, respectively. The sensible answer turns on an

---

2 Muriel Jaeger, *Liberty versus Equality* (Nelson Discussion Series), pp. 11, ff.

3 The Labour Party, *The Old World and The New Society*.

4 Laski, *Liberty in The Modern State*, Pelican Edition, pp. 39, 40.

analysis of the impact of planning upon different *kinds* of freedom. A limited plan might wholly destroy certain freedoms: while a plan of much more comprehensive scope might leave other freedoms quite untouched. Here it is clear that Miss Jaeger on the one side, and Professor Laski and the Labour Party on the other, are thinking about different kinds of freedom. Neither side denies that economic planning can fill the belly. The Left asserts that when the belly is full we are free from the necessity of filling it: the opposition replies that the price of filling it is the surrender of the freedom to use this freedom as we wish. Both *could* be right. If they are, the simultaneous enjoyment of economic, civil and political freedoms is impossible. That at least makes the problem important.

In the background of this controversy there lies one further distinction which is quite fundamental. That is the distinction between those effects on freedom which are inherent in any kind of plan, and those which are related to the content of a particular plan, or to the particular method of its operation. If Miss Jaeger is right and *any* plan is incompatible with the chief economic, political and civil freedoms, then the problems concerned with the differences between one plan and another are not worth discussing. We are sunk anyway. If, on the other hand the mere technique of planning is not necessarily destructive of these freedoms, it certainly does not follow that all the problems of freedom under planning are settled. To show, for instance, that the government can effectively determine economic priorities without recourse to compulsory direction of labor is not the same as to show that any actual economic plan will be either wise or popular or conducive to freedom. To show that planners need not exercise certain powers is not the same as to show that they will not. To show that it is possible to plan for good is not the same as to show that it is impossible to plan for evil.

READING 34

The Planned Economy: Con

THE PLANNED ECONOMY controversy has as one of its chief figures Friedrich A. von Hayek. Professor Hayek in the following reading takes the position that a planned economy can be run only by dictatorial methods. These dictatorial methods absolutely necessitate loss of freedom on the part of individuals. He points out that freedoms cannot be increased or maintained by curtailing them either economically or otherwise. And further, curtailments to freedom, i.e., dictatorial government, tend to grow and mushroom and give rise to further loss of liberty.

Friedrich A. von Hayek (1899-   ) is a famous Austrian economist, formerly Professor of Economics at the University of Vienna and Professor of Economics at the University of London. Although his chief economic work has been on money and monetary theory, he is probably most widely known for his writing in opposition to the planned economy. The reading is from *The Road to Serfdom*, by Friedrich A. von Hayek (Chicago: University of Chicago Press; copyright 1944 by The University of Chicago; 250 pp.), Chapter VII, "Economic Control and Totalitarianism," pp. 88-100. Reprinted by permission of The University of Chicago.

Most planners who have seriously considered the practical aspects of their task have little doubt that a directed economy must be run on more or less dictatorial lines. That the complex system of interrelated activities, if it is to be consciously directed at all, must be directed by a single staff of experts, and that ultimate responsibility and power must rest in the hands of a commander-in-chief whose actions must not be fettered by democratic procedure, is too obvious a consequence of underlying ideas of central planning not to command fairly general assent.

The consolation our planners offer us is that this authoritarian direction will apply "only" to economic matters. One of the most prominent economic planners, Stuart Chase, assures us, for instance, that in a planned society "political democracy can remain if it confines itself to all but economic matter." Such assurances are usually accompanied by the suggestion that, by giving up freedom in what are, or ought to be, the less important aspects of our lives, we shall obtain greater freedom in the pursuit of higher values. On this ground people who abhor the idea of a political dictatorship often clamor for a dictator in the economic field.

The arguments used appeal to our best instincts and often attract the finest minds. If planning really did free us from the less important cares and so made it easier to render our existence one of plain living and high thinking, who would wish to belittle such an ideal? If our economic activities really concerned only the inferior or even more sordid sides of life, of course we ought to endeavor by all means to find a way to relieve ourselves from the excessive care for material ends and, leaving them to be cared for by some piece of utilitarian machinery, set our minds free for the higher things of life.

Unfortunately, the assurance people derive from this belief that the power which is exercised over economic life is a power over matters of secondary importance only, and which makes them take lightly the threat to the freedom of our economic pursuits, is altogether unwarranted. It is largely a consequence of the erroneous belief that there are purely economic ends separate from the other ends of life. Yet, apart from the pathological case of the miser, there is no such thing. The ultimate ends of the activities of reasonable beings are never economic. Strictly speaking, there is no "economic motive" but only economic factors conditioning our striving for other ends. What in ordinary language is misleadingly called the "economic motive" means merely the desire for general opportunity, the desire for power to achieve unspecified ends. If we strive for money, it is because it offers us the widest choice in enjoying the fruits of our efforts. Because in modern society it is through the limitation of our money incomes that we are made to feel the restrictions which our relative poverty still imposes upon us, many have come to hate money as the symbol of these restrictions. But this is to mistake for the cause the medium through which a force makes itself felt. It would be much truer to say that money is one of the greatest instruments of freedom ever invented by man. It is money which in existing society opens an astounding range of choice to the poor man—a range greater than that which not many generations ago was open to the wealthy. We shall better understand the significance of this service of money if we consider what it would really mean if, as so many socialists characteristically propose, the "pecuniary motive" were largely displaced by "noneconomic incentives." If all rewards, instead of being offered in money, were offered in the form of public distinctions or privileges, positions of power over other men, or better housing or better food, opportunities for travel or education, this would merely mean that the recipient would no longer be allowed to choose and that whoever fixed the reward determined not only its size but also the particular form in which it should be enjoyed.

Once we realize that there is no separate economic motive and that an economic gain or economic loss is merely a gain or a loss where it is still in our power to decide which of our needs or desires shall be affected, it is also easier to see the important kernel of truth in the general belief that economic matters affect only the less important ends of life and to understand the contempt in which "merely" economic considerations are often held. In a sense this is quite justified in a market economy—but only in such a free economy. So long as we can freely dispose of our income and all our possessions, economic loss will always deprive us only of what we regard as the least important of the desires we were able to satisfy. A "merely" economic loss is thus one whose effect we can still make fall on our less important needs, while when we say that the value of something we have lost is much greater than its economic value, or that it cannot even be estimated in economic terms, this means that we must bear the loss where it falls. And similarly with an economic gain. Economic changes, in other words, usually affect only the fringe, the "margin," of our needs. There are many things which are more important than anything which economic gains or losses are likely to affect, which for us stand high above the amenities and even above many of the necessities of life which are affected by the economic ups and downs. Compared with them, the "filthy lucre," the question whether we are economically somewhat worse or better off, seems of little importance. This makes many people believe that anything which, like economic planning, affects only our economic interests cannot seriously interfere with the more basic values of life.

This, however, is an erroneous conclusion. Economic values

are less important to us than many things precisely because in economic matters we are free to decide what to us is more, and what less, important. Or, as we might say, because in the present society it is *we* who have to solve the economic problems of our lives. To be controlled in our economic pursuits means to be always controlled unless we declare our specific purpose. Or, since when we declare our specific purpose we shall also have to get it approved, we should really be controlled in everything.

The question raised by economic planning is, therefore, not merely whether we shall be able to satisfy what we regard as our more or less important needs in the way we prefer. It is whether it shall be we who decide what is more, and what is less, important for us, or whether this is to be decided by the planner. Economic planning would not affect merely those of our marginal needs that we have in mind when we speak contemptuously about the merely economic. It would, in effect, mean that we as individuals should no longer be allowed to decide what we regard as marginal.

The authority directing all economic activity would control not merely the part of our lives which is concerned with inferior things; it would control the allocation of the limited means for all our ends. And whoever controls all economic activity controls the means for all our ends and must therefore decide which are to be satisfied and which not. This is really the crux of the matter. Economic control is not merely control of a sector of human life which can be separated from the rest; it is the control of the means for all our ends. And whoever has sole control of the means must also determine which ends are to be served, which values are to be rated higher and which lower—in short, what men should believe and strive for. Central planning means that the economic problem is to be solved by the community instead of by the individual; but this involves that it must also be the community, or rather its representatives, who must decide the relative importance of the different needs.

The so-called economic freedom which the planners promise us means precisely that we are to be relieved of the necessity of solving our own economic problems and that the bitter choices which this often involves are to be made for us. Since under modern conditions we are for almost everything dependent on means which our fellow-men provide, economic planning would involve direction of almost the whole of our life. There is hardly an aspect of it, from our primary needs to our relations with our family and friends, from the nature of our work to the use of our leisure, over which the planner would not exercise his "conscious control."

The power of the planner over our private lives would be no less complete if he chose not to exercise it by direct control of our consumption. Although a planned society would probably to some extent employ rationing and similar devices, the power of the planner over our private lives does not depend on this and would be hardly less effective if the consumer were nominally free to spend his income as he pleased. The source of this power over all consumption which in a planned society the authority would possess would be its control over production.

Our freedom of choice in a competitive society rests on the fact that, if one person refuses to satisfy our wishes, we can turn to another. But if we face a monopolist we are at his mercy. And an authority directing the whole economic system would be the most powerful monopolist conceivable. While we need probably not be afraid that such an authority would exploit this power in the manner in which a private monopolist would do so, while its purpose would presumably not be the extortion of maximum financial gain, it would have complete power to decide what we are to be given and on what terms. It would not only decide what commodities and services were to be available and in what quantities; it would be able to direct their distribution between districts and groups and could, if it wished, discriminate between persons to any degree it liked. If we remember why planning is advocated by most people, can there be much doubt that this power would be used for the ends of which the authority approves and to prevent the pursuits of ends which it disapproves?

The power conferred by the control of production and prices is almost unlimited. In a competitive society the prices we have to pay for a thing, the rate at which we can get one thing for another, depend on the quantities of other things of which by taking one, we deprive the other members of society. This price is not determined by the conscious will of anybody. And if one way of achieving our ends proves too expensive for us, we are free to try other ways. The obstacles in our path are not due to someone's disapproving of our ends but to the fact that the same means are also wanted elsewhere. In a directed economy, where the authority watches over the ends pursued, it is certain that it would use its powers to assist some ends and to prevent the realization of others. Not our own view, but somebody else's, of what we ought to like or dislike would determine what we should get. And since the authority would have the power to thwart any efforts to elude its guidance, it would control what we consume almost as effectively as if it directly told us how to spend our income.

Not only in our capacity as consumers, however, and not even mainly in that capacity, would the will of the authority shape and "guide" our daily lives. It would do so even more in our position as producers. These two aspects of our lives cannot be separated; and as for most of us the time we spend at our work is a large part of our whole lives, and as our job usually also determines the place where and the people among whom we live, some freedom in choosing our work is, probably, even more important for our happiness than freedom to spend our income during the hours of leisure.

No doubt it is true that even in the best of worlds this freedom will be very limited. Few people ever have an abundance of choice of occupation. But what matters is that we have some choice, that we are not absolutely tied to a particular job which has been chosen for us, or which we may have chosen in the past, and that if one position becomes quite intolerable, or if we set our heart on another, there is almost always a way for the able, some sacrifice at the price of which he may achieve his goal. Nothing makes conditions more unbearable than the knowledge that no effort of ours can change them; and even if we should never have the strength of mind to make the necessary sacrifice, the knowledge that we could escape if we only strove hard enough makes many otherwise intolerable positions bearable.

This is not to say that in this respect all is for the best in our present world, or has been so in the most liberal past, and that there is not much that could be done to improve the opportunities of choice open to the people. Here as elsewhere the state can do a great deal to help the spreading of knowledge and information and to assist mobility. But the point is that the kind of state action which really would increase opportunity is almost precisely the opposite of the "planning" which is now generally advocated and practiced. Most planners, it is true, promise that in the new planned world free choice of occupation will be scrupulously preserved or even increased. But there they promise more than they can possibly fulfill. If they want to plan, they must control the entry into the different trades and occupations, or the terms of remuneration, or both. In almost all known instances of planning, the establishment of such controls and restrictions was among the first measures taken. If such control were universally practiced and exercised by a single planning authority, one needs little imagination to see what would become of the "free choice of occupation" promised. The "freedom of choice" would be purely fictitious, a mere promise to practice no discrimination where in the nature of the case discrimination must be practiced, and where all one could hope would be that the selection would be made on what the authority believed to be objective grounds.

There would be little difference if the planning authority confined itself to fixing the terms of employment and tried to regulate numbers by adjusting these terms. By prescribing the remuneration, it would no less effectively bar groups of people from entering many trades than by specifically excluding them. A rather plain girl who badly wants to become a saleswoman, a weakly boy who has set his heart on a job where his weakness handicaps him, as well as in general the apparently less able or less suitable are not necessarily excluded in a competitive society; if they value the position sufficiently they will frequently be able to get a start by a financial sacrifice and will later make good through qualities which at first are not so obvious. But when the authority fixes the remunerations for a whole category and the selection among the candidates is made by an objective test, the strength of their desire for the job will count for very little. The person whose qualifications are not of the standard type, or whose temperament is not of the ordinary kind, will no longer be able to come to special arrangements with an employer whose dispositions will fit in with his special needs: the person who prefers irregular hours or even a happy-go-lucky existence with a small and perhaps uncertain income to a regular routine will no longer have the choice. Conditions will be without exception what in some measure they inevitably are in a large organization —or rather worse, because there will be no possibility of escape. We shall no longer be free to be rational or efficient only when and where we think it worth while; we shall all have to conform to the standards which the planning authority must fix in order to simplify its task. To make this immense task manageable, it will have to reduce the diversity of human capacities and inclinations to a few categories of readily interchangeable units and deliberately to disregard minor personal differences.

Although the professed aim of planning would be that man should cease to be a mere means, in fact—since it would be impossible to take account in the plan of individual likes and dislikes—the individual would more than ever become a mere means, to be used by the authority in the service of such abstractions as the "social welfare" or the "good of the community."

That in a competitive society most things can be had at a price—though it is often a cruelly high price we have to pay—is a fact the importance of which can hardly be overrated. The alternative is not, however, complete freedom of choice, but orders and prohibitions which must be obeyed and, in the last resort, the favor of the mighty.

It is significant of the confusion prevailing on all these subjects that it should have become a cause for reproach that in a competitive society almost everything can be had at a price. If the people who protest against having the higher values of life brought into the "cash nexus" really mean that we should not be allowed to sacrifice our lesser needs in order to preserve the higher values, and that the choice should be made for us, this demand must be regarded as rather peculiar and scarcely testifies to great respect for the dignity of the individual. That life and health, beauty and virtue, honor and peace of mind, can often be preserved only at considerable material cost, and that somebody must make the choice, is as undeniable as that we all are sometimes not prepared to make the material sacrifices necessary to protect those higher values against all injury.

To take only one example: We could, of course, reduce casualties by automobile accidents to zero if we were willing to bear the cost—if in no other way—by abolishing automobiles. And the same is true of thousands of other instances in which we are constantly risking life and health and all the fine values of the spirit, of ourselves and of our fellow-men, to further what we at the same time contemptuously describe as our material comfort. Nor can it be otherwise, since all our ends compete for the same means; and we could not strive for anything but these absolute values if they were on no account to be endangered.

That people should wish to be relieved of the bitter choice which hard facts often impose upon them is not surprising. But few want to be relieved through having the choice made for them by others. People just wish that the choice should not be necessary at all. And they are only too ready to believe that the choice is not really necessary, that it is imposed upon them merely by the particular economic system under which we live. What they resent is, in truth, that there is an economic problem.

In their wishful belief that there is really no longer an economic problem people have been confirmed by irresponsible talk about "potential plenty"—which, if it were a fact, would indeed mean that there is no economic problem which makes the choice inevitable. But although this snare has served socialist propaganda under various names as long as socialism has existed, it is still as palpably untrue as it was when it was first used over a hundred years ago. In all this time not one of the many people who have used it has produced a workable plan of how production could be increased so as to abolish even in western Europe what we regard as poverty—not to speak of the world as a whole. The reader may take it that whoever talks about potential plenty is either dishonest or does not know what he is talking about. Yet it is this false hope as much as anything which drives us along the road to planning.

While the popular movement still profits by this false belief, the claim that a planned economy would produce a substantially larger output than the competitive system is being progressively abandoned by most students of the problem. Even a good many economists with socialist views who have seriously studied the problems of central planning are now content to hope that a planned society will equal the efficiency of a competitive system; they advocate planning no longer because of its superior productivity but because it will enable us to secure a more just and equitable distribution of wealth. This is, indeed, the only argument for planning which can be seriously pressed. It is indisputable that if we want to secure a distribution of wealth which conforms to some predetermined standard, if we want consciously to decide who is to have what, we must plan the whole economic system. But the question remains whether the price we should have to pay for the realization of somebody's ideal of justice is not bound to be more discontent and more oppression than was ever caused by the much-abused free play of economic forces.

We should be seriously deceiving ourselves if for these apprehensions we sought comfort in the consideration that the adoption of central planning would merely mean a return, after a brief spell of a free economy, to the ties and regulations which have governed economic activity through most ages, and that therefore the infringements of personal liberty need not be greater than they were before the age of laissez faire. This is a dangerous illusion. Even during the periods of European history when the regimentation of economic life went furthest, it amounted to little more than the creation of a general and semipermanent framework of rules within which the individual preserved a wide free sphere. The apparatus of control then available would not have been adequate to impose more than very general directions. And even where the control was most complete it extended only to those activities of a person through which he took part in the social division of labor. In the much wider sphere in which he then still lived on his own products, he was free to act as he chose.

The situation is now entirely different. During the liberal era the progressive division of labor has created a situation where almost every one of our activities is part of a social process. This is a development which we cannot reverse, since it is only because of it that we can maintain the vastly increased population at anything like present standards. But, in consequence, the substitution of central planning for competition would require central direction of a much greater part of our lives than was ever attempted before. It could not stop at what we regard as our economic activities, because we are now for almost every part of our lives dependent on somebody else's economic activities. The passion for the "collective satisfaction of our needs," with which our socialists have so well prepared the way for totalitarianism, and which wants us to take our pleasures as well as our necessities at the appointed time and in the prescribed form, is, of course, partly intended as a means of political education. But it is also the result of the exigencies of planning, which consists essentially in depriving us of choice, in order to give us whatever fits best into the plan and that at a time determined by the plan.

It is often said that political freedom is meaningless without economic freedom. This is true enough, but in a sense almost opposite from that in which the phrase is used by our planners. The economic freedom which is the prerequisite of any other freedom cannot be the freedom from economic care which the socialists promise us and which can be obtained only by relieving the individual at the same time of the necessity and of the power of choice; it must be the freedom of our economic activity which, with the right of choice, inevitably also carries the risk and the responsibility of that right.

INDEX